ULTIMATE LAS VEGAS AND BEYOND

SECOND EDITION

"Tells you what there is to do on the Strip and off, even venturing into the nearby National Parks."

—*Los Angeles Times*

"This book covers everything . . . . Odds are 10 to 1 that the most useful information for neophyte gamblers will be the explanations of how casino games work, including tips on strategy."

—*Newsday*

"Las Vegas is portrayed as more than a row of gambling halls. The book contains the sort of data that a new resident, not just a visitor, could use."

—*Las Vegas Review-Journal*

"Perfect for big players, slot machine junkies, desert rats and Native American history buffs alike."

—*Arizona Senior World*

"Covers the usual fare—hotels, restaurants, casinos and gambling tips—but provides a bonus with coverage far beyond the city. The side trips cover everything from Death Valley to Laughlin to the Grand Canyon and Utah's national parks. If that sounds like a lot of territory for a 220-page book, you're right."

—*San Diego Union-Tribune*

ULTIMATE LAS VEGAS AND BEYOND

SECOND EDITION

David Stratton

RAY RIEGERT, LESLIE HENRIQUES

Executive Editors

GLENN KIM

Illustrator

ULYSSES PRESS

Published by: Ulysses Press
3286 Adeline Street, Suite 1
Berkeley, CA 94703

Library of Congress Catalog Card Number 94-60467
ISBN 1-56975-016-5

Printed in the U.S.A. by the George Banta Company

10 9 8 7 6 5 4 3 2

Managing Editor: Claire Chun
Editors: Zippy Collins, Joanna Pearlman
Editorial Associates: Jennifer Wilkoff, Ellen Nidy, Lee Micheaux, Mark Rosen, Doug Lloyd
Proofreader: Bruce Bender
Cartographers: Wendy Ann Logsdon, Phil Gardner
Cover Designers: Bonnie Smetts, Leslie Henriques
Indexer: Sayre Van Young
Cover Photography: Front cover by Larry Hamill; back cover by Lee Foster

Distributed in the United States by Publishers Group West, in Canada by Raincoast Books, and in Great Britain and Europe by World Leisure Marketing

Printed on recycled paper

For My Parents,
from Whom I Continue to Learn

Acknowledgments

There are many talented people who contributed to producing this book. My heartfelt thanks to the professional staff at Ulysses Press: Publishers Ray Riegert and Leslie Henriques, who saw the possibilities in a somewhat hazy book proposal and brought the entire project into clear focus; to editors Zippy Collins (second edition) and Joanna Pearlman (first edition) for a copy editing job well-done. Special recognition goes to Jennifer Wilkoff, Ellen Nidy, Claire Chun, Lee Micheaux, Mark Rosen, Doug Lloyd and Bruce Bender for outstanding production and editorial support. I also want to extend a special thank you to Ed Silberstang for his advice and guidance with the gambling chapter.

Close to home I want to thank Cynthia for her unwavering support and encouragement, as well as her thoughtful, constructive criticism.

Contents

Maps

Notes from the Publisher

An alert, adventurous reader is as important as a travel writer in keeping a guidebook up-to-date and accurate. So if you happen upon a great restaurant, discover an intriguing locale or (heaven forbid) find an error in the text, we'd appreciate hearing from you. Just write to:

Ulysses Press
3286 Adeline Street, Suite 1
Berkeley CA 94703

It is our desire as publishers to create guidebooks that are responsible as well as informative. We hope that our guidebooks treat the people, country and land we visit with respect. We ask that our readers do the same.

Best of Las Vegas and Beyond

Casinos
Barbary Coast *(Page 107)*
Caesars Palace *(Page 108)*
Golden Nugget *(Page 110)*
Las Vegas Club *(Page 110)*
Palace Station *(Page 111)*

Family Attractions
Luxor Hotel *(Strip Area, page 24)*
Excalibur Hotel *(Strip Area, page 26)*
MGM Grand Hotel and Theme Park *(Strip Area, pages 26–28)*
Circus Circus Hotel *(Strip Area, page 30)*
Lied Discovery Children's Museum *(Downtown, page 60)*

Hotels
Carriage House *(Strip Area, pages 35–36)*
Alexis Park *(Strip Area, page 36)*
Caesars Palace *(Strip Area, page 37)*
Golden Nugget *(Downtown, pages 62–63)*
Cal-Neva Lodge Resort *(Lake Tahoe, page 249)*

Nightspots
The Metz *(Strip Area, page 54)*
Cleopatra's Barge *(Strip Area, page 55)*
French Quarter Lounge *(Downtown, page 75)*
Hurricane *(Greater Las Vegas, page 97)*
Dick Clark's Bandstand Club *(Reno, page 241)*

Production Shows
Mystere *(Treasure Island, page 56)*
Siegfried & Roy *(The Mirage, page 56)*
Splash *(Riviera Hotel, pages 56–57)*
Starlight Express *(Las Vegas Hilton, page 57)*
Enter The Night *(Stardust Hotel, page 57)*

Restaurants

Michael's *(Strip Area, page 44)*
Pegasus *(Strip Area, page 48)*
Andre's *(Downtown, page 66)*
Middle Eastern Bazaar *(Greater Las Vegas, page 91)*
Le Moulin *(Reno, page 237)*

Sightseeing Attractions

Caesars Palace *(Strip Area, pages 28–29)*
Liberace Museum *(Greater Las Vegas, page 78)*
Clark County Heritage Museum *(Greater Las Vegas, pages 82–83)*
Wilbur D. May Center *(Reno, page 233)*
Vikingsholm *(Lake Tahoe, page 246)*

Shopping

The Forum Shops *(Strip Area, pages 51–52)*
Vignettes *(Strip Area, pages 52–53)*
Gamblers General Store *(Downtown, page 70)*
Ray's Beaver Bag *(Downtown, page 70)*
Spy Factory *(Greater Las Vegas, page 96)*

State Parks and Recreational Areas

Red Rock Canyon *(Side Trips from Las Vegas, pages 144, 146–48)*
Mount Charleston *(Side Trips from Las Vegas, pages 149–52)*
Corn Creek *(Side Trips from Las Vegas, page 154)*
Lake Mead *(Side Trips from Las Vegas, page 157)*
Valley of Fire *(Side Trips from Las Vegas, pages 169–70)*

Tops in Tawdry

Drive-through at A Little White Chapel *(Page 12)*
Emerald City *(Strip Area, page 26)*
Vegas World Hotel *(Strip Area, page 32)*
The Bonanza Gift Shop *(Strip Area, page 54)*
The Gun Store *(Greater Las Vegas, page 99)*

ONE

Las Vegas Dreaming

No other American city has the flash-card recognition of Las Vegas. Mention its name and you evoke quicksilver images of luxurious resort hotels, high-stakes gamblers, fast-paced production shows and the frantic pursuit of adult entertainment 24 hours a day, 365 days a year. Las Vegas is America's answer to Oscar Wilde's Europe of a century ago, a city that is "vibrantly decadent" and "a creation of fantasy." It's probably the most fun, albeit sinful, place on earth since God torched Sodom and Gomorrah.

Yet this is a city that defies its very existence. Visitors to Las Vegas discover a masterpiece of bricolage in the middle of a geographic purgatory, a land seemingly unfit for habitation and possibly best suited as a place of exile. Las Vegas is an anomaly, standing out of the southern Nevada wilderness like a glittering gold hood ornament on a rusty pickup truck: It gets your attention but it looks out of place.

Las Vegas is here mainly because its architects broke with moral convention and reshaped the vices of an isolated, male, frontier society into a major tourist attraction. In short, they discovered that sins worth committing are sins worth marketing.

The result: sales commissions that are staggering. The gambling and tourism industries generate more than $12 billion in revenue a year. The only institution that makes money faster is the U.S. Mint.

Critics of the city say Las Vegas defies social convention because it produces prosperity without production and exists to satisfy the human appetites for wealth, speculation, pleasure and amusement. But if ours is indeed a society where the ultimate commercial truth is making a quick buck on insider trading, then Las Vegas is a logical extension, if not a caricature, of that society, because the ultimate commercial truth here is making a quick buck on an inside straight. And the difference between Wall Street and Las Vegas, it's been said, is largely a matter of interior decoration.

Perhaps Tom Wolfe was right when he described Las Vegas as an epoch, a historic combination of nature—the Mojave Desert—and art—the neon trendiness of the hotels. Mario Puzo saw the city as "one of the most creditable achievements of our society. Decadent society though it may be."

Whatever the reasons, Las Vegas has become the largest city founded in the 20th century. It is also an unforgettable experience for its visitors. Whether strolling along the Strip or wandering through a casino, you have the distinctly urban feeling of being onstage or, perhaps, in the midst of a prison riot.

While Las Vegas exists because of legalized gambling, most visitors come here simply to experience Las Vegas, to have their senses bombarded by its flamboyance, its extravagance—and, maybe, break a few rules along the way. Las Vegas is a world apart, a land of paradoxes and high contrast. It refuses to accept the labels that apply to other cities—trendy, aloof, brash, defiant—because it is all of these and more. There are no curfews in this city, and no school nights. Like the frontier tent city that preceded it, there are no questions asked, and none answered. There are no raised eyebrows, wrong ancestries, improper wardrobes or deficient accents in Las Vegas. This is a place where visitors can loosen their collective belts and let everything hang out.

Although the city has gained a reputation as an adult amusement park, it is also a vital metropolitan hub for some 850,000 people, about the population of San Francisco but spread over an area 20 times larger. From the air it looks like any other neo-Southwestern city sprawling toward the horizon. Yet, in many ways, it is still a small frontier town that reveres its Wild West heritage.

Ultimate Las Vegas and Beyond escorts you through the brightly lit fantasy world of the casinos, resort hotels, celebrity showrooms, production extravaganzas, all-you-can-eat buffets and other attractions that have made Las Vegas an entertainment capital.

You'll venture into the city's newest "virtual reality" megaresorts, with their amusement parks, interactive arcades and high-tech attractions. As commercial gambling spreads across the country, Las Vegas keeps pace by rapidly reinventing itself, and the newest version is a species of electronic expressionism somewhere between *Blade Runner* and *The Wizard of Oz*.

This guidebook takes you beyond the neon, where you'll discover the city's best and most unusual restaurants, piano bars, sports taverns, nightclubs and shopping opportunities, often hidden in the jumbled cityscape.

You'll find out how you can waterski in the morning and snow ski in the afternoon; where to buy a slot machine or blackjack table; where the local dealers and keno runners gather after work; what to do with the

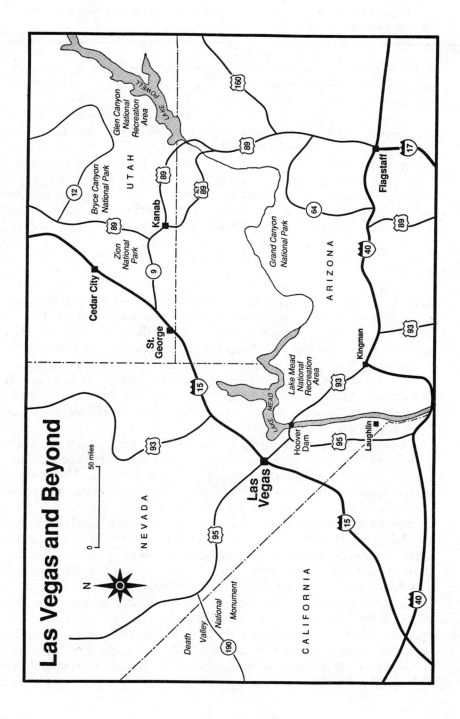

Las Vegas and Beyond

Las Vegas, which means "the meadows," was named by early Spanish explorers for the area's artesian springs.

---

kids when they've run out of video-game quarters; where to see a concert or play; and many more things that tourists seldom discover, even if they have the time to search for them.

This guide also showcases the vast wilderness that surrounds the city, a wilderness harsh and cruel in some places, but always fascinating and beautiful. In the nearby desert, you can still experience the tranquillity that greeted Kit Carson and other pioneers who passed this way before.

Ultimate Las Vegas and Beyond takes you through the entire Las Vegas experience, with a focus on quality and value, the exemplary and the unique. Take a break from the casinos and explore the city. It will be worth it. You might go home empty-handed, but you won't go home empty.

History

Las Vegas is one of our country's most modern cities—it didn't exist before the 20th century. Some say it never really existed before Benjamin "Bugsy" Siegel built the Flamingo Hotel in 1946, when the town finally decided to throw over its hokey Wild West image for ultra-modern neon.

But even before the Sands, the Dunes and the Sahara, Las Vegas was an oasis for desert travelers. Primitive tribes of nomadic Indians settled the area beginning around 2500 B.C. These Archaic Indians were scattered throughout what is now southern Nevada and remained for about 2000 years, or until the Anasazi arrived.

The Anasazi ("ancient ones") were one of the most advanced Native American civilizations. They cultivated land southeast of Las Vegas and built a metropolis—Pueblo Grande—near what is now Overton. They hunted with bows and arrows, wove intricate baskets, created black-and-white pottery and established trading networks with other tribes in the Southwest.

But the Anasazi abandoned the area around the year 1000 for reasons not fully understood. Archaeologists have speculated that they left because of natural disasters such as droughts, floods or epidemics. But experts in Native American culture believe the Anasazi moved south and established a civilization later known as the Hopi.

At about the same time, members of the Paiute tribe moved into southern Nevada from the northeast. The Paiutes were peaceful and free spirited; they roamed the area, cultivating squash and corn and hunting whatever game was available. Less sophisticated than their predecessors, the Paiutes lived in makeshift wickiups and had little or no formal structure to their society.

Except for a few traders, explorers and gold and silver prospectors, the earliest white settlers were the Mormons, who established a camp here in 1855. But the area's isolation, harsh summer heat and crop failures drove the would-be colonists back to Utah in 1858.

The area continued to be a mere watering hole until 1905, when the Union Pacific Railroad set up a connection point between Salt Lake City and Los Angeles. That was also the year the town's site was established. Incorporation followed a few years later.

Las Vegas remained largely a tent city until gambling was legalized in 1931 following a 22-year hiatus. At the same time, the residency requirement for divorce was reduced from three months to six weeks.

During the 1930s Las Vegas tied its tourism fortunes to Boulder Dam, located about 25 miles south of the city. The project, the largest undertaking of its kind, took five years to complete and attracted visitors from around the world. Royalty from Europe and Asia, as well as Hollywood's own nobility—Clark Gable, Cary Grant, Shirley Temple and Katharine Hepburn, to name a few—often used Las Vegas as a jumping-off point for visiting Boulder Dam. (The name was changed to Hoover Dam in 1947.)

In the meantime, Reno was becoming the acknowledged capital both of gambling and of the quickie divorce. Then, in the early 1940s, Californian Thomas E. Hull built the luxurious Hotel El Rancho at a site some two-and-one-half miles south of Las Vegas in what appeared to be desert wasteland. The town would never be the same.

The new hotel, with its swimming pool (the first in Las Vegas), cottages, restaurants, bars, casinos and live entertainment, began to attract Hollywood's rich and famous. Through its doors passed such notables as Joan Crawford, Ava Gardner, Howard Hughes and Cary Grant.

Two years later the plush Hotel Last Frontier opened down the highway from Hotel El Rancho, and the Strip began to take shape as a kind

---

MARRIAGE CAPITAL

Because of Nevada's liberal marriage laws, about 1 in 20 of the nation's weddings are performed here, and most of these take place in Las Vegas. All you need to get a marriage license is proof of age, a birth certificate or driver's license, the $35 filing fee and a potential spouse. If you're under 18, you must have a notarized consent from your parent or guardian. **The Marriage Bureau** *(200 South Third Street; 702-455-3156) is open seven days a week (24 hours a day on weekends and holidays).*

But just remember: The two busiest days of the year for Las Vegas wedding chapels are Valentine's Day and New Year's Eve.

of Wild West theme park, complete with one-armed bandits, showgirls and around-the-clock gambling.

A dramatic change came in '46 when Benjamin "Bugsy" Siegel built his fabulous Flamingo Hotel—a tangerine, magenta, pink and fuchsia resort that was a dead ringer for a South American parrot. The Flamingo was followed in rapid succession by the Thunderbird, Desert Inn, Sahara, Sands, Riviera, Dunes, Hacienda, Tropicana and Stardust, all elegant pleasure domes strung out along a three-mile section of the old Los Angeles Highway. From that time on, visitors couldn't get enough of this exotic, eccentric city that had the feel of a year-round fraternity party staged by Ringling Brothers.

LAS VEGAS TODAY   Although Las Vegas is an around-the-clock city, it's easy to find a place to sleep. There are currently more than 87,000 hotel rooms in Las Vegas, the most of any American city. The city also is home to 13 of the 15 largest hotels in the world.

Hotel reservation desks are kept busy. In 1970, about 6.8 million visitors came to Vegas; there were more than 20 million visitors in 1990. By the year 2000, it's estimated that Las Vegas will have 115,000 guest rooms, attract 29 million visitors and generate $17 billion in gaming revenue annually.

As the tourism industry has grown, so has the city. While the city itself has a population of about 300,000, most of Las Vegas, including the famed Strip, is in an unincorporated area of Clark County. Today, more than 850,000 people live in the greater Las Vegas metropolitan area, a number that is growing by 3000 to 4000 a month.

Many are attracted by the affordable housing, low cost of living, recreational facilities, relaxed attitudes and year-round sunshine. Another incentive, largely a result of the taxes on gaming revenue, is a nearly tax-free lifestyle. There is no state personal income tax here, no inheritance tax and no corporate income tax.

While Las Vegas may sound like utopia, the fast-growing city has its problems. The existing road and highway system hasn't been able to handle the increased population, and traffic congestion is developing, especially on east-west thoroughfares.

The availability of water is of major concern to Las Vegas, especially as Southern California communities increase their demand for Colorado River water. Government entities have curtailed the building of artificial lakes and fountains in some of the city's planned developments and are considering other conservation and rationing measures.

Nevada is ranked among the lowest states in several educational categories, and the suicide rate is double the national average. Health-care costs and auto insurance rates are among the nation's highest, as are the rates of alcoholism and lung cancer.

In spite of its problems, Las Vegas remains a fascinating place to live and work. There's always a feeling that something is happening all around you, even though that something may not be exactly what you had in mind.

When you visit Las Vegas, I hope you'll take the time to delve below the surface, rather than skim along from one casino to another, nourished by 50-cent shrimp cocktails. Discover the various layers of the Las Vegas region, and you will be alternately charmed and perplexed, enchanted and horrified, but never bored.

Climate

Las Vegas enjoys an average of more than 312 days of sunshine every year—the most of any U.S. city. You'll seldom need an umbrella, as average rainfall totals less than three inches per year.

The most comfortable weather occurs during spring and fall. The typical daytime temperatures for March, April and May are in the 70s and 80s, with nighttime temperatures in the 40s and 50s.

The summer months are the hottest, with daytime temperatures averaging about 102 degrees but reaching peaks of 112 to 115 degrees. The nights are usually pleasant, with lows normally in the 70s. The late summer months are, oddly enough, the wettest months, and subject to sudden, unexpected thunderstorms. The electrical storms can be spectacular, but the possibility of flash flooding is a real danger, and care should be taken when driving in desert areas.

September, October and November bring welcome relief from the scorching summer months, with daytime temperatures dropping from the 90s to the 70s. Winter is normally dry, although it has been known to snow in Las Vegas on rare occasions. Daytime temperatures can be a blustery 60 degrees with lows at night at or below freezing.

Here are the average daily maximum and minimum temperatures for Las Vegas:

	Avg. High Temp. (F)	Avg. Low Temp. (F)
January	60	28
February	66	33
March	71	39
April	80	44
May	89	51
June	98	60
July	102	68
August	102	66
September	95	57
October	84	46
November	71	35
December	60	30

Between 1951 and 1962, the United States detonated more than 120 atomic bombs above ground at the Nevada Test Site 70 miles north of Las Vegas.

Calendar

JANUARY

Side Trips   The town of Jean, Nevada, near the California border is the starting point for the **World Championship Hare and Hound Motorcycle Race**, a 150-mile cross-country desert race.

Reno–Tahoe   The nation's top skiers flock to South Lake Tahoe when Heavenly Valley holds its month-long series of races and events known as the **Winter Celebration**.

FEBRUARY

Downtown   Vintage cars take center stage at Cashman Field's **Autorama Antique Car Show**.

MARCH

The Strip   Top women golfers compete in the **LPGA International Golf Tournament** at the Desert Inn Golf Course.

Downtown   Be sure to wear green for the **St. Patrick's Day Parade** down Fremont Street. Regional artists and craftspeople display and sell their work at Cashman Field's **Arts and Crafts Festival**.

Greater Las Vegas   In Henderson, discover the history and artistry of Southwestern Native Americans at the Clark County Heritage Museum's **Native American Arts Festival** (March or early April). Events include demonstrations, performances, lectures and Native American foods and crafts. Dance to the waltzes and polkas of Johann Strauss at Las Vegas Symphony's annual **Afternoon in Old Vienna** at the Charleston Heights Arts Center.

Side Trips   Swing your partner and do-si-do at Boulder City's **Hoover Dam Square Dance Festival**.

APRIL

The Strip   Looking for a mint-condition Model T? Try the **Antique Auto Auction** at the Imperial Palace Hotel. Children can hunt for Easter eggs and visit **Bunny Village** at the Riviera Hotel.

Downtown   Table stakes are $1 million at Binion's Horseshoe Hotel's **World Series of Poker**.

Greater Las Vegas   The region's best artists converge in Las Vegas to compete for cash prizes in the Clark County Library's **Festival of the Arts and Art-A-Fair**. In addition to the juried art competition, you'll find arts and crafts, kids' activities, music, dance, theater, food and entertainment. The **Henderson Industrial Days** offer a car show, concert, beauty pageant and chili cook-off. Top players from the Senior PGA Tour compete in the **Las Vegas Senior Golf Classic** at Summerlin Country Club.

Side Trips   Stunt flying and vintage planes are featured at the **Angel Plane Airfest** at the Boulder City Airport. In Logandale, the **Clark County Fair** gets a blue ribbon for its livestock shows, crafts, food competition, rodeos, ferris wheels and pig racing.

MAY

The Strip   Tantalize your taste buds at the **Greek Food Festival** at the Sahara Hotel. Former top pros tee off for the **Senior Classic** golf tournament at the Desert Inn Country Club.

Greater Las Vegas   **Elks Helldorado Days & Rodeo** at the Thomas and Mack Center is the city's longest-running event and features a professional rodeo, carnival, parade, street dance and chili cook-off. Barbecued ribs and rhythm-and-blues are the fare at the **Clark County Craft Fair & Rib Burn-Off** in Sunset Park.

Side Trips   Celebrate the **Spring Jamboree & Street Festival** with a parade, arts and crafts, food booths, a dog show and a golf tourney in Boulder City.

JUNE

Greater Las Vegas   Every Saturday night relax and enjoy **Jazz in the Park**, a series of free concerts featuring local, national and international jazz greats at county parks.

Reno–Tahoe   The long-running **Reno Rodeo** continues to attract many of the world's finest riders to the Reno Livestock Events Center in late June. Retracing the original route of Lake Tahoe's Pony Express, the **Highway 50 Association Wagon Train** is a mile-long series of 16 covered wagons slowly heading from South Lake Tahoe to Placerville. The **Valhalla Summer Arts and Music Festival**, held through September at the Tallac Historic Site near Camp Richardson on the lake's southern shore, exhibits regional artists and hosts live jazz and classical music Tuesday and Thursday nights.

JULY

Downtown   The Las Vegas Symphony Orchestra presents its **Fourth of July Family Pops Concert** at Cashman Field Center.

Greater Las Vegas   Anything from Shakespeare to Noel Coward is presented **Live!** in the city's Jaycee, Lorenzi and Angel parks.

Side Trips   Celebrate the Fourth at **Damboree Days** with a parade and concert in Boulder City. Beat the summer heat during Laughlin's **River Days**, which include a golf tournament, a fireworks display and rubber duck races along the Colorado River.

Reno–Tahoe   Sprawling throughout the northern-shore resort town of King's Beach, the **Pro Arts Festival** is the place to shop for handcrafted wares made by local artisans during July and August.

AUGUST

The Strip   Philatelists will love the **International Stamp Show** at the Sahara Hotel.

Greater Las Vegas   Toe-tappin' bluegrass and country music are featured at the **Sundown-Hoedown Concert Series** in Jaycee Park.

Reno–Tahoe   The first weekend of the month, Reno welcomes **Hot August Nights**, a festival of classic cars and rock-and-roll performers from the '50s and '60s. The Reno Livestock Events Center hosts the **Nevada State Fair**, with the usual carnival games and live entertainment complemented by livestock competitions and exhibits. The **Dragon Boat Festival** at Zephyr Cove celebrates Asian culture with food, crafts, and races of fancifully decorated Chinese boats.

SEPTEMBER

The Strip   You don't have to be Italian to love the **San Genaro Festival** at the Sahara Hotel parking lot. Festivities include a beauty pageant, live entertainment and plenty of food booths.

Greater Las Vegas   The **Clark County Basque Festival**, held in a different location each year, celebrates with dancing, contests, food and a boat exhibition. Visit Jaycee Park in Las Vegas for the **Craftworks Market**, a juried craft show and sale featuring 150 artists, live entertainment, food booths and hands-on children's activities.

Side Trips   Hydroplanes skim across Lake Mead at the **Las Vegas Cup Unlimited Hydroplane Races**.

Reno–Tahoe   An unusual spectacle descends on—or rather ascends from—Reno on the second weekend of September when **The Great Reno Balloon Race** occurs. Fanatics of speedier airborne craft may prefer watching some of the world's fastest planes race at the **National Championship Air Races**. Skywriting and aerobatics are also part of the festivities.

OCTOBER

Downtown   For an old-fashioned carnival, try the **Las Vegas Jaycees State Fair** at Cashman Field.

Greater Las Vegas   The PGA-sanctioned **Las Vegas Invitational Golf Tournament** has one of the tour's richest purses. In North Las Vegas, watch hot-air balloon races (don't blink) at Fairshow, which also features craft booths, exhibits, a food fair, a bluegrass festival, a chili cook-off and a carnival.

Side Trips   Masterpieces alfresco are the fare at Boulder City's **Art in the Park** exhibition and sale.

NOVEMBER

Downtown   Arts and crafts fill the Cashman Field Center for the **Harvest Festival**.

Greater Las Vegas   Canines and their owners compete at Dog Fancier's Park in Las Vegas for the **Strut Your Mutt Day** contest and exhibition. The annual **76+4 Trombones Concert** features Carl Fontana at Ham Hall of the University of Nevada, Las Vegas (UNLV).

DECEMBER

Downtown   Fremont Street turns into Times Square for Las Vegas' traditional **New Year's Eve Celebration**.

Greater Las Vegas   The country's best broncobusters gather for the **National Finals Rodeo** at the Thomas and Mack Center. Football fans can take in the **Las Vegas Bowl** at the Sam Boyd Silver Bowl, which hosts champs from the Mid-America and Big West conferences. Enjoy an **Old-Fashioned Christmas Celebration** with carolers, crafts, door prizes and a catered feast at the Clark County Heritage Museum.

Side Trips   Christmas lights sparkle at Lake Mead Marina's **Harbor Parade of Lights**.

Packing

For most of the year, pack light and casual. Dress styles are informal, so all you'll need in the way of clothing are some shorts, lightweight shirts or tops, cool pants and something relatively casual for a special event that might call for dressing up. Don't forget a swimsuit and sunscreen.

Warm clothing—an extra sweater, a lined jacket—are required during the winter months (from mid-December to late February) when nighttime temperatures often dip into the 30s.

If you intend to do a lot of exploring on foot, carry good, soft, comfortable, lightweight shoes. If you plan to visit some of the scenic recreational areas surrounding Las Vegas, wear a hat to protect yourself from the sun.

Visitor Information

Several agencies provide free information for visitors. The **Las Vegas Convention and Visitors Authority** (3150 Paradise Road, Las Vegas, NV 89109; 702-892-0711) can supply you with maps, brochures and calendars of events for Las Vegas. The **Nevada Commission on Tourism** (Capital Complex, Carson City, NV 89710; 800-638-2321) is another excellent source of information on scenic attractions, recreation and historic sites. The **Las Vegas Chamber of Commerce** (711 East Desert Inn Road, Las Vegas, NV 89109; 702-735-1616) will send you its brochures and guide to local services.

A number of free publications for visitors highlight what's happening in town—entertainment, dining, dancing, sports and events. **What's On** (4425 South Industrial Road, Las Vegas, NV 89103; 702-891-8811) spotlights celebrity performers and has listings and ads (and a few coupons) for shows, lounges and restaurants, plus television and movie times. It is found in most of the city's hotel and motel rooms, but you can also write ahead for a copy. **Showbiz** (800 South Valley View, Las Vegas, NV 89107; 702-383-7185) has a similar format plus information on galler-

---

OH, WE'RE GOING TO THE CHAPEL

*Las Vegas, known for its "theme" resorts and outrageous behavior, carries its unique brand of excess over to its wedding emporiums. Nuptials take place in such diverse settings as the **Little Church of the West** (3960 Las Vegas Boulevard South; 702-739-7971), resembling a western movie set, or the **Las Vegas Wedding Gardens** (200 West Sahara Avenue; 702-387-0123), which features an indoor garden chapel, complete with running waterfall, or **A Little White Chapel** (1301 Las Vegas Boulevard South; 702-382-5493), with its "Minister on Wheels" who will come to you to perform the wedding. If you're in a hurry, there's a Drive-Up Wedding Window where you can exchange vows without leaving the front seat of your car or truck.*

Looking like adorable miniature churches decorated with neon angels or bells outside, most of the 50 or so wedding chapels in town are open around the clock. A simple civil ceremony with a justice of the peace runs about $50. Additional services are offered à la carte: $75 to rent a gown; $25 for an organist; $30 for flowers; and so on. A full-blown celebration might cost about $500 and include rings, photographer (still and video), tuxedo rental, wedding cake and reception.

Las Vegas has more convention and trade-show space than any other city in the United States. On average, the city hosts between 30 and 50 conventions a month.

ies, museums and other nongaming attractions. **Today in Las Vegas** (3225 McLeod Drive, Suite 203, Las Vegas, NV 89121; 702-385-2737) is a weekly magazine with restaurant, show and casino information, and is usually found in casinos and hotel gift shop racks.

For an up-to-date report on Las Vegas' best bargains, consider the **Las Vegas Advisor** published by Huntington Press (5280 South Valley View Boulevard, Suite B, Las Vegas, NV 89118; 702-597-1884), a 12-page monthly newsletter filled with hints on where to get the best dining and entertainment deals. Its monthly "Top Ten" lists bargains ranging from the best steak dinner and breakfast buffet to the largest shrimp cocktails and half-price pasta specialties. Also included are gambling tips and ratings of the various slot and video poker clubs. You can subscribe to the *Advisor* or purchase single copies at the Gamblers Book Club (630 South 11th Street, Las Vegas; 702-382-7555).

Getting There

BY CAR

Several major highways lead to Las Vegas. From the Southern California area, take **Route 15** northeast across the Mojave Desert straight to Las Vegas (about 270 miles from Los Angeles).

If you're traveling north from Arizona, take **Route 93**, which is also the choice if you're driving south from Reno, Lake Tahoe or Northern California.

Motorists from Utah and points east will use **Route 15**, which is the main artery through Las Vegas. The major hotels and the convention center all have exits along Route 15.

BY AIR

McCarran International Airport handles more passengers, per capita, than any other airport in the world. The ultramodern facility, complete with slot machines, is about eight miles from the Strip resorts, five miles from the convention center and 12 miles from downtown Vegas. It is served by 17 domestic and foreign airlines including Air Canada, Air Nevada, American Airlines, America West, American Trans Air, Clark Air, Continental Airlines, Delta Air Lines, Hawaiian Air, Northwest

---

With more than 600 daily flights, McCarran International Airport is the 17th busiest facility in the United States.

Airlines, Scenic Airlines, Sky West, Southwest Airlines, Sun Country Airlines, TWA, United Airlines and USAir.

City buses serve the airport, or you can take a **Gray Line** (702-384-1234) shuttle to your Strip or downtown destination.

BY TRAIN

Amtrak (800-872-7245) makes two stops a day on its "Desert Wind" run between Los Angeles and Salt Lake City. The depot is adjacent to the Union Plaza Hotel at 1 Main Street in downtown Las Vegas.

BY BUS

It may not be the quickest way to travel, but taking the bus is usually the least expensive. **Greyhound Bus Lines** (200 South Main Street; 800-231-2222) has a station adjacent to the Union Plaza Hotel in downtown Las Vegas.

Local Transportation

BY BUS

The bus system, **Citizens Area Transit** (702-228-7433), runs buses 24 hours a day from the Hacienda Hotel at the south end of Las Vegas Boulevard (the Strip) to the downtown hotels and to the shopping malls. The Strip-downtown buses run every 15 minutes from 7 a.m. to midnight. Then it's every half-hour until 3 a.m., and every hour from 3 a.m. to 7 a.m. Discounts are available to seniors with a Medicare card.

Another inexpensive way to move up and down the Strip is the **Las Vegas Strip Trolley** (702-382-1404), a classic replica of a San Francisco trolley. It runs daily about every 30 minutes from 9:30 a.m. to 2 a.m., and stops at the main entrances of most hotels. The fare is $1.

TAXIS

Taxis are plentiful but clustered mainly around the hotels and airport. It's often difficult to flag one, so, if you're away from your hotel, it's best to call. The basic rate is $2.20, plus $1.50 per mile. An additional 20 cents per person is charged for the fourth and fifth riders. **Desert Cab** (702-736-1702), **Whittlesea Blue Cab** (702-384-6111) and **Yellow and Checker Cab** (702-873-2227) are the principal operators in the city.

LIMOUSINES

If you want to arrive in style, there are a number of limousine services in town. Most stretch limos feature a wet bar, stereo, television, telephone, moon roof, intercom and, of course, chauffeur. The average cost for a limo and driver is about $22 per hour. A stretch limo will cost between $30 and $40 per hour. A super stretch is available for about $60 an hour. Operators include **Bell Transportation** (702-736-4428), **Presidential Limousine** (702-731-5577) and **Lucky 7 Limousine** (702-739-6177).

CAR RENTALS

Perhaps the best way to see Las Vegas is to drive. The city is laid out in a north-south and east-west grid, with the Strip serving as the main north-south artery, so finding your destination in town is not difficult. A car will also allow you to visit some of the nearby sights, such as Lake Mead, Hoover Dam, Boulder City and Red Rock Canyon, which are all less than a half-hour's drive from the city.

Several rental car companies offer discounts to seniors, usually 10 percent off with an AARP card. Check with **Ajax Car Rental** (702-798-7200), **Value Rent a Car** (702-733-8886), **Budget Car Rental** (702-736-1212), **Dollar Car Rental** (702-739-8408), **Payless Car Rental** (702-739-8488), **Thrifty Car Rental** (702-736-8227) and **Valley Rent A Car** (702-732-8282).

Lodging

Las Vegas is famous for its theme resorts—fantasy-inspired mini-cities containing all the amenities (restaurants, nightlife, recreational facilities) to keep guests from wandering off to other properties. But there are also a number of fine nongambling hotels, mostly in the convention center area, designed with the business traveler and family in mind, all offering first-class accommodations. I've included the best of these neighborhood hotels, located away from the Strip and other tourist areas.

It usually isn't difficult to find a place to stay in a city with more than 87,000 hotel rooms. But during some conventions and holiday weekends the hotels sell out, so it's a good idea to have a reservation before you arrive.

Even if a hotel sells out and you failed to make a reservation, it's often possible to obtain a room. Some guests who have booked rooms never arrive, so you can sometimes find accommodations by approaching hotels after 6 p.m. It's a little risky, especially with your family waiting in an overheated car, but you can often get a room at the last minute.

No matter where you stay you'll find hotel prices among the country's lowest, running nearly half those of other resort and convention cities. Weekday rates often run 20 to 25 percent lower than on weekends. Ask the hotel about its prices for Monday through Thursday arrival.

In *Ultimate Las Vegas and Beyond*, I've chosen the best or most unusual accommodations the city has to offer. To help you match your budget, I've rated them according to price. Rates listed are for high season, weekend, so if you're looking for low-season, weekday or corporate bargains, it's a good idea to inquire.

Budget hotels are generally less than $50 per night for two adults and two children; the rooms are clean and comfortable but lack luxury. *Moderate* hotels run from $50 to $90 and generally provide larger rooms, plusher furniture and more amenities. At a *deluxe* hotel, expect to spend between $90 and $130 and receive a well-appointed room with upscale amenities. For the finest rooms in town, try an *ultra-deluxe* hotel, which will have plush furnishings and all the amenities, and run over $130.

Camping

A few of the hotels provide RV parking and campgrounds for visitors with their own bed and board. The largest are **Circus Circus Hotel & Casino** (2880 Las Vegas Boulevard South; 702-794-3757) and the **Hacienda Hotel** (3950 Las Vegas Boulevard South; 702-739-8911), both on the Strip. The **California Hotel** (12 Ogden Avenue; 702-388-2602) and the **Silver Nugget Casino** (2240 Las Vegas Boulevard North; 702-649-7439) provide similar facilities downtown. **Sam's Town** (4040 South Nellis Avenue; 702-454-8056) has a large RV park about five miles east

---

TIME-SHARE VACATIONS IN LAS VEGAS

Las Vegas has two time-share resorts on the Strip that offer condominium-style accommodations—the Jockey Club (3700 Las Vegas Boulevard South; 702-798-3500) and the Polo Towers (3745 Las Vegas Boulevard South; 702-261-1000). There are also "right to use" time-share vacations at the Sahara Hotel's Safari Club and the Hacienda's Gold Key Club. For information about exchanging your time-share for a vacation in a Las Vegas time-share, contact Interval International (6262 Sunset Drive, Miami, FL 33143; 305-666-1861, 800-622-1861, fax 305-665-2546).

of the Strip, and the new **Boomtown Hotel** (3333 Blue Diamond Road; 702-263-7777) has an RV park three miles south of the Strip off Route 15.

Other campgrounds include **American Campgrounds** (3440 Las Vegas Boulevard North; 702-643-1222); the **Good Sam Hitchin' Post Camper Park** (3640 Las Vegas Boulevard North; 702-644-1043); and the **KOA Las Vegas Resort Kampgrounds** (4315 Boulder Highway; 702-451-5527).

Restaurants

The hotel dining rooms in Las Vegas, particularly the all-you-can-eat buffets, have gained a worldwide reputation for serving inexpensive food. Often overlooked, however, are the hundreds of other restaurants that offer exciting, innovative and oftentimes award-winning cuisine. I've included the best of the hotel restaurants, as well as some exemplary and unusual neighborhood eateries.

The restaurants are grouped by location, with each establishment described as budget, moderate, deluxe or ultra-deluxe in price. Dinner entrées at *budget* restaurants usually cost $8 or less. These include many of the hotel dining rooms and café-style neighborhood restaurants. *Moderate* restaurants range between $8 and $16 for a dinner entrée and typically offer a more varied menu, nicer surroundings and a slower pace. *Deluxe* establishments price their entrées from $16 to $24 and feature sophisticated cuisine, plush decor and more personalized service. *Ultra-deluxe* dining rooms, where $25 will only get you started, include the gourmet dining rooms at the upscale hotels and a few five-star gems along the way.

Most restaurants, except for the upscale, ultra-deluxe dining rooms, have very casual dress requirements, so, even dressed in Bermuda shorts and sneakers you can expect to be seated nearly everywhere.

Shopping

If Las Vegas is truly "Sin City," then shopping here is an arena for all seven Deadly Sins: Avarice and Gluttony, of course; Sloth in the afternoon sun; Pride when you discover a "find" others have overlooked; Envy and Wrath when you hesitate on a set of bargain-priced bone china and lose it to another sharp-eyed shopper; even Lust, for the upscale malls are as much promenades as marketplaces.

Shopping around Las Vegas is a form of entertainment and relaxation, and a great way to get to know the city. The choices range from upscale boutiques and emporiums such as Gucci's, Ungaro's, Saks Fifth Avenue and Neiman-Marcus, to offbeat clothing stores, discount bookstores and hip art galleries.

The history and culture of the region are reflected in the Southwestern and Indian art, crafts and jewelry sold at several well-stocked shops. Local rock and gem dealers specialize in quartz crystals and polished jewelry mined in nearby states. Las Vegas has its own antique guild, made up of two dozen shops, most within a few blocks of each other. Their treasures range from Victorian jewelry and collectibles to jukeboxes, German clocks and retro-chic clothing. There's also a cartel of vintage music stores, selling an intriguing array of albums and tape recordings such as the early Beatles and Fats Waller. A growing Asian population has been the inspiration for shops specializing in Chinese, Japanese and Korean art, as well as crafts and curios.

If you prefer to take home gambling memorabilia, you can pay a visit to one of several dealers who recondition and sell slot machines. You can also buy craps and blackjack tables, roulette wheels, cards, dice, chips—even authentic clothing worn by card dealers, keno runners and croupiers.

This city, unlike, say, San Francisco or Washington, D.C., is spread over a vast area, and there is no "North Beach" or "Georgetown" neighborhood ideal for browsing. So Las Vegas shopping excursions take a little planning. I've identified the city's best shopping destinations—the malls, commercial centers and unique specialty shops—and grouped them by geographic location.

Family Travelers

Once known strictly as an adult playground, Las Vegas is evolving into a travel destination suitable for the entire family. Theme hotels such as the

---

THE LEGACY OF HOWARD HUGHES

A few weeks after Howard Hughes slipped into town on November 27, 1966, he began buying hotels like they were game pieces on a Monopoly board. He also bought an airport, a television station, a huge ranch and 2700 mining claims across the state. Within three years the enigmatic billionaire had invested $300 million in Nevada and become the state's biggest property owner.

Hughes brought more than his wealth to town. He brought corporate respectability to a city that was trying to overcome the stigma of "Bugsy" Siegel, Tony Corneros, Sam Giancana and the dubious Teamsters Union Pension Fund. Because of Hughes' squeaky-clean business reputation, other financiers followed his lead, and new hotels with the MGM, Hilton, Ramada and Holiday Inn trademarks popped up along the Strip. By 1970 the tarnished image of Las Vegas as a mob-connected city was beginning to fade.

Luxor, Treasure Island, MGM Grand, Excalibur and Circus Circus feature attractions just for kids, and several facilities cater to the younger generation. Las Vegas offers a children's museum, zoological park, water park, chocolate factory, a miniature golf course and dozens of other attractions geared to children. These and other activities are described in more detail throughout this book.

An excellent source of information on activities for children is **Las Vegas Kidz Magazine** (4082 Aduana Court, Las Vegas, NV 89103; 702-252-0404), a monthly publication listing southern Nevada activities and events for children. A 180-page book, *Things to Do with Kidz in Las Vegas*, is also available from the same publisher, or at Waldenkids bookstores.

Most hotels in Las Vegas will arrange for babysitters, or you can try the **Las Vegas Babysitting Agency** (1900 Ginger Tree Lane; 702-457-3777), **Around the Clock Child Care** (3867 South Valley View; 702-365-1040), or **Sandy's Sitter Service** (953 East Sahara Avenue; 702-731-2086). Each agency specializes in hotel service and is licensed and bonded. There's even a **Youth Hotel** (3000 Paradise Road; 702-732-5705) at the Las Vegas Hilton featuring meals, adult supervision, indoor and outdoor playgrounds, and girls' and boys' dormitories. Parents who are guests of either the Las Vegas Hilton or the Flamingo Hilton can drop off their children (ages 3 to 18) for anywhere from an hour to a whole weekend (reservations required).

Here are a few general guidelines for traveling with children. Book airline reservations with a travel agent. Agents can reserve bulkhead seats on airlines and determine which flights are least crowded. Bring everything you need on board—diapers, food, toys and extra clothes for kids and parents alike.

Always allow extra time for getting places. Book your accommodations well in advance, and make sure the hotel or motel has the extra crib or cot you require.

A first-aid kit is always a good idea. Ask your pediatrician for special medicines and dosages for colds and diarrhea.

Travelers With Disabilities

Because Las Vegas is a modern city, its facilities—hotels, casinos, restaurants and other buildings—have been built or modified with the disabled in mind. Many hotel-casinos even offer free wheelchairs for guests. The Citizens Area Transit bus system features vehicles that are wheelchair accessible, and the Department of Motor Vehicles provides special parking permits for the disabled. (Disabled drivers from California are allowed to use their permits in Nevada.)

Silver Safari Youth Excursions (3661 South Maryland Parkway; 702-737-6680, 800-245-0028) offers chaperoned tours and expeditions for kids between Memorial Day and Labor Day.

For information on Las Vegas facilities, contact the **Nevada Association for the Handicapped** (6200 West Oakey Boulevard, Las Vegas, NV 89102; 702-870-7050). And **Southern Nevada Sightless** (1001 North Bruce Street, Las Vegas, NV 89101; 702-642-0100) provides general information and transportation assistance.

Information resources for travelers with disabilities include: the **Society for the Advancement of Travel for the Disabled** (347 Fifth Avenue, Suite 610, New York, NY 10016; 212-447-7284), **Travel Information Center** (Moss Rehabilitation Hospital, 12th Street and Tabor Road, Philadelphia, PA 19141; 215-329-5715), **Mobility International USA** (P.O. Box 3551, Eugene, OR 97403; 503-343-1284) and **Flying Wheels Travel** (P.O. Box 382, Owatonna, MN 55060; 800-533-0363). For general travel advice contact **Travelin' Talk** (P.O. Box 3534, Clarksville, TN 37043; 615-552-6670), a networking organization.

Senior Travelers

Because of the city's 24-hour entertainment, inexpensive dining and lodging costs, and outdoor activities such as golf, tennis and water sports, Las Vegas is an ideal destination for older travelers. But, since the city's predisposition is toward low prices for everyone, senior discounts are the exception. Nevertheless a few hotels offer special concessions for seniors. Be sure to ask your travel agent when booking reservations, or check with the **Las Vegas Convention and Visitors Authority** (3150 Paradise Road; 707-733-2244).

The **American Association of Retired Persons** (AARP) (1909 K Street, NW, Washington, DC 22049; 202-872-4700) offers members travel discounts and provides escorted tours. For those 60 and over, **Elderhostel** (75 Federal Street, Boston, MA 02110; 617-426-7788) offers educational programs about southern Nevada.

Be extra careful about health matters. Bring any medications you use, along with the prescriptions. Consider carrying a medical record with you—including your current medical status and medical history, as well as your doctor's name, phone number and address. Also be sure to confirm that your insurance covers you away from home.

Foreign Travelers

PASSPORTS AND VISAS   Most foreign visitors are required to obtain a passport and tourist visa to enter the United States. Contact your nearest United States embassy or consulate well in advance to obtain a visa and to check on any other requirements.

It is the policy of the United States government to complete customs and immigration formalities at the first point of arrival in the United States, even though such entry point may be only an intermediate stop en route to your destination.

CUSTOMS REQUIREMENTS   Foreign travelers are allowed to carry in: 200 cigarettes (or 100 cigars) and $400 worth of duty-free gifts, including one liter of alcohol (you must be 21 years of age to bring in alcohol). You may bring in any amount of currency, but you must fill out a form if you bring in more than U.S. $10,000. Carry any prescription drugs in clearly marked containers. (You may have to produce a written prescription or doctor's statement for the customs officer.) You are not permitted to bring meat or meat products, seeds, plants, fruit and narcotics into the United States. Contact the **United States Customs Service** (1301 Constitution Avenue, Northwest, Washington, DC 20229; 202-566-8195) for further information.

DRIVING   If you plan to rent a car, you should obtain an international driver's license before arriving in Nevada. Some rental companies require both a foreign license and an international license. Many car rental agencies require a lessee to be 25 years of age; all require a major credit card.

CURRENCY   United States money is based on the dollar. Bills come in six denominations: $1, $5, $10, $20, $50 and $100. Every dollar is divided into 100 cents. Coins are the penny (1 cent), nickel (5 cents), dime (10 cents) and quarter (25 cents). Half-dollar and dollar coins are often used in the casinos. You may not use foreign currency to purchase goods and services in the United States. You may, however, exchange your currency at many of the major banks and hotels. Other locations include: **American Express Financial Services** in Caesars Palace (3570 South Las Vegas Boulevard; 702-731-7705); **Foreign Money Exchange** (3025 South Las Vegas Boulevard; 702-791-3301); and **America Foreign Exchange** in the Hilton Hotel (3000 Paradise Road; 702-892-0100). You should consider buying traveler's checks in dollar amounts. You may also use credit cards affiliated with an American company such as Interbank, Barclay Card or American Express.

ELECTRICITY   Electric outlets use currents of 110 volts, 60 cycles. For appliances made for other electrical systems, you will need to use a transformer or other adapter.

TWO

The Strip Area

The famed Las Vegas Strip is a mecca of sights and sounds that vary from
the sublime to the exotic, from the outrageous to the bewildering. Here
you can gape at the largest resort hotels in the world or at the world's
largest collection of tacky souvenirs.

You can watch cigars being made, leave offerings at a Brahma shrine,
or visit a church where gamblers pray for luck—or salvation—and leave
casino chips in the collection basket. You can marvel at soaring neon
architecture or the handcrafted treasures of Southwest Native Americans. You can take an ersatz archaeological ride, explore a replica of
King Tut's tomb or watch buccaneers wage a mock sea battle.

Of the world's 13 largest resort hotels, all are located on the Strip,
except the Hilton Hawaiian Village in Waikiki. The most recent editions—
Luxor, Treasure Island and the MGM Grand—opened over a ten-week
span in late 1993, adding more than 10,000 guest rooms to the city's
roster. More important, the resorts' themes and attractions—packaged
by designer-label architects and special effects masters—signaled the
town's commitment to offering a wider range of interactive, family-
friendly entertainment.

Most of the year, you can take in the sights on foot any time of day.
During July and August, the hottest summer months, try the cooler
hours of morning and evening. A walking tour of the entire Strip is
easily a six-mile hike, so you might want to take it in two or three doses.
And be sure you have comfortable walking shoes.

The weary-if-not-wise who want an overview before setting off on
foot might consider a guided tour. The ubiquitous **Gray Line Tours**
(1550 Industrial Road; 702-384-1234), **Guaranteed Tours** (3734 Las

The diamond-shaped "Welcome to Fabulous Las Vegas" sign south of the Hacienda Hotel has been greeting visitors since the early 1950s.

Vegas Boulevard South; 702-369-1000) and **Ray and Ross Transport** (300 West Owens Avenue; 702-646-4661) offer daytime tours of city sights and nightlife after dark.

At the southern end of the Strip, at Tropicana Boulevard, is the pyramid-shaped **Luxor Hotel** (3900 Las Vegas Boulevard South; 702-262-4000), which carries its Egyptian theme throughout the 47-acre, 2526-room resort. The entrance is guarded by a sandstone obelisk etched with hieroglyphics that towers over Karnak Lake, a lagoon surrounded by reeds, palm trees, rock formations and statues of pharaohs. The hotel's porte cochere is a ten-story sphinx that crouches above a rock-and-stone entrance. At night, green laser beams from the sphinx's eyes strike the obelisk and lake, causing the water to boil and rise in a screen-like fountain, on which video holograms of ancient Egypt are projected.

The 30-story (350-foot) pyramid is shrouded in dark glass, with its apex containing a 40-billion-candlepower beacon (the world's strongest), which sends a shaft of light more than ten miles into space at night. Inside, the pyramid's atrium is large enough to stack nine Boeing 747s, and features three levels of dining, entertainment and gambling. Guest rooms are built into the pyramid's sloping walls and are reached by "inclinators," elevators that rise at a 39-degree angle, leaving passengers feeling like they're on an enclosed ski lift. A narrow, 1700-foot canal—the river Nile—encircles the interior of the pyramid, which is tastefully decorated with deep-red carpeting, sandstone walls, faux palm trees, Egyptian statues and hieroglyphic-inscribed tapestry.

For a peek into Egypt's past, visit **King Tut's Tomb and Museum** (admission), an accurate reproduction of Howard Carter's 1922 find, often called the archaeological discovery of modern history. After you watch a five-minute video of Tutankhamen's life, guides escort you through the tomb's antechamber, burial chamber and treasury room, where you'll see more than 500 replicas of mummies, Egyptian furniture, a chariot, pottery, baskets, jewelry, linens and other artifacts. For those impressed, the gift shop sells Egyptian antiquities and keepsakes.

For a more hands-on excursion through time, try **Secrets of the Luxor Pyramid** (admission), a simulated adventure trilogy designed by special effects guru Douglas Trumbull (*Blade Runner*, *2001: A Space Odyssey* and *Close Encounters of the Third Kind*). The two-hour show has a kind of *Star Wars* meets *Indiana Jones* story line, enhanced by motion simulators, 3-D projectors, a time machine and a steeply-raked theater with a seven-story screen.

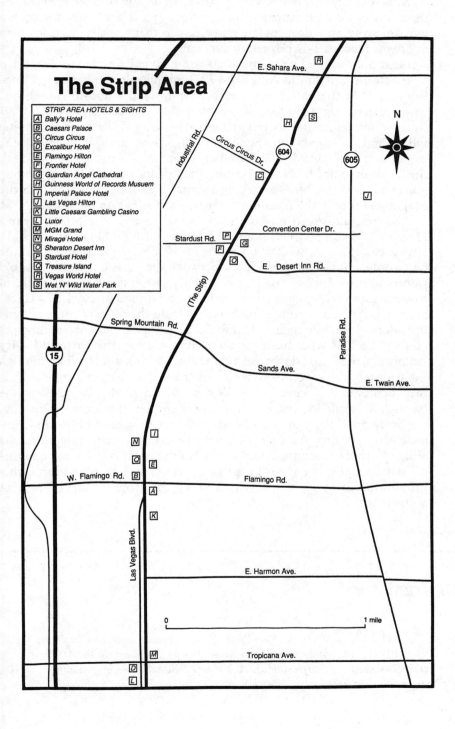

The Strip Area

STRIP AREA HOTELS & SIGHTS
- A Bally's Hotel
- B Caesars Palace
- C Circus Circus
- D Excalibur Hotel
- E Flamingo Hilton
- F Frontier Hotel
- G Guardian Angel Cathedral
- H Guinness World of Records Musuem
- I Imperial Palace Hotel
- J Las Vegas Hilton
- K Little Caesars Gambling Casino
- L Luxor
- M MGM Grand
- N Mirage Hotel
- O Sheraton Desert Inn
- P Stardust Hotel
- Q Treasure Island
- R Vegas World Hotel
- S Wet 'N' Wild Water Park

E. Sahara Ave.

Industrial Rd.

Circus Circus Dr.

604

605

Convention Center Dr.

Stardust Rd.

E. Desert Inn Rd.

(The Strip)

Paradise Rd.

Spring Mountain Rd.

15

Sands Ave.

E. Twain Ave.

W. Flamingo Rd.

Flamingo Rd.

Las Vegas Blvd.

E. Harmon Ave.

0   1 mile

Tropicana Ave.

N

Kids will enjoy Luxor's **VirtuaLand**, an arcade of Sega Enterprises' most advanced amusement games, including a flight simulator with a gyro-moving, spherical cockpit and race cars that actually twist and turn as drivers react to 3-D images on a screen.

Next door to the Luxor, the 4000-room **Excalibur Hotel** (3850 Las Vegas Boulevard South; 702-597-7777) is built to resemble an old English castle. At the entrance are turrets, spires and a 265-foot-high bell tower that stands guard over the moat. Inside, in addition to a 100,000-square-foot casino and six restaurants, there are a Renaissance shopping village and a dungeon "fun zone" for kids, complete with video arcade, games and a Magic Motion Simulator that takes you on the high-tech thrill ride of your life. Not to be outdone by pirate battles and exploding volcanos, a 51-foot fire-breathing robotic dragon battles a Merlin the Magician robot in the Excalibur's moat, every night on the hour.

The emerald-green monolith across the street is the **MGM Grand Hotel** (3799 Las Vegas Boulevard South; 702-891-1111), the world's largest resort hotel, with 5005 rooms, a *Wizard of Oz* theme, and the city's only amusement park. Enter between the paws of an 88-foot gold stucco lion to discover the Emerald City, a six-story crystal castle of towering, twinkling spires, surrounded by a haunted forest, 12,000 blossoming poppies and animated characters from the *Wizard of Oz*, all under a domed rainbow ceiling of fluffy clouds, complete with silver linings, of course. To find what lies over the rainbow, enter the **Emerald City** (admission), and stroll down the Yellow Brick Road, which winds through the haunted forest, complete with eerie trees that suggest tormented human figures and a wisecracking Wicked Witch of the West. Continue through a cornfield where you'll find friendlier characters—Dorothy, the Scarecrow, the Tin Woodsman and the Cowardly Lion—who serenade you with songs and dialogue from the classic motion picture. Enter the Wizard's inner sanctum, a golden portal lined with magic books, mystical statues and other wizardly artifacts, and complete your tour with a motion simulator trip to Oz, which ends as the professor flies off in a hot air balloon.

THE STRIP

*The stretch of Las Vegas Boulevard from Sahara Avenue south was originally Highway 91, commonly known as the Los Angeles Highway. In the 1950s it was nicknamed the **Strip**—after L.A.'s famed Sunset Strip—by gambling executive Guy McAfee, a former Los Angeles police officer.*

Believe it or not, Vegas has more churches per capita than any other American city.

Kids also like the MGM Grand's **Oz Midway** with its candy-colored, swirling carnival motif. In addition to time-tested arcade games such as ring tossing, target shooting and ball rolling, you'll find wizardly challenges like the Ruby Slippers Pitch, a horse race game with a horse of a different color, a haunted forest squirt gun game and Wack-E-Witch, where contestants try to whack a wicked witch with airballs fired from an "EXT Terminator" gun. There are also a motorcycle game in which riders are video-linked so they can compete against each other and eight virtual reality games, complete with head-monitor helmets that can be linked so players can enjoy the same game.

At the rear of the MGM Grand Hotel, **Grand Adventures Theme Park** (3799 Las Vegas Boulevard South; 702-891-7979; admission) contains 33 acres of adventure rides, shows, theme streets, shops and restaurants. Built by Duell Corporation—the architect of non-Disney theme parks such as Sea World and Six Flags Magic Mountain—Grand Adventures was inspired by MGM's famous back lot in Los Angeles. Allow five to six hours for the rides and shows, with less walking than in most theme parks—it's about one-tenth the size of Disneyland. The park is divided into theme areas with movie-set streets and buildings, artificial lakes and rivers and plenty of strolling cartoon and *Wizard of Oz* characters. The best rides and attractions include:

Lightning Bolt: This indoor roller coaster ride lasts only a minute, but its special effects are great, hurtling you through "outer space," a meteor shower, gas nebulas, the Black Hole and the eerie Altered Space. Appropriately, the ride touches down on Las Vegas at Night, a miniature sculpture of the Strip's skyline.

Deep Earth Exploration: Burrow beneath the Nevada Test Site, where dozens of nuclear bombs were detonated during the 1950s, in a motion simulator capsule enhanced by high-tech audiovisual effects and state-of-the-art animation. Rock slides, cavern gorges, a crystallized frozen lake with menacing mutant creatures, a molten lava bed and an erupting volcano make the trip memorable.

Back Lot River Tour: A hapless tour guide "inadvertently" steers your boat through a lava flow, a monster-infested swamp and a war zone, where a helicopter gunship takes a few shots at you with an M-80.

Haunted Mine: Ride an ore car through an ancient Indian mine haunted by skeletons, ghosts, booby traps and robotic rats. The blacklight effects, dynamite blasts and animated creatures are convincing, although the giant spider generates more laughs than screams.

Grand Canyon Rapids: Churn through white-water rapids and a Lost Cavern in a free-floating, nine-seat inner tube. Curiously, the rafting trip ends with a bank robbery in which robots shoot at each other.

Dueling Pirates: Breakaway masts, exploding towers, sharks, stunts and swashbuckling swordplay thrill audiences in the outdoor Pirate's Cove Theater.

You're in the Movies: Audience members are selected, costumed and given their scripts for performances that are electronically mixed with pre-filmed scenes for this high-tech version of Coney Island photo cutouts.

Magic Screen Theater: The Three Stooges show (produced by Moe Howard's grandson Jeffrey Scott) is a combination of live-action look-alikes and vintage video clips for a nostalgic visit with the famous slapstick trio.

The park also features sidewalk street dancers, strolling gunfighters, and a lagoon where you can rent miniature radio-controlled boats. Take a break and relax at the Rio Grande Cantina, an outdoor garden with live entertainment, or refuel at a gourmet coffee and pastry shop, pizzeria, ice-cream parlor or fast-food eatery (there are half a dozen).

Bally's Hotel (3645 Las Vegas Boulevard South; 702-739-4111) was originally built as the MGM Grand in 1973. The hotel was the site of the city's worst disaster in 1981, when a fire swept through it, killing 87 people and injuring 700. The hotel reopened nine months later with a new sprinkler system (they previously weren't required) and other safety devices. Bally's bought the hotel in 1986 and retained the Hollywood motif. Downstairs, past the huge casino, is a shopping arcade, the largest of any in a hotel, with several art galleries, a Hollywood memorabilia shop and a delightful ice-cream parlor.

Moving north along the Strip, plan a stop at **Caesars Palace** (3570 Las Vegas Boulevard South; 702-731-7110). Notice that the people-moving sidewalks on either side of the entrance carry you into but not out of the casino. As the walkway glides between faux Roman aque-

---

THE TRAVELER'S GUARDIAN ANGEL

*Of the many churches in Las Vegas, the **Guardian Angel Church** (302 East Desert Inn Road; 702-735-5241), a huge A-frame cathedral with flying buttress support columns attracts the largest percentage of tourists for worship. It's not certain whether worshipers come to pray for luck or for forgiveness, but the priest, Father Anderson, is known to occasionally lay down a bet himself, usually on football.*

There's no apostrophe in "Caesars" Palace because its developer, Jay Sarno, wanted every guest to feel like a Caesar.

---

ducts, booming martial music heralds your arrival, and a recorded voice assures you the slot machines are friendly.

To the right of the main fountain—the one Evel Knievel's son vaulted with his motorcycle in 1989—is a **Brahma Shrine**, where visitors from the East actually worship and leave offerings of fruit and flowers. The bronze statue of Brahma, with four beneficent faces at the center, is flanked by hundreds of carved elephants.

Inside, the **Omnimax Theater** is a gigantic dome designed to surround movie audiences with sound and pictures. The futuristic theater features 98 speakers and several projection screens, even on the ceiling, creating an incredible movie experience.

At the north end of the Caesars Palace casino is **The Forum Shops** (3500 Las Vegas Boulevard South; 702-893-4800), which follows the hotel's Roman motif of marble statues, arches and columns, and fountains with dancing jets of water. But the mall ventures even further into the realm of make-believe with a hand-painted ceiling that reproduces the Mediterranean sky, changing color to reflect the time of day. Accompanied by smoke and music, lasers make four Roman statues "come to life" during a five-minute show twice an hour.

Next door is the **Mirage Hotel** (3400 Las Vegas Boulevard South; 702-791-7111), famous for its erupting volcano atop a 54-foot-tall artificial mountain. The spectacle, which you can watch from the sidewalk, takes place every half hour after dark, spewing fire and smoke onto the mountain's waterfalls and palm trees and into the surrounding lagoon. Walk indoors, and behind the registration desk you'll find a 20,000-gallon aquarium containing multicolored fish and pygmy sharks. If the air feels heavy at the casino entrance that's because of the tropical rainforest, climate-controlled for the orchids, Canary Island date palms and other tropical plants. Maintaining the forest costs $1 million per year. A short walk from the atrium is a glass-enclosed habitat for Siegfried and Roy's white tigers.

The Mirage's sister hotel, **Treasure Island** (3300 Las Vegas Boulevard South; 702-894-7111, 800-627-6667) fronts the Strip with a replica of an 18th-century sea village, surrounded by rock cliffs, shrubs, palm trees, and nautical artifacts, all perched atop Buccaneer Bay, a bluewater lagoon. Two fully rigged ships—a pirate galleon and a British frigate—moored and anchored in the bay, play out for a mock sea battle every 90 minutes beginning in the late afternoon. The show fills the sidewalk with onlookers, who marvel at the cannons blazing, masts top-

---

If all the glass tubing used in Las Vegas neon signs were straightened and laid out end to end, it would stretch for 15,000 miles.

---

pling, powder kegs exploding and stunt actors leaping into the lagoon. The hotel's pirate theme continues inside with 18th-century bas-relief art on the ceilings, overflowing treasure chests on the walls and black carpet decorated with colorful images of jewels, gold doubloons and rope chains. Kids become buccaneers in **Mutiny Bay**, an arcade disguised as a dark, cavernous castle, with skeletons in stone alcoves, treasure chests filled with gold pieces and jewelry, and piped-in sounds of a pirate village.

Across the street is **Little Caesars Gambling Casino** (3665 Las Vegas Boulevard South; 702-734-2827), whose sports book is a throwback to the old days of the smoke-filled gambling hall. Despite its size, the casino has a reputation for "no-limit" betting. It is here that Bob Stupak, flamboyant owner of the Vegas World Hotel, bet $1 million on the 1989 Super Bowl, and won.

Magicians are a staple in nearly two dozen Vegas shows and lounge acts, and you can sample a history of the magical art at the **Magic and Movie Hall of Fame** (3555 Las Vegas Boulevard South; 702-792-0777; admission) in O'Shea's Casino. The 20,000-square-foot hands-on museum is home to a fascinating collection of turn-of-the-century arcade games, movie memorabilia and sleight-of-hand artifacts used by magic's past masters. Among the vintage arcade games are mechanical fortune-tellers, strength testers and a hand-crank magic show in which an onstage magician performs a disappearing act with a female assistant. You'll also find the leather straitjacket and milk can that Houdini escaped from while he was submerged and handcuffed, a replica of the famous Chinese torture cell, a life-size cutout of Harry Kellar next to the levitation table he used to "float" Princess Karnak, and Sevais Le Roy's "cremation" coffin.

Car buffs will like the **Imperial Palace Hotel Auto Collection** (3535 Las Vegas Boulevard South; 702-731-3311; admission) next door, displaying more than 200 antique, classic and special-interest cars. Included are a 1947 Tucker (one of just 51 manufactured before the company went out of business), the 1939 Mercedes Benz that was custom-built for Adolf Hitler, the 1939 Alfa Romeo given by Benito Mussolini to his mistress, a 1910 Thomas Flyer and a 1954 Corvette.

The Bambino loved a good cigar. You can watch experts produce handmade ones at **Don Pablo Cigar Company** (3025 Las Vegas Boulevard South, Suite 117; 702-369-1818). Using a variety of leaves from five foreign countries, the master cigar traders, who learned their craft on plantations in Cuba, produce about 500 "ropes" a day. Custom blends and other tobacco are available for sale.

It's an easy walk to the midway at **Circus Circus** (2880 Las Vegas Boulevard South; 702-734-0410), replete with carnival games and circus acts. The midway is open to all.

Protected by a climate-controlled, pink-glass dome, **Grand Slam Canyon** (2880 Las Vegas Boulevard South; 702-734-0410; admission) at Circus Circus is a five-acre amusement park set amid lush vegetation, a 90-foot waterfall, faux Native American cliff dwellings, Flintstone-style mountain peaks, and animated spitting dinosaurs stuck in fake tar pits. Rides include a double-loop, double-corkscrew roller coaster (the only one of its kind indoors), a water-flume ride and two tubular slides. There's also a replica of a stratified fossil wall and a collection of pretend dinosaur bones. The most popular attraction is Hot Shots laser tag, played with noninjury laser guns in a black-lit room.

Movie buffs can glimpse Hollywood's Golden Age at the **Debbie Reynolds Hollywood Hotel & Movie Museum** (305 Convention Center Drive; 702-734-0711), which displays memorabilia from Reynolds' fabled MGM prop and costume collection. In the hotel lobby, Baccarat crystal chandeliers (from *The Great Waltz*) glow above marble-topped consoles (from *Camille* and *Marie Antoinette*), a brocade, high-backed ottoman (from *Grand Hotel*) and Harold Lloyd's vintage Steinway player piano, one of only four in existence. Stroll along the "Hollywood Walk of Fame" with life-size, costumed figures of Laurel and Hardy, and Mae West in an elegant, black velvet evening gown, low-cut, of course. Among the tableaux and exhibits in Reynolds' **Movie Museum** (admission) are Elizabeth Taylor's headdress from *Cleopatra*, Shirley Temple's dress from *The Littlest Rebel*, Doris Day's mermaid costume from *Glass Bottom Boat*, Esther Williams' sequinned, blue-and-silver swimsuit from *Deep in My*

SIGN LANGUAGE

*Most of Las Vegas' famous neon signs were created and built by the **Young Electric Sign Company** (5119 Cameron Street; 702-876-8080), which has been putting the glitter into Glitter Gulch since the 1940s. YESCO, as it is called, built the city's first neon sign for the old Boulder Club downtown—a 40-foot-high, freestanding sign with vertical letters. Later came the famous Vegas Vic cowboy over the Pioneer Club. Other neon masterpieces include the 222-foot-high Sahara Hotel sign and Circus Circus' Lucky the Clown, the largest neon sign in terms of square footage. Other YESCO bright spots include the signs at Binion's Horseshoe, the Fremont, Four Queens, the Sands, Bally's and the Tropicana.*

Heart, and Bob Hope's gold lamé and rhinestone-studded tuxedo from *Here Come the Girls.*

Even if you haven't read the book, you might want to see the show at the **Guinness World of Records Museum** (2780 Las Vegas Boulevard South; 702-792-3766; admission). Consisting of displays, replicas, videos and interactive computers, the museum highlights world's records: the tallest, fattest, oldest and most married man; the most poisonous jellyfish; the most tattooed woman; and some of the strange events that shaped Las Vegas, such as the swim-up craps table and the time a nuclear bomb was shot from a cannon.

The only nonhotel chapel on the Strip, the **Candlelight Wedding Chapel** (2855 Las Vegas Boulevard South; 702-735-4179), is a quaint, A-frame chalet with a steeple, knotty-pine walls, vaulted ceilings, white pews, arched windows and a marble altar. Despite its less-than-romantic location—it's flanked by a car rental agency and the Circus clowns—more weddings are performed here than at any other chapel in the city.

During the summer months, the 26-acre **Wet 'n' Wild Water Park** (2601 Las Vegas Boulevard South; 702-737-3819; admission) is a great place to cool off. You can swim or float on rafts in the lagoons and Lazy River, or challenge the world's tallest water slide (76 feet), the water roller coaster or the 500,000-gallon wave-making machine. The park also includes a snack bar, picnic grounds, a gift shop and a children's playground.

Technically, the Strip ends at Sahara Avenue, with the stretch of Las Vegas Boulevard running to downtown a kind of no-man's-land. Appropriately, it is here you will find Bob Stupak's **Vegas World Hotel** (2000 Las Vegas Boulevard South; 702-382-2000), which takes gaudy to new heights—beyond the atmosphere. The lobby area looks like a set from *Star Wars.* There's a 40-foot ceiling decorated with a fiber-optic replica of the solar system, complete with skylab and life-size model astronauts. Near the keno machines at the rear entrance you'll find $1 million displayed in a glass booth. The towering concrete "tripod" adjacent to the hotel is Stupak's new Stratosphere Tower, which will be the tallest structure in the country at 1012 feet when completed in mid-1995. Planned amenities include a revolving restaurant, observation decks and four wedding chapels.

Lodging

The first hotel motorists from California see upon entering the city is **Vacation Village** (6711 Las Vegas Boulevard South; 702-897-1700, 800-338-0608, fax 702-361-6726), a low-profile, Southwestern-style, 360-room resort about three miles south of the actual Strip. Because it is so far from the action, the hotel relies on budget-priced accommodations and food to attract guests. The bright and airy rooms feature Southwestern patterns and pastels, light-wood furniture and a plastic saguaro cactus for atmosphere. Hotel amenities include four restaurants, three bars, a cabaret lounge and an outdoor pool overlooking the surrounding desertscape.

With its new 700-room tower, the **Hacienda Hotel** (3950 Las Vegas Boulevard South; 702-739-8911, 800-634-6713, fax 702-891-8240) has outgrown its "motor court" image and now successfully competes with the larger hotels. The resort's decor reflects a Southwest theme, with adobe arches, Mexican tile and Aztec carpeting in the lobby. The tower rooms are similarly decorated, while the original 450 garden rooms are more motel-like with tired tan-and-brown color schemes, and wood and faux-leather furnishings. The hotel features a good steak house and a theater for live entertainment. The pool area is one of the nicest in town; it's landscaped with towering palm trees and lush plants and features a tropical bar and poolside service. Budget.

The Egyptian-theme **Luxor** (3900 Las Vegas Boulevard South; 702-262-4000, 800-288-1000, fax 702-262-4452) features 2526 rooms and suites that cling to the inside walls of the 30-story, pyramid-shaped hotel. Each room has a sloped wall and bank of windows with views of the Strip and surrounding mountains, and a door that opens to overlook the pyramid's interior atrium. The Egyptian-inspired decor features medium brown wooden furniture etched with Egyptian characters. There's a touch of elegance in the registration area with its seamless onyx counter decorated with gold Egyptian designs, softly lit palm-tree sculpture and brightly colored murals of Egyptian street scenes. After check-in, hotel guests are ferried by barge along an interior canal to the pyramid's four "inclinators," which transport them at a 39-degree angle to the upper floors. Hotel amenities include a pool, seven restaurants, a 100,000-

---

HOWARD HUGHES' HIDEAWAY

*From 1966 to 1970, the **Desert Inn** was where billionaire Howard Hughes hid from the world. In 1970, when he and his nongambling Mormon entourage were asked to give up the ninth-floor penthouses customarily reserved for high rollers, Hughes bought the hotel for $13.25 million.*

You can tour Hughes' two-room penthouse, but you need to mentally remove the plush furnishings to get a sense of the spartan surroundings in which the reclusive billionaire spent four years of his life. On your visit, you'll learn how Hughes lived behind sealed windows, with just a few cots and piles of newspapers as his decor.

The 5005-room MGM Grand, the world's largest resort hotel, has more employees—7700—than guest rooms.

---

square-foot casino, a cluster of shops, an action adventure trilogy that uses virtual reality technology and special effects, a full-sized replica of King Tut's tomb, and a nightly production show in an 1100-seat showroom. Moderate.

Next door, the 4032-room **Excalibur** (3850 Las Vegas Boulevard South; 702-597-7777, 800-937-7777, fax 702-597-7040) is connected to its cousin, Luxor, by a bullet-shaped tram. The hotel's medieval castle theme is reflected in the fantasyland spires, drawbridge walkway (over a moat), cobblestone foyer and rock-walled atrium graced by a three-story-high fountain. The massive registration desk is flanked by suits of armor and decorated in red-on-red carpeting and wall coverings. The rooms are done in bold reds, blues and greens, and feature dark wood furniture and wrought-iron fixtures. Amenities include seven restaurants, two production shows, a motion simulator theater, a shopping arcade, carnival games for kids, two pools and a 100,000-square-foot casino. Like its other cousin, Circus Circus, the Excalibur caters mostly to families and is usually packed. Moderate.

An island paradise might best describe the **Tropicana Hotel** (3801 Las Vegas Boulevard South; 702-739-2222, 800-634-4000, fax 702-739-2469). At the entrance to the 1900-room resort are two 35-foot-tall Maori gods, a waterfall, outrigger canoes, palm trees, a lagoon and a Polynesian long-house, which often hosts Hawaiian entertainment. Between the hotel's twin towers is a five-acre water park featuring three pools, a 110-foot waterslide, five spas, two lagoons, tropical plants and exotic flowers. The rooms are decorated with colorful prints and wood-and-bamboo furnishings. Among the amenities offered are three restaurants, a comedy club, a small cluster of shops and the long-running Folies Bergere production show. One of the Folies showgirls will escort you on a Backstage Tour (admission) of the sets, scenery and "feather room" where the elaborate costumes are kept. Exhibits and displays on the 40-minute tour also tell the history behind Folies Bergere, which began its Vegas run in 1959. Moderate to deluxe.

Built at a cost of $1 billion, the **MGM Grand Hotel** (3799 Las Vegas Boulevard South; 702-891-1111, 800-929-1111, fax 702-891-3036) is the world's largest, with 5005 rooms and suites honeycombed in four emerald-green towers. The massive lobby features a brass registration desk, behind which sits an 80-panel video screen that flashes panoramic images of desert scenes, baseball stadiums and advertisements. Waiting guests can sit beneath a circular dome adorned with gold panels and bright red ceiling, while high rollers can follow the red carpet to a glassed VIP registration area. Most of the moderate- to deluxe-priced guest rooms follow the hotel's *Wizard of Oz* motif, with emerald carpeting, gold-crown moldings, red poppy linens and prints of scenes from the movie. Of the hotel's 750 suites, about half are really oversized rooms with a sofa and two TVs; others perch on the 29th floor, fill 3000 square feet in a split-level design and are served by one butler and up to 27 telephones. Hotel amenities include a pool area the size of four football fields, nine restaurants, two headliner theaters, a 15,000-seat events arena, tennis courts and a 33-acre theme park. Families will like the King Looey Youth Activity center, a day-care facility open to the 3- to 16-year-old children of hotel guests. In addition to adult supervision, the center has every toy imaginable, from Duplo building blocks for preschoolers to Ping-Pong and Super Nintendo for preteens.

The **Ramada Hotel San Remo** (115 East Tropicana Avenue; 702-739-9000, 800-522-7366, fax 702-736-1120) offers affordable elegance. A high-arched ceiling and crystal chandeliers in the casino help the hotel live up to its Southern Riviera namesake. The 711 rooms in the twin silver-and-gold towers are modern affairs with plush blue carpeting and dark hardwood furniture. Hotel amenities include five restaurants, a large pool and a Parisian-style cabaret. Moderate.

Because it doesn't have a casino, the **Carriage House** (105 East Harmon Avenue; 702-798-1020, 800-777-1700, fax 702-798-1020, "Attn: Reservations") is often overlooked by visitors. But the 140-room hotel offers some of the best accommodations in the city. The tasteful, moderately priced rooms are among the best buys in town and feature plush

---

THE RIGHT STUFF

*Located between the Strip and downtown, **Vegas World** (2000 Las Vegas Boulevard South; 702-382-2000, 800-634-6277, fax 702-383-4750) suggests a "Lost in Space" theme. On one tower facade is a mural featuring a space-walking astronaut tethered to a roulette-wheel/space station. Another wall has drawings of the lunar surface, Saturn and other planets. Perched over the casino are models of Titan and Vanguard missiles. Inside, astronauts and lunar modules dangle from the casino's ceiling, which faithfully reproduces the night sky, complete with fiber-optic stars. It gets even better in the guest rooms: plush silver carpeting, silver wallpaper, gray-and-white-patterned spreads and curtains, and chrome-and-white table and chairs—all suggesting the inside of Skylab. The hotel has two restaurants, a pool and a 1200-seat showroom. Vegas World is definitely worth visiting, if not for the budget-priced accommodations, then to reaffirm your belief that anything is possible.*

carpeting, midwest tile, grass-paper wall covering, ivory enamel furniture and overstuffed sofas and love seats. The relaxing lobby is decorated in cool grays and blues and furnished with provincial sofas and tables. The ninth-floor restaurant, Kiefer's, offers unobstructed views of the city and the MGM Grand Hotel and Theme Park. Outside, the tennis court, pool and sundeck are landscaped with pine trees.

When the **Alexis Park** (375 East Harmon Avenue; 702-796-3300, 800-582-2228, fax 702-796-4334) was built in 1985, critics predicted the nongambling resort would never survive. The critics are now eating humble pie: The Alexis Park proved that a Las Vegas hotel without a casino could not only survive but also prosper. Situated on 20 acres of lush greenery, streams and waterfalls, the Mediterranean-style villa in white stucco and red tile is one of the city's showplaces. The lobby suggests European elegance with its Spanish tile floor, overstuffed chairs, French telephones and striped canopies over the onyx-topped registration desk. The 500 ultra-deluxe-priced suites are available in ten floor plans. Furnishings range from Victorian (pecan armoires, flower-print ottomans, mahogany dining sets) to Southwest modern (adobe walls, club chairs, macramé wallhangings). Some have fireplaces and jacuzzis. Recreational facilities include three swimming pools, tennis courts and health spa. The four-star Pegasus restaurant, coffee shop and lounge round out the amenities.

From the outside, the **St. Tropez Hotel** (455 East Harmon Avenue; 702-369-5400, 800-666-5400, fax 702-369-5400, "Attn: Room Reservations") looks like a Palm Springs resort, with its pink stucco walls, red tile roof, palm trees and lush landscaping. Inside, the mission-style hotel features luxurious rooms at moderate prices. Most are decorated in soft

---

THE BEAT GOES ON

Shortly after Mirage Resorts blew up the defunct Dunes Hotel to signal the opening of its Treasure Island resort in late 1993, it announced a joint venture with Gold Strike Casinos to build a new 3000-room low-roller resort on 43 acres at the south end of the 164-acre Dunes site. Mirage also plans a more luxurious, Fontainbleau-style resort for the Flamingo Road end of the property. And Sheraton has unveiled plans for the Desert Kingdom, a $750 million, 3500-room megaresort to be built on 34 acres adjacent to its Desert Inn. It will incorporate the fantasyland amenities found in the new theme resorts—a free outdoor show, spires and turrets, hands-on entertainment, even a river running through the property. When completed in early 1997, the new hotels will add about 10,000 rooms to the city, pushing the total to nearly 100,000.

pastels with dark wood furniture and overstuffed couches. Some have four-poster canopy beds with country quilts, Roman tubs, jacuzzis and VCRs. The inviting pool area is surrounded by trees and gardens.

A throwback to Las Vegas of the 1950s is the 200-room **Holiday Inn Boardwalk** (3750 Las Vegas Boulevard South; 702-735-1167, 800-465-4329). The neon-lit, winged marquee in front is original, as are the jukebox and vintage slot machines in the cramped casino. But the budget-priced rooms are clean and tastefully decorated, and the grill and counter serve up bargain-priced breakfasts and burgers. There's nothing fancy here, but it's an easy walk to the major Strip hotels.

Fitness lovers will enjoy the recreational facilities at the 1100-room **Aladdin Hotel** (3667 Las Vegas Boulevard South; 702-736-0111, 800-634-3424, fax 702-734-3583). Its rooftop recreation center features lit tennis courts, a large pool and a snack bar. Famous for its spectacularly lit porte cochere, the hotel also boasts a casino highlighted by oversized lead-glass chandeliers. Most of the rooms are spacious, with wheat-colored upholstery and linen, white wood furniture and brass accessories. Hotel amenities include five restaurants, a shopping arcade, a comedy club, a production show and a 7000-seat performing arts theater. Prices are in the moderate range.

Bally's Hotel (3645 Las Vegas Boulevard South; 702-739-4111, 800-634-3434, fax 702-794-2413) originally opened in 1973 as the MGM Grand Hotel and retains its Hollywood roots. Guest rooms have brass stars on the door, and photos of legendary MGM stars grace the hallways. The 2832 spacious rooms—probably the largest in Las Vegas—are primarily decorated in California modern: overstuffed furniture and mushroom coffee tables. Amenities of the 26-story hotel include six restaurants, two showrooms, a 40-store shopping arcade, a movie theater, a large pool area, tennis courts and a health club. Moderate.

Turn-of-the-century San Francisco is the motif at the **Barbary Coast Hotel** (3595 Las Vegas Boulevard South; 702-737-7111, 800-634-6755). If you can get one of the hotel's 200 rooms, you'll be charmed by the Victorian wallpaper and paintings, floral carpeting, etched mirrors and lace curtains. Some even have four-poster brass beds. The hotel's busy casino is accented by crystal globe chandeliers and Tiffany-style stained glass. For fine dining, Michael's is one of the best restaurants in town. Moderate.

The grandeur that was once Rome can be found today at **Caesars Palace** (3570 Las Vegas Boulevard South; 702-731-7110, 800-634-6661, fax 702-731-7172). Marble statues, Roman fountains and toga-clad cocktail waitresses help the megaresort realize its Roman-opulence theme. The deluxe-priced rooms have plush carpets, mirrored walls, velvet chaise lounges and platform beds. The resort also offers six restaurants, cocktail lounges, a cluster of upscale shops, a "surround-sound" movie theater and a pool courtyard accented by manicured shrubbery.

The Mirage Hotel has played host to some unusual foreign guests, but none so exotic as the five bottle-nosed dolphins in its saltwater lagoon.

Expansions to the **Flamingo Hilton** (3555 Las Vegas Boulevard South; 702-733-3111, 800-732-2111, fax 702-733-3353) have increased the room count to 3500, making it one of the ten largest hotels in the world. As you might expect, it caters to plenty of tour groups and is usually crowded and bustling. The facade facing the Strip is decorated with neon-pink flamingos against a mirrored backdrop. The theme is carried throughout the hotel, but the rooms have a Hilton influence—done in conservative blues and greens with wood-and-rattan furnishings. Moderate.

The small, blue-roofed pagoda at the front of the **Imperial Palace Hotel** (3535 Las Vegas Boulevard South; 702-731-3311, 800-634-6441, fax 702-735-8578) is only the tip of the iceberg of this sprawling 2700-room complex, located behind a modest Strip facade. The hotel has an Oriental theme, with an entry marked by crystal, jade, bamboo and carved wood accents. The rooms are decorated in cool colors with cane-and-rattan furnishings. Restaurants, a pool, a rock impersonator production show and a vintage auto museum round out the amenities. Budget to moderate.

What was once the world's largest Holiday Inn is now **Harrah's Las Vegas** (3475 Las Vegas Boulevard South; 702-369-5000, 800-634-6765, fax 702-369-5008). Although Harrah's has owned and operated the 1725-room resort since 1983, the name was changed in 1992 to enhance the corporation's image in the gaming industry. Designed as a giant riverboat, the main building looks like the deck of a Mississippi paddle wheeler, complete with twin red smokestacks and bow. The lobby features deep red carpeting and a dark wood registration desk accented by brass lanterns. The modern rooms contain plush teal carpeting, peach print upholstery, white wood furniture and blue bamboo-style chairs. Amenities include restaurants, bars, a health club, a pool and a theater with a magic show. Moderate.

With its gold-mirrored facade glistening in the desert, the **Mirage Hotel** (3400 Las Vegas Boulevard South; 702-791-7111, 800-627-6667, fax 702-791-7446) stands out among Strip hotels. It is also a major tourist attraction. Nearly half the visitors to Las Vegas find their way to the 100-acre, 3054-room complex. Conceived as a Polynesian-theme resort, this hotel is now Jungleland gone wild. Outside the entrance there's a lagoon with waterfalls and grottoes, as well as an erupting volcano. In back, five bottle-nosed dolphins reside in a special saltwater habitat. Inside, you'll find a rainforest atrium with 60-foot-tall palms, orchids and other exotic plants. Behind the marble-and-brass registration desk is a wall-length, 20,000-gallon aquarium that's home to sharks, rays and other sea life. And there's more: The pool area features tree-lined islands, grottoes, waterfalls and lagoons. The deluxe-priced rooms are done in tropical color schemes and contain rattan-and-cane furnishings and floor-to-ceiling headboards crafted from white louvered panels. The resort offers five restaurants and the Siegfried and Roy magic show, the most expensive production show in town. And guests can play golf on the former Dunes course, which, along with the hotel, was acquired by Mirage Resorts in 1993.

Long John Silver would approve of **Treasure Island** (3300 Las Vegas Boulevard South; 702-894-7111, 800-944-7444, fax 702-894-7446), a pirate-theme hotel with a 60-foot skull and crossbones over the reader-board marquee. Like the Mirage, its cousin next door, the hotel is built in a Y-shaped configuration with three coral-colored, 36-story towers. Inside, there's a glint of gold throughout the lobby, which features black corkscrew pillars, marble floors covered with Oriental rugs and a chandelier made of gold-plated skulls and bones. Waiting guests will enjoy the pirate-theme murals behind the onyx registration desk. The 2900 rooms are decorated with light carpeting, brass fixtures, white-washed wood furniture, 17th-century nautical paintings and floor-to-ceiling windows. Hotel amenities include a spa with sauna, whirlpool and exercise room, a beauty salon, a pool area with a 200-foot slide and cabanas covered with blue awnings, two wedding chapels, golf privileges at the Mirage Country Club, and a 1500-seat theater that is home to Cirque du Soleil's "Mystere." Moderate to deluxe.

Once known as the hangout for the "Rat Pack" during the 1960s, the **Sheraton Desert Inn** (3145 Las Vegas Boulevard South; 702-733-4444, 800-634-6906, fax 702-733-4676) is now famous for its 18-hole golf course. Other recreational facilities at the 200-acre resort include ten tennis courts, a jogging track, a workout room and a European spa. The 821 guest rooms are among the best on the Strip, featuring chaise lounges, armoires and country English furnishings, all in cool lavenders or quiet pastels. Rounding out the hotel's amenities are five restaurants, three bars, a shopping arcade and two production theaters. Deluxe.

The Stardust Hotel (3000 Las Vegas Boulevard South; 702-732-6111, 800-634-6757, fax 702-732-6257) recently opened a 1500-room, 32-story tower, bringing its guest room total to 2300. Another 1500-room monolith is planned for the mid-1990s. The new rooms, among the better buys on the Strip, are decorated with earth-tone carpets, red and black upholstery, glass or marble tables and wicker furniture. Downstairs, there are six restaurants, eight bars, two pools, a cluster of shops and two production showrooms. Moderate.

Just a dice roll from the Strip, **Sun Harbor Budget Suites** (1500 Stardust Road; 702-732-1500, 800-752-1501, fax 702-732-2656) offers apartment-style units in the budget price range. The one-bedroom suites are somewhat cramped but tastefully decorated in dark blue and pastel shades and furnished with light-wood tables, rattan lamps and herculon couches. The kitchens come complete with utensils and china. The garden complex has a pool, well-equipped workout gym, spa and tennis court. Gambling is limited to a few slot machines. There are daily and weekly rates both in the budget range.

When the **Riviera Hotel** (2901 Las Vegas Boulevard South; 702-734-5110, 800-634-6753, fax 702-794-9451) opened in 1955, it changed the face of the Strip. Not only was it the first high-rise (nine stories), but it also broke with the city's dude-ranch architecture. Today, the 2200-room megaresort's claim to fame is its entertainment: four production shows run continuously. Coupled with its huge gambling casino, the hotel is always bustling. Fortunately, the moderately priced rooms are far from the din of the casino and feature rich blue and black velour upholstery, dark wood furnishings and magnificent views of the city. Other amenities include four restaurants, two lit tennis courts, an Olympic-sized pool and a mini shopping arcade.

The first thing most people notice at **Circus Circus** (2880 Las Vegas Boulevard South; 702-734-0410, 800-634-3450, fax 702-734-5847) is the pink-and-white, clown-shaped marquee out front. Then it's the tent-shaped casino under a pink-and-white big top. Inside, there are free circus acts, a carnival midway, arcade games and 2800 budget-priced rooms. Put it all together and you have the number-one hotel choice for families with children, which makes the place a perpetual three-ring scene. Thankfully, the rooms are off the midway. The decor features soft blue carpeting, light-wood furniture and just a few hot-air balloons painted on the walls. Hotel amenities include a surprisingly good steak house, swimming pools, a wedding chapel, a 421-space RV park and a dome-enclosed mini amusement park.

Marking the northern boundary of the Strip is the **Sahara Hotel** (2535 Las Vegas Boulevard South; 702-731-2111, 800-634-6666, fax 702-791-2027). An expansion and renovation helped revitalize the aging resort and made it a popular destination for tour groups and conventioneers. Both new and renovated rooms have a sunny disposition, with tan carpeting and drapes, earth-tone upholstery and wooden desks with brass lamps. Tower rooms have views, of course, but some of the nicest are the older bungalow rooms near the pool. Hotel facilities include two pools, one with landscaped gardens and a thatched-hut bar, five restaurants and a cabaret lounge. Moderate.

Adjacent to the convention center, the **Las Vegas Hilton** (3000 Paradise Road; 702-732-5111, 800-732-7117, fax 702-732-5584) is favored by conventioneers and business travelers. Remote from the Strip, the 3174-room hotel is a self-contained resort with 13 restaurants, a celebrity showroom, lounges, a shopping arcade and a ten-acre outdoor recreation deck that features six tennis courts, a putting green, shuffleboard and a large pool area. The 100-foot registration desk and lobby area is separated from the step-down casino, decorated with tropical colors, Grecian bas-reliefs, crystal chandeliers and neon rainbows. The large rooms feature upholstered easy chairs, marble-topped dressing tables, wood-frame mirrors and deep closets. Colors tend toward cool blue and green pastels. The hotel's colorful, 362-foot plumed marquee is the world's tallest sign, and its 77,000 lights, 6000 feet of red neon and electronic message board consume 3 million watts of power. Deluxe.

The nongambling **Crown Plaza Suites Hotel** (4255 Paradise Road; 702-369-4400, 800-465-4329, fax 702-369-3770) is an eclectic cross between a Southwestern-style resort and a corporate office building. Three five-story towers are decorated with chrome and mirrors on some facades, stucco and red panels on the others. Inside, the lobby area is dominated by a tile-and-marble waterfall and a futuristic, crayon-colored mobile hanging from the elevated ceiling. The 202 suites are tastefully done with upholstered easy chairs, dark wood furniture and glass-topped tables, in colors ranging from boardroom mauve to Irish green. Hotel amenities include a restaurant, pool and jacuzzi. Deluxe.

Since the late 1980s, a new breed of hotel has popped up in the convention center area. Fashioned like garden townhouse apartments, these nongambling resorts are geared toward corporate travelers, conventioneers and families. They feature spacious units, some with full kitchens, bedrooms and even grocery service. Here are three of the best:

The **Courtyard by Marriott** (3275 Paradise Road; 702-791-3600, 800-321-2211, fax 702-796-7981) is popular with business travelers because of the fax machines, meeting rooms and large work desks in the 149 guest rooms. The comfortable lobby is accented by light wood-and-brass fixtures and features a marble fireplace and club chairs. The deluxe-priced rooms have plush carpeting, textured wall coverings and dark wood furniture. The outdoor pool is surrounded by lush landscaping and, coupled with the pavilion in the courtyard, provides the setting for a relaxing tête-a-tête after a full day.

A ROOM WITH A VIEW

*One of the best views of the Strip is from **Kiefer's** (105 East Harmon Avenue; 702-739-8000) atop the Carriage House Hotel. Grass wallpaper, rattan club chairs and dozens of plants create a tropical atmosphere in the heart of the desert. You'll dine on moderately priced spicy Louisiana seafood gumbo, steak au poivre, veal saltimbocca or the house specialty, orange roughy Oscar—filets topped wiht crabmeat and asparagus spears and finished with béarnaise sauce.*

Next door, the Tudor-style **Residence Inn** (3225 Paradise Road; 702-796-9300, 800-331-3131, fax 702-796-9562), also by Marriott, features spacious condolike units designed to accommodate guests on extended visits. All of the 192 deluxe-priced rooms and suites are tastefully decorated and feature earth-tone color schemes, Danish modern furnishings, balconies or patios, modern art, large bathrooms, and kitchens complete with microwaves and dishwashers. The quiet lobby features wing chairs for relaxing around the fieldstone fireplace. Rounding out the hotel amenities are a pool, three spas and a grocery shopping service.

Surrounded by tall palm trees and lush landscaping, **La Quinta Inn** (3970 Paradise Road; 702-796-9000, 800-531-5900, fax 702-796-3537) is a 228-room, Mediterranean-style building with white stucco walls, red tile roof and black ironwork. The lobby, which is somewhere between a Swiss château and a country farmhouse, features exposed-beam ceilings, tile floor, arched windows and leather wing chairs. The step-up dining room, which doubles as a reading room or den, features open-beam ceilings, English country wood tables and chairs, and a cozy fireplace. The three-story building contains 228 rooms decorated with a French country flavor and featuring plush teal carpeting, pastel upholstered furniture, light-wood tables and chairs, balconies, VCRs, microwaves, refrigerators and whirlpool tubs. The courtyard is heavily landscaped with trees, plants and pathways around a fountain and pool. Moderate to deluxe.

Restaurants

Often overlooked because it is at the southern end of the Strip away from the other hotels, is the Hacienda Hotel's **Charcoal Room** (3950 Las Vegas Boulevard South; 702-739-8911). Soft lighting, brick-lined

---

A TOUCH OF SOUTHERN FRANCE

*For a romantic hideaway only a block off the Strip, visit **Pamplemousse** (400 East Sahara Avenue; 702-733-2066). This intimate, candlelit bistro is located in a converted house. There is no menu; the waiter simply recites the daily specials. You start with a "French Riviera" salad: a large basket of fresh vegetables and a vinaigrette house dip. Among appetizer choices are fresh scampi, scallops, soft-shell clams, escargots, shallots and an outstanding fettucine. Entrée choices may include prime New York filet, milk-fed white veal, Norwegian salmon with orange curry sauce, or roast Wisconsin duckling with cranberry sauce, cream of garlic sauce, green peppercorns or fresh fruit. Deluxe to ultra-deluxe.*

walls and cozy booths create an intimate setting for the deluxe-priced cuisine, which includes steaks, veal chops, seafood and a 40-ounce prime rib. The restaurant is famous for its black bean soup, ladled ceremoniously from a black iron kettle and accented with a spot of sherry, sliced egg, onion and lemon wedges.

At the Luxor Hotel you can dine with pharaohs at **Isis** (3900 Las Vegas Boulevard South; 702-262-4000), an exquisite room guarded by twin caryatid statues at its entrance and adorned inside with Egyptian artifacts, a black ceiling embedded with gold stars and a glass-encased gold statue of Selket at the center. Specialties include salt- and freshwater seafood, veal, steaks and poultry dishes. Deluxe to ultra-deluxe.

Seldom overlooked, judging by the overflow crowds, are the restaurants in the **Excalibur Hotel** (3850 Las Vegas Boulevard South; 702-597-7777). Two restaurants follow the hotel's medieval village theme and serve cuisine ranging from bargain-priced prime rib and Yorkshire pudding at **Sir Galahad's** to lobster thermidor at the ultra-deluxe **Camelot**. Despite its whimsical name, **Lance-a-Lotta-Pasta** is an old world spaghetti house with Corinthian columns, colorful canopies and Egyptian palms, and **Wild Bill's** is a bunkhouse-style steak house where you can gnaw on a 20-ounce T-bone or rack of barbecue ribs. Both moderate.

Sample a taste of Piccadilly Circus at **Sir Reginald's Steak House** (3799 Las Vegas Boulevard South; 702-891-1111) in the MGM Grand, a British-style pub that fuses dark woods, deep hunter greens, etched-glass dividers between private booths and a man-sized, tuxedo-clad bloodhound—Sir Reginald—standing next to a gown-wearing fox. The specialty here is charbroiled steaks, on and off the bone, including a 20-ounce New York sirloin. Deluxe to ultra-deluxe. Also worth mentioning at the MGM Grand are Mark Miller's **Coyote Café**, a clone of his popular Santa Fe, New Mexico, eatery, that specializes in moderately priced Southwestern dishes, and **Wolfgang Puck's Café**, which serves up designer pizzas and pastas at moderate prices.

For elegant dining, walk across the street to the venerable **Rhapsody** (3801 Las Vegas Boulevard South; 702-739-4460) restaurant in the Tropicana Hotel. Since the early 1960s this softly lit, art deco dining room has been serving award-winning French cuisine such as breast of capon *estragon* and roast duckling *à l'orange*. Other favorites are châteaubriand *bouquetière* and rack of lamb *printanière*. Diners enjoy a view of the five-acre water park, and harpists add to the ambience during the dinner hour and Sunday brunch. Deluxe to ultra-deluxe.

For exotic seafood and spicy-hot Cajun specialties, try **Fisherman's Port** (3667 Las Vegas Boulevard South; 702-736-0111) in the Aladdin Hotel. In dark-paneled booths with nautical trim you can pique your palate on blackened redfish, catfish or New York steak. More timid diners can feast on broiled salmon and Maine lobster. Moderate. If you prefer gourmet Asian cuisine in an opulent setting, **Sun Sun** restaurant features deluxe-priced Chinese, Vietnamese and Korean specialties. And for hearty appetites **Wellington's Steakhouse** challenges diners with a huge T-bone steak and all-you-can-eat barbecue ribs at moderate prices.

At the Flamingo Road intersection, sometimes called "Times Square" because of its cluster of hotels, Bally's Hotel (3645 Las Vegas Boulevard South; 702-739-4111) features fine Continental cuisine at **Seasons**, a deluxe-priced restaurant decorated with period furniture and tapestries to create a 19th-century Parisian atmosphere. The house specialties are steak tartare, filet mignon and fresh Maine lobster. If your palate craves something Italian, take the marble staircase to **Al Dente**, a softly lit, gourmet Italian restaurant that serves moderately priced pizzas, pastas and salads. For more traditional fare, the ultra-deluxe-priced **Bally's Steakhouse** serves a wide variety of steaks, from a 12-ounce New York sirloin to a 24-ounce porterhouse, as well as other beef dishes. The room's dark woods, large chandeliers and secluded booths create the ambience of a private New York club.

The first time I walked into **Battista's Hole in the Wall** (4041 Audrie Lane; 702-732-1424), the young host put his arm around my shoulder and said, "Let's eat!" This is a fun, friendly Italian restaurant, with a wandering accordion player who guarantees he can play a tune connected with anyone's hometown. Among the appetizers, the calamari and steamed clams are the best. The pasta is homemade and includes lasagna, manicotti and fettucine. Specialties are the veal (picante, marsala, milanese, bolognese and parmigiana), steak and chicken. Dinners include all the wine you can drink and a cup of cappuccino. Moderate to deluxe.

Michael's (3595 Las Vegas Boulevard South; 702-737-7111), one of the finest restaurants in the city, is located across the street in the Barbary Coast Hotel. The elegant dining room features finely upholstered decor and a stained-glass dome ceiling that creates a feeling of turn-of-the-century San Francisco. Among the house favorites on the ultra-deluxe-priced menu are imported fresh Dover sole, rack of lamb, veal *française* and châteaubriand for two. In addition to a number of tempting pastries, Michael's serves a complimentary tray of fruit slices dipped in white and dark chocolate at the end of the meal. For fast, round-the-clock dining, the budget-priced **Victorian Room** features beef, chicken and fish dishes, as well as Chinese cuisine. The "Midnight Teaser" breakfast, served from midnight to 7 a.m., is one of the town's best buys at 95 cents.

Next door at the Flamingo Hilton Hotel (3555 Las Vegas Boulevard South; 702-733-3111), the moderately priced **Flamingo Room** has an art deco look with its brass-edged glass panels, leaf-patterned chairs and metal flamingos. The house specialty is the Flamingo Barbecue featuring roast pork loin, beef ribs, chicken, corn on the cob and a five-bean casserole. Of the three dining levels, the terrace overlooking the pool and garden area is the best. While the hotel is famous for its Miami modern decor, its most popular restaurant is the Old West-style **Beef Baron**, decorated with longhorn chandeliers, mounted deer heads and vintage rifles. The deluxe-priced fare features prime rib, rack of lamb and châteaubriand. For a Chinese feast, try the moderately priced **Peking Market**, where the nine-course dinner includes lemon chicken, Mongolian beef, seafood, Chinese vegetables and banana fritters.

For a touch of Roman decadence, head for the award-winning restaurants at Caesars Palace (3570 Las Vegas Boulevard South; 702-731-7110). The ultra-deluxe-priced **Palace Court** is adorned with lush green plants, objets d'art and a magnificent stained-glass ceiling. Distinctive appetizers include caviar, French onion soup and smoked Scottish salmon carved tableside. The specialties are steak Diane, rack of lamb, breast of duck and prime sirloin. For a Roman banquet complete with toga-clad wine goddesses and belly dancers, **Bacchanal** serves a lavish, seven-course feast in a garden setting around a fountain. Fixed price is about $65 per person. If you prefer gourmet Chinese cuisine, take the brass-railed staircase to **Empress Court**, which offers the best in Cantonese and Mandarin cooking. The house specialty on the ultra-deluxe-priced menu is Peking duck, prepared tableside by a white-gloved carver who transforms the entire duck into filling for small rolled crêpes covered with a rich hoisin sauce.

Next door at the **Mirage Hotel** (3400 Las Vegas Boulevard South; 702-791-7111) you can dine in a tropical rainforest at **Kokomo's**. Cooled by the mist of a cascading waterfall and nestled among banana trees, royal palms, orchids and other exotic flowers, guests can choose from seafood, beef, lamb and pork specialties. For an appetizer try the crab-meat taco with pineapple salsa, and save (or make) room for the Oreo peanut butter cheese cake. Prices are deluxe to ultra-deluxe.

Spago Restaurant & Café (3500 Las Vegas Boulevard South; 702-369-6300) at the Forum Shops reproduces Wolfgang Puck's famous Hollywood hangout with a California chic decor of warm wood panels, beamed ceiling, marble pedestal tables and rattan-backed chairs. Among Puck's specialties are a duck sausage and spicy chicken pizza, Peking duck spring roll, steamed Maine lobster with saffron fettuccine and basil, almond-ginger-crusted salmon and Sonoma lamb tacos with Wolfgang's fresh tomato salsa. Moderate to deluxe.

For a touch of old New Orleans, step across the street to **Joe's Bayou** (3475 Las Vegas Boulevard South; 702-369-5000) in Harrah's Hotel. The dining room is accented by tin shanty walls, and features moderately priced Cajun and Southern specialties such as blackened fish and barbecued chicken, pork ribs and chops. The house favorite is the sampler, with generous portions of chicken, shrimp, frog's legs, fried catfish and barbecued ribs.

Taste the pirate's life at **The Plank** (3300 Las Vegas Boulevard South; 702-894-7111) in Treasure Island. Resembling a ship's library, the dining room is decorated with bookcases, antiquarian books, brass wall sconces, dark wood tables and chairs with velour upholstery. Specialties from the mesquite grill include lobster, shrimp scampi, scallops and the Edwardian combination of lamb chop and lobster tail. Deluxe to ultra-deluxe.

Regency Ristorante (3355 Las Vegas Boulevard South; 702-733-5000) at the Sand Hotel is where Hollywood's "Rat Pack" of the 1960s once hung out. Today it's a bright and airy trattoria with white-washed wood furnishings and a modern purple and burgundy color scheme. Among the ultra-deluxe priced Italian specialties are seafood lasagna made with shrimp, lobster and crab, classic veal marsala, veal chops and fresh seafood including Dover sole, Norwegian salmon and orange roughy.

One of the few restaurants offering authentic dim sum is **Chin's** (3200 Las Vegas Boulevard South; 702-733-8899) in the Fashion Show Mall. Lots of glass and polished metal beams accent this upscale Chinese restaurant popular with the business lunch crowd. The dim sum lunch is fancy and appetizing—shrimp puffs, minced chicken, spicy chicken and sweet rice buns filled with chicken, beef or pork. Among the innovative entrées are strawberry chicken, spicy Manila clams in the shell, and raspberry and strawberry shrimp with fruit sauce. Moderate to deluxe.

If Northern Italian food is your favorite, try **Ristorante Italiano** (2901 Las Vegas Boulevard South; 702-734-5110) in the Riviera Hotel. In an atmosphere accented by dark woods, rich upholstery and subdued colors, choose your appetizer from a well-stocked antipasto cart, then feast on a number of seafood, chicken and steak dishes, or try the house specialty—*vermicelli salsa bellavista*, a combination of crabmeat, shrimp, prosciutto and vegetables on a bed of pasta. Deluxe to ultra-deluxe.

The popular choice of meat-eaters since 1960 is the noisy and always-crowded **Flame Restaurant** (1 Desert Inn Road; 702-735-4431), where the walls are lined with photos of the celebrities and athletes who have preceded you. Start by selecting your steak from a tray before it is cooked on an open grill. Choose from rib eye, porterhouse, New York cut, top sirloin, brochette of beef or filet mignon. Other entrées include seafood, prime rib and lobster tail. Get a flavor of the Howard Hughes days by talking to waiters who worked his table. Deluxe.

A gathering place for Asian high rollers is **Ho Wan** (3145 Las Vegas Boulevard South; 702-733-4547) in the Sheraton Desert Inn. Ancient Chinese clay pictures, tapestries and artifacts decorate this upscale dining room where Hong Kong–trained chefs specialize in seafood dishes like steamed trout with ginger and scallions and exotic soups such as bird's nest, shark's fin and seaweed with cabbage. Ultra-deluxe.

For a taste of the fabulous '50s, visit **Ralph's Diner** (3000 Las Vegas Boulevard South; 702-732-6111) in the Stardust Hotel. Budget-priced burgers, fries, malts, shakes and blue plate specials are the fare. Dancing waitresses often be-bop to jukebox oldies across the checkerboard floor. If you prefer to dine in 1890s elegance, **William B's Steakhouse** features a turn-of-the-century motif, with its polished mahogany wall panels, etched glass, brass fixtures and sepia-toned photographs. Traditional American cuisine includes prime rib, steaks, fish, veal, rack of lamb and a classic onion soup. Moderate to deluxe.

Some of the best budget-priced Mexican food can be found at **Margarita's Cantina** (3120 Las Vegas Boulevard South; 702-794-8200) in the Frontier Hotel. Colorful booths and Mexican decor in a bright, open setting create a cheerful dining experience. Specialties of the house are *pollo en mole, carne asada* and shrimp in Mexicali sauce. Steaming tortillas served immediately after you're seated are a nice touch.

No-nonsense dining is the ticket at **Alias Smith & Jones** (541 East Twain Avenue; 702-732-7401). Oak tables, captain's chairs and a cozy fieldstone fireplace add to the homey feeling. Specialties include steak Oscar topped with Alaskan crab, beef stroganoff and beef ribs. Breakfast lovers should try the create-your-own omelette served with homemade corn bread. Budget to moderate.

In a city short on delis, **Bagelmania** (855 East Twain Avenue; 702-369-3322) is a welcome find. The New York–style deli features nine varieties of bagels served with lox or nova, sturgeon, sable, chub, herring, white fish or just plain cream cheese. Sandwiches are mainstream deli: corned beef, pastrami, roast beef, ham and turkey. Budget.

The **House of Lords** (2535 Las Vegas Boulevard South; 702-732-2111) in the Sahara Hotel follows an English grill motif with rich wood paneling and diamond-tufted leather booths. The house specialty is whole Dover sole topped with a zesty mix of capers, shrimp and mushrooms. The perfect accompaniment is the spinach salad, prepared tableside with a warm bacon vinaigrette. Other popular dishes include single- or double-cut porterhouse, rack of lamb and châteaubriand for two. Deluxe to ultra-deluxe.

If you like your steaks large, thick and juicy, bring a hearty appetite to **The Steak House** (2880 Las Vegas Boulevard South; 702-734-0410) in the Circus Circus Hotel. Don't let the high-wire acts and throngs of kids on the midway discourage you; The Steak House is a quiet, oak-paneled dining room where you can enjoy mesquite-broiled New York sirloin, porterhouse or filet mignon at moderate-to-deluxe prices.

Next door to the Convention Center, the Las Vegas Hilton Hotel (3000 Paradise Road; 702-732-5801) has five international restaurants topped by **Le Montrachet**, an intimate, European-style room accented by soft peach lighting, elegant floral arrangements and formal table settings. The ultra-deluxe-priced fare is served by an attentive staff and features poached filet of John Dory, medallions of venison and rack of lamb. You can make a gourmet meal of such appetizers as chilled foie gras of duck, pheasant breast mousse and the hot duck and spinach salad. All the desserts are works of art, notably the white espresso ice cream shaped as a swan.

For the ultimate in fine dining, it's **Pegasus** in the Alexis Park Hotel (375 East Harmon Avenue; 702-796-3300), where dark glass panels, mirrored walls, silver champagne stands and a custom crystal chandelier help create a sophisticated ambience. Imaginative appetizers include lobster medallion with quail egg, red caviar in sauce imperial and mushrooms baked in puff pastry. The house specialty is lobster prepared with black truffles and wine in a bordelaise sauce and served flaming. A harpist adds to the romantic atmosphere during the dinner hour. Ultra-deluxe.

Fresh fish in a cannery-style bar and grill is the fare at **Famous Pacific Fish Co.** (3925 Paradise Road; 702-796-9676). With its open, air-duct ceilings and nautical decor, this noisy restaurant appears transplanted from Monterey's Cannery Row. The specialty is fresh, mesquite-broiled seafood such as salmon, swordfish, tiger shrimp and Dungeness crab. Moderate to deluxe.

Alpine Village (3003 Paradise Road; 702-734-6888) has been celebrating Oktoberfest since the early 1950s. The entire staff dresses Bavarian-style and marches to the beat of a German band. There's a rathskeller downstairs, along with a piano bar and sandwich shop. The menu features schnitzels, bratens and potato pancakes. The house specialty is wiener schnitzel—veal breaded with egg and cracker meal, sautéed and topped with a poached egg, capers, anchovies and mushroom sauce. Moderate.

The **Beijing** restaurant (3900 Paradise Road; 702-737-9618) resembles an Asian gallery. Most of the rare art works, embroidered silk pictures, jade, cloisonné and ivory carvings are for sale. Signature dishes at moderate prices include the sweet-and-sour pineapple duck, fish steak with plum or curry sauce, lobster with electronic eyes and sizzling steak and tender shrimp with pine nuts. In addition, there is a unique selection of vegetarian dishes, including the "banquet," consisting of kung pao "chicken" and imitation pork.

Northern Indian cuisine prepared in tandoori ovens is the specialty at **Shalimar** (3900 Paradise Road; 702-796-0302). Appetizers include *samosa* (deep-fried pastry stuffed with vegetables), tandoori-cooked chicken *tikka*, marinated lamb kabob and *seckh* kabob. The chicken curries are prepared with almonds, spinach, dried fruit, sautéed onions and scallions. Seafood curries are made with prawns and fresh fish. Complete vegetarian dinners with eggplant, cauliflower, okra, spinach and tomatoes are also offered. Basmati rice, imported from Punjab, is prepared with saffron and vegetables. Moderate.

Brazilian-style cooking is featured at **Yolie's Steakhouse** (3900 Paradise Road; 702-794-0700), where you can eat in the high-ceilinged dining room or on the rooftop terrace. The fixed-price house specialty begins with soup or salad, then continues with a procession of waiters bearing sausage Ipanema, turkey breast wrapped in bacon, young spring chicken, New York sirloin, brisket of beef and leg of baby lamb. Side dishes include fried potatoes, polenta, bananas, vegetables and rice. If you prefer to order from the menu, try scampi, orange roughy, rack of lamb for two or daily seafood specials. Moderate.

Visitors to **Ginza** (1000 East Sahara Avenue; 702-732-3080) will discover a colorful Far East setting behind the anemic storefronts of Sahara Avenue. The sushi bar features octopus and tuna. Entrées are pork, beef, chicken and seafood. The specialty is yosenabe, a Japanese bouillabaisse with shrimp, crab, fish and clams served in a covered stone bowl. Moderate.

Another popular Japanese restaurant is **Kabuki** (1150 East Twain Avenue; 702-733-0066). In addition to a sushi bar and traditional teriyaki and tempura dishes, there's an intriguing selection of broiled squid legs, dried whitefish on ground radish, squid with smelt eggs and three kinds of rice balls wrapped in seaweed. For the less adventurous, the house specialty is the Love Boat dinner for two—sushi, beef teriyaki, yakitori, mixed tempura, tea and ice cream. Budget to moderate.

One mile east of the Strip, the Commercial Center Shopping Plaza, located at 953 East Sahara Avenue, has developed into a mini-Chinatown. In addition to interesting shopping opportunities, there are a few fine Asian restaurants. **Seoul Korean BBQ** (702-369-4123) specializes in thin-sliced barbecued beef, boneless short ribs, yellow corvina, *saury*, *adka* or sliced chicken—all prepared over gas-fired braziers. Or you can opt for one of the popular "food bowls" such as sliced pork or seafood casserole with kimchi. If you burn easily, ask for the mild seasoning— the Korean hot, spicy sauces are just that. Budget to moderate.

If you prefer Japanese cuisine, **Tokyo** (Commercial Center Shopping Plaza; 702-735-7070) features two large hibachi tables, a 14-seat tatami room and a sushi bar. There are dozens of entrée choices, but the best bet is cooking your own dinner on the tabletop hibachi—beef, chicken, seafood and vegetables on skewers—served with soup, pickles, rice, dessert and green tea. Start with one of the many interesting appetizers: Octopus with vinegar seasoning and fish cakes with hot green mustard are two of the best. Budget to moderate.

Moving along the Pacific Rim, **Lotus of Siam** (Commercial Center Shopping Plaza; 702-735-4477) offers inexpensive Thai cuisine served in a quiet setting featuring traditional Thai art. The food is milder than most experienced diners expect. The secret is blending each course with seasonings—ginger, lemongrass, fish sauce, lime leaves and hot red and green peppers—to create varying degrees of sweet, sour, bitter or salty flavors. Appetizers include *mee krob* (the national dish of Thailand), a semisweet combination of fried crispy rice stick and shrimp. The chicken, beef, seafood and catfish entrées are served with a spicy red curry sauce, and the traditional noodle dishes—wide Thai or rice noodles—are served with seafood, beef or chicken. Budget.

Rounding out the Commercial Center restaurants is **Dickinson's Wharf** (702-732-3594), where the specialty is a festive New England clambake: house salad or chowder, a one-and-one-half pound steamed whole lobster, a half-dozen steamed clams, corn on the cob and choice of pasta, rice or potato. The year-round fare includes Maine lobster broiled or stuffed with crabmeat, lobster Newburg, sole, stuffed flounder, salmon steak, orange roughy, and swordfish. Moderate to deluxe.

Sushi lovers must visit **Nippon** (101 Convention Center Drive; 702-735-5565), where they can feast on 30 varieties of raw fish in the restaurant's long, narrow dining room or cozy sushi bar. The house specialty is the *nabe yaki udon*—fish cake, cabbage, shrimp tempura, onion, mushrooms and udon noodles, all served in an iron kettle. Beef sukiyaki and shrimp tempura with vegetables are also recommended. Moderate.

One of the better Italian delis in town is **Café Milano** (3900 Paradise Road; 702-732-2777), which features a cozy storefront dining area and ice-cream parlor. The best selections on the menu are lasagna and *penne pomodoro, arabiata* (tomato, garlic, red pepper) with meatball plus spaghetti *aglio colio* and carbonara. Also popular are the cannelloni stuffed with veal and ricotta cheese, and antipasto misto with salami and cheese. The ice-cream parlor has a huge selection of Italcream gelato and tartufo. A good bet is the refreshing lemon Italian ice. Budget.

For more formal Italian dining, try **La Strada** (4640 Paradise Road; 702-735-0150). It offers subdued lighting, quiet booths, mirrored walls, and a pianist performing nightly. The antipasto platter of calamari, gazpacho, chicken liver pâté and buffalo mozzarella makes a great beginning. Moderately priced entrées include chicken and veal dishes and seafood choices such as calamari provençal, scampi Napoleone, Norwegian salmon, sautéed orange roughy and mussels peasant style.

Shopping

Nearly every major hotel has a gift shop selling expensive men's and women's clothing, jewelry and gifts. But **Bally's** (3645 Las Vegas Boulevard South; 702-739-4111) has 40 shops in its promenade, the largest in the city. In addition to high-fashion boutiques—**Marshall Rousso** (702-736-6124) for women, **Mort Wallin** (702-736-1313) for men—you can find Far East arts and crafts at **Arts of Asia** (702-733-6114), or discover authentic Indian and Southwestern art and jewelry at the Indian-owned **TePee** (702-735-5333). The **Brass and Copper Shop** (702-736-4050) offers intriguing, though expensive decorative housewares and gifts. There's also an **MGM Movie Set Photo Studio** (702-731-2945), where you can have your picture taken in various western costumes.

Though not as large as the Bally's arcade, Appian Way at Caesars Palace (3570 Las Vegas Boulevard South; 702-731-7110) is home to some of the world's most exclusive shops. Designer women's shoes from France are sold at **Del Monaco Shoe Salon** (702-735-1300), while **Cuzzen's** (702-732-1331) caters to the well-heeled man. **Gucci's** (702-731-1724), famous for its crocodile shoes and handbags, is worth exploring, even if you don't buy one of its purses or a pair of $900 loafers. Exclusive jewelers such as **Cartier** (702-733-6652) and **Ciro** (702-369-6464) are also part of this scaled-down Rodeo Drive.

Among the shops worth visiting at The Forum Shops (3500 Las Vegas Boulevard South) is **Bebe** (702-735-8885), a New York–style designer boutique specializing in moderately priced form-fitting suits with hot pants, linen jumpsuits and black leather vests with crystal pleats. For ultrachic (and ultraexpensive) women's wear it's the **French Room** (702-796-0511) and **Gianni Versace** (702-796-7222), where you might stumble upon a sequinned, snakeskin bodysuit or a beaded leather jacket. More conservative and reasonably priced attire such as linen and silk skirts and suits can be found at the **Express** (702-892-0424). Men can walk next door to **Structure** (702-892-0422) and find excellent prices on linen shirts and slacks and silk shirts and ties. If you're tired of clothes and interested in autographed sports and show biz memorabila, try **Field of Dreams** (702-792-8233).

SHOPPING ESPRIT

*Las Vegas is a haven for souvenir T-shirts, coffee mugs, snow domes and salt and pepper shakers, but the gift shops at the new theme resorts offer original though pricier mementos of your visit. For upscale artifacts try the shops at **Treasure Island** (3300 Las Vegas Boulevard South; 702-894-7111), where you'll find Moroccan chests inlaid with stone and camel bone and intricately patterned ceramic platters, bowls, pitchers and Tiffany-style vases. At **Excalibur** (3850 Las Vegas Boulevard South; 702-597-7777), you can choose from medieval reproductions of Spanish weaponry, wizard sculptures, chess sets, paintings, lamps, pewter shields and axes. For gifts with a tropical flavor visit the **Mirage** (3400 Las Vegas Boulevard South; 702-791-7111) for a complete collection of carved fish from Bali, South Sea totems and feathered dolls. The shops at **Luxor** (3900 Las Vegas Boulevard South; 702-262-4000) specialize in Egyptian-made ceramic vases, hand-tooled leather boxes, hand-blown perfume bottles, games and Christmas ornaments. You can also buy reproductions of the jewelry, papyrus scrolls and other treasures found in King Tut's tomb.*

A fun spot to visit is **Boogie's Diner** (702-892-0860), where you can grab a sandwich or buy a leather-and-denim jacket, a sequined sweatsuit or any number of items from the Aspen-based boutique. For athletic wear it's **Just for Feet** (702-791-3482), which features the largest selection of tennis shoes in town. You can even try out a pair of Air Jordans on the shop's wood-floored basketball court. No mall is complete without a sweet shop, and there are two among the Forum Shops: the **Sweet Factory** (702-732-3877) for colorful confections and the **Chocolate Chariot** (702-735-2639) for hand-dipped chocolate apples.

An unusual gift store is **West of Santa Fe** (702-737-1993), which sells genuine Southwestern and Native American art and jewelry. In addition to the Zuni turquoise and Hopi silver jewelry and bolos, there are hand-carved fetishes, kachina dolls, feathered headdresses, pottery and blankets.

The jewel of the city's shopping malls is the **Fashion Show Mall** (3200 Las Vegas Boulevard; 702-369-8382), which has 144 shops—mostly upscale—on two enclosed levels. Located along the Strip (between the Mirage and the Frontier hotels), this is where the tourists shop. The mall is anchored by five major department stores, including Neiman Marcus and Saks Fifth Avenue, but some of the more interesting finds are at the smaller boutiques. For instance, have you ever found yourself in a shop where every item grabs your attention? Where everything looks like it was tastefully and painstakingly selected just for you? **Vignettes** (702-737-7707) is that type of shop, an enchanting little boutique that sells trendy house furnishings and classy gifts.

Ultraviolet rays are on everybody's mind, especially in the desert, so, along with a thick coat of SPF 30 why not keep shady under a fashionable floppy? **I Love Hats** (702-731-3770) sells everything from western Stetsons to strokers caps and berets.

LEATHER FOR THE STARS

*If you're into leather, clothing that is, **North Beach Leather** (Caesars Forum, 702-733-0035; and the Fashion Show Mall, 702-731-0630) sells nifty men's and women's apparel designed by San Francisco's Michael Hoban, who originally started his business making jackets for the San Francisco Police Department and Hell's Angels. Today they're worn by celebrities such as Arsenio Hall, Cher and Dolly Parton. Incidentally, this is the shop where Elvis spent $17,000 on his first visit and another $21,000 over the next few weeks. Many of his selections were gifts for friends. Ask manager Joseph De Nucci at the Fashion Show Mall store to tell you the story.*

If you're in need of some Irish luck, stop at O'Shea's Casino (3555 Las Vegas Boulevard South; 702-792-0777) and try the gift shop, which is overflowing with shamrock pins, shirts, caps, four-leaf clovers—all in white and emerald green.

The mall is a great place to feed your foot fetish. **San Remo** (702-731-3778) and the **Brass Boot** (702-731-6502) sell quality shoes for men, while **Norman Kaplan** (702-733-6303) and **Joyce Selby** (702-733-1740) offer the same for women. **Rocky Mountain** (702-733-3436) sells outdoor hiking and walking shoes. For fun footwear, try **Bianca** (702-369-0048).

Among the two dozen women's fashion boutiques located in the mall are the glitzy but tasteful **Lillie Rubin** (702-735-2131) for extravagant evening gowns and **Laise Adzer** (702-735-6392) for an upscale Third World look. For Australian outback wear, stop by **Koala Blue** (702-734-9777).

Quality men's apparel is sold at **Steve Gordon's** (702-369-8990), **Amici** (702-369-9133) and **Uomo-Uomo Sport** (702-735-4200), where you can still buy a designer linen suit for less than $500.

The Fashion Show Mall is home to several excellent commercial art galleries that often host exhibits of the work of artists such as Picasso and Dali. **Minotaur** (702-737-1400) and **Centaur** (702-737-0004) galleries also carry works by people-pleasing artists like Erté and Leroy Neiman. History buffs will want to stop at the **Gallery of History** (702-731-2300), which specializes in rare manuscripts, letters and photographs of notables the likes of Abraham Lincoln, Marilyn Monroe, John Lennon and Babe Ruth.

For gadget lovers there's **Future Tronics** (702-734-6464) featuring high-tech toys and electronic gizmos, while real kids can find treasures galore at **Karl's Toys & Hobbies** (702-735-7442).

Before you leave the Fashion Show Mall, visit the **Antique Emporium** (702-733-4949). This small shop is crammed with vintage Wurlitzer jukeboxes, popcorn machines, soft-drink dispensers, neon signs, old jewelry—all reconditioned to mint working condition.

Located next door at **Bethany's Celebrity Doll Museum** (1775 East Tropicana Avenue in the Liberace Plaza; 702-798-3036) you can see Barbie originals, *Wizard of Oz* characters, and historical and motion picture figures.

The **Country Village Gift Shop** in the Frontier Hotel (3120 Las Vegas Boulevard South; 702-794-8200) has quirky, modern-day souvenirs displayed in antique hutches that are real collector's items, embellished with ornate carvings of fruits and flowers and curlicue legs signed by their talented maker.

Nightlife

A great place to cut a rug is **The Metz** (3765 Las Vegas Boulevard South; 702-739-8855), which features 20,000 watts of musical power linked to a mesmerizing light display, a huge dancefloor, private booths and a balcony overlooking the Strip. Cover.

Peter Jackson's *Winds of the Gods* (3900 Las Vegas Boulevard South; 702-262-4000) at the **Luxor Hotel** plays twice nightly in a dirt-floored, hockey-rink-shaped arena. The Egyptian-based extravaganza features angry pharaohs, belly dancers, flying mummies, tomb robbers, chariot races and a cast of animals from Noah's Ark. Cover.

The 1700-seat **Grand Theatre** (3799 Las Vegas Boulevard South; 702-891-1111) at the MGM Grand Hotel features tiered seating in semi-circles for front-facing views of the city's largest stage. The theater hosts headliners such as Frank Sinatra and is the setting for a new stage production to be announced. Also at the MGM Grand, the red and black **Hollywood Theatre** (702-891-1111) has an old-fashioned movie house entrance and 630 seats in a horseshoe arrangement around the stage. It plays host to familiar names such as Kenny Loggins, Smokey Robinson, Randy Travis, Tom Jones and the Righteous Brothers. Rounding out the hotel's theater complexes, is the **Grand Garden** (702-891-1111), a 15,000-seat arena with three tiers of retractable turquoise seats that can be removed for conventions and exhibitions. Barbra Streisand opened the theater, but it is most frequently used for sporting events and title fights. Cover charge at all theaters.

The **MGM Grand** (3799 Las Vegas Boulevard South; 702-891-1111) is also a great place to sip a drink between shows. The **Betty Boop Lounge** features a wall-length mural of the perky cartoon character perched atop a garden of flowers, while a robotic Foster Brooks slurs one-liners and party jokes. If you get tired of sitting, stroll over to the **Turf Club Lounge** or **Center Stage Lounge**, where you can dance until dawn to live music.

SHOP 'TIL YOU DROP

*At the top of the Strip, stop and browse at **Bonanza: World's Largest Gift Shop** (2400 Las Vegas Boulevard South; 702-384-0005), right across the street from the Sahara Hotel. Even if you don't buy anything, you'll be amazed by the selection of souvenirs: dice clocks, jewelry, T-shirts, moccasins, plaques, tumblers, X-rated gags, wind-up animals, cacti, toys, UNLV paraphernalia, fudge and aspirin. Who knows, you may find the perfect gift for that hard-to-shop-for uncle.*

The **Aladdin Hotel** (3667 Las Vegas Boulevard South; 702-736-0240) offers a number of choices, including *Country Tonight*, a delightful mix of new and traditional country music, dancing and "Hee-Haw" comedy. The **Theater for the Performing Arts** hosts major concerts with performers such as Stevie Wonder, Sting and Rod Stewart, and Broadway productions such as *Cats*. Cover charges for all shows.

The **Jubilee Theater** at Bally's (3645 Las Vegas Boulevard South; 702-739-4567) features the long-running *Jubilee*, a musical extravaganza with a huge cast of dancers and dazzling stage effects ranging from sinking the *Titanic* to a World War I aerial dogfight. Right next door, the 1400-seat **Celebrity Room** features headliners such as George Carlin, Lionel Ritchie and the Oak Ridge Boys. **Catch a Rising Star** is a New York–style comedy/music club showcasing stand-up comedians, singers and variety acts twice nightly. Table seating surrounding the stage puts guests within teasing distance of the comic. Cover charge for all shows.

Big-name entertainers such as Diana Ross, David Copperfield, the Beach Boys and the Pointer Sisters perform regularly in the four-tiered **Circus Maximus Room** at Caesars Palace (3570 Las Vegas Boulevard South; 702-731-7333); cover charge. For one-on-one encounters, it's **Cleopatra's Barge** featuring dancing to live bands, usually rock or rhythm-and-blues. The lively lounge is more like a crayon-colored Viking vessel, but it floats in real water and bobs when the dancefloor action picks up.

For a Strip tavern, the **Peppermill** (2985 Las Vegas Boulevard South; 702-735-7635) is surprisingly restrained. Candlelit tables and a fireplace surrounded by plush sofas create the feeling of a living room cocktail party. The waitresses' long evening gowns are a refreshing change from the skimpy outfits worn at the nearby casinos. If you're hungry, a full menu is served around the clock in the dining room.

For a quiet drink, the **Winner's Circle Lounge** at the Desert Inn (3145 Las Vegas Boulevard South; 702-733-4566) is an intimate piano bar with dark wood tables, rattan chairs and an oak bar.

Debbie Reynolds stars in her own production at her newly opened **Hollywood Hotel & Movie Museum** (305 Convention Center Drive; 702-734-0711). Joining her is longtime friend Rip Taylor for an evening of song, dance, stand-up comedy and vintage film clips. Cover.

King Arthur's Tournament at the Excalibur (3850 Las Vegas Boulevard South; 702-597-7600) is a medieval dinner show in a multitiered theater that features jousting, magic acts, singers and laser special effects. You can also eat your chicken dinner with your fingers. Cover.

The **Flamingo Hilton** (3555 Las Vegas Boulevard South; 702-733-3100) offers *City Lites*, an eclectic blend of dance, magic, novelty acts and ice-skating numbers. Cover charge for the dinner and cocktail shows. Or you can dance in the **Casino Lounge** to artists such as Earl Turner, Joe Frank and the Irish Show Band; cover.

Cirque de Soleil's *Mystere* (3300 Las Vegas Boulevard South; 702-894-7111) at Treasure Island is an eclectic blend of abstract and performing art, performed in a 1500-seat theater built to the French-Canadian circus troupe's specifications. Surreal masks and costumes coupled with seductive lighting and an original musical score transport the acrobats, clowns, aerialists, dancers, stilt walkers, bungee jumpers and body balancers into the realm of primal theater. Easily one the city's best production shows. Cover.

Lance Burton, one of Las Vegas' most popular magicians, performs regularly in the **Fiesta Showroom** at the Hacienda Hotel (3950 Las Vegas Boulevard South; 702-891-8231). The illusionist supplements his feats with specialty acts and beautiful (are you surprised?) dancers. The early evening show has no nudity and admits children. One of the few rooms with a no-smoking policy. Cover.

For more wizardry, try *Spellbound—A Concept of Illusion* in the **Commander's Theater at Harrah's** (3475 Las Vegas Boulevard South; 702-369-5222). The extravaganza features a husband-and-wife magic team combining pyrotechnics, dance and gravity-defying illusions. Their levitations and saw-a-woman-in-half stunt are interesting variations on traditional tricks. As always, the backdrop includes lavish sets, dazzling costumes and leggy dancers. Cover.

The Imperial Palace (3535 Las Vegas Boulevard South; 702-794-3261) hosts one of Las Vegas' most consistent hits, Legends in Concert in its Imperial Theater. The show features accomplished impersonators who re-create the talents of Elvis Presley, Roy Orbison, Buddy Holly, Liberace, the Blues Brothers and more. A Krypton red laser and projection system creates mystifying patterns and special effects. Cover.

A good place to pick up sports betting tips is **Art's Place** (532 East Sahara Avenue; 702-737-1466). Swings in the Dow have no effect on this sports bar's clientele, but teams that fail to beat the point spread can whip the local crowd into a frenzy. You can sit at the large, circular bar or at the booths and tables surrounding it. The place is famous for its barbecued ribs and half-pound burgers. Either would go well with the Anchor Steam beer on tap.

Siegfried & Roy command the most for any show in town—more than $75 a ticket. But the illusionists' show at **The Mirage** (3400 Las Vegas Boulevard South; 702-792-7777) is always packed and features space-age magic acts and exotic white tigers.

The **Riviera Hotel** (2901 Las Vegas Boulevard South; 702-794-9301) has more continuously running production shows than any other hotel. Topping the list is the award-winning *Splash*, variety entertainment for the entire family. In addition to the signature mermaid aquacade, the show features daredevil motorcyclists, magic acts, music, dance and an outstanding exotic bird trainer. Children admitted to early show only. *An Evening at La Cage* stars Frank Marino as a catty Joan Rivers. Other impressionists become replicas of show stars in this kinky though solid production. *Crazy Girls: Sensuality, Passion and Pudgy!* is a bawdy Parisian fantasy show with an emphasis on topless showgirls. **An Evening at the Improv** is a comedy club featuring established and up-and-coming comedians. Cover charge for all shows.

For a piano bar, **Patricia's Lounge** (208 East Sahara Avenue; 702-791-0107) can be a noisy, lively little establishment, but it calms down when Mary Oliver sits down at the piano and wraps a Cole Porter song around her little finger—you know she's for real.

The **Sahara Hotel** (2535 Las Vegas Boulevard South; 702-737-2111) is the frequent home of Rich Little and his *Copy Cats* revue, and the permanent roost of Kentry Kerr's *Boy-lesque*, a cabaret-style revue starring female-impersonators. Cover.

The **Copa Room** at the Sands Hotel (3355 Las Vegas Boulevard South; 702-733-5453) features *Viva Las Vegas*, a potpourri of music, comedy, dance and specialty acts for afternoon audiences. Cover.

Enter the Night at the **Stardust Hotel** (3000 Las Vegas Boulevard South; 702-732-6325) is an illusion-filled, high-tech extravaganza of modern and erotic dancers, gymnasts and skaters who jump in and out of laser lights. Cover. The music and dancing in the **Starlite Lounge** focuses on the '50s and '60s, so be prepared to do the twist and shout.

Andrew Lloyd Webber's *Starlight Express* at the **Las Vegas Hilton** (3000 Paradise Road; 702-732-5755) is a Broadway-style production that tells the musical tale of Rusty, the steam locomotive that "could," an Elvis-impersonating diesel and a more modern Electra—all on roller skates. Included in the show are 19 musical pieces that span rock, pop, jazz, gospel, rap and country. The songs are enhanced by a 1600-light stage show, lasers, a projection screen and costumes that cost between $10,000 and $20,000. Highlights of the show include roller skate race scenes that run through the audience and a soulful song called "Poppa's Blues." Cover.

The **Tropicana Hotel** (3801 Las Vegas Boulevard South; 702-739-2411) features one of the city's pioneer extravaganzas, the *Les Folies Bergere*—patterned after the famous French revue with lines and lines of feathered-and-sequined showgirls. The quintessential production show takes place in the **Tiffany Theatre**, which has a no-smoking policy. **The Comedy Stop** features contemporary comedians and variety acts. Both shows have a cover.

THREE

Downtown

Las Vegas gambling was born on Fremont Street in the 1930s, and much of that frontier atmosphere remains. The area known as Glitter Gulch also boasts the country's best collection of neon lighting—just check out the landmark Vegas Vic and Sassy Sally signs, along with those decorating the Four Queens, Binion's Horseshoe and Union Plaza hotels, and the Lady Luck, Pioneer Club and Lucky Lucy's gambling halls.

The area also has the best collection of street people. Wandering the sidewalks are the Runyonesque types that made Las Vegas famous: derelicts, touts, beggars, thieves and barkers who shout come-ons for casinos.

Fremont Street is frequently blocked off for local parades, including the St. Patrick's Day, Helldorado Days, Nevada Days Celebration, National Finals Rodeo and Christmas parades (check the Calendar in Chapter 1 for more information). It is also the site of an annual New Year's Eve Party where thousands of frenzied revelers crowd into the street below the Union Plaza Hotel, imagining they're in Times Square.

Rising above the Pioneer Club (25 East Fremont Street; 702-386-5000) is the famous **Vegas Vic** sign, the city's oldest neon sign. The waving, "Howdy Partner" cowboy has been greeting visitors since 1951. Across the street is its better half, **Sassy Sally**, a neon cowgirl perched precariously over Sassy Sally's Casino (32 East Fremont Street; 702-382-5777), famous for its Belt-Bustin' Barbecue Ribs and foam-hatted cowgirls handing out coupons.

The only Las Vegas hotel without a neon sign is the **Golden Nugget** (129 East Fremont Street; 702-385-7111). The posh, white-marble resort has everything else, however, including the world's largest gold nugget—a 36-pounder—in a display case just outside the gift shop.

Another hotel worth visiting is **Binion's Horseshoe** (128 East Fremont Street; 702-382-1600), where you can have your photo taken with $1 million in cash. The hotel boasts a no-limit gambling policy, and it is the site of the annual World Series of Poker, which guarantees at least $1 million to the winner. The bronze statue of a cowboy on horseback at the corner of Casino Center and Ogden Avenue is of Benny Binion, founder of the Horseshoe. He was convicted of second degree murder (in Texas) and served time for income tax evasion. He never held public office, but he is considered one of the city's foremost founding fathers and original gambling visionaries. His family continues to operate the Horseshoe as one of the few successful noncorporate resorts in Las Vegas.

If you're looking for a change in luck, go to the **Lucky Forest Museum** in Fitzgerald's Hotel & Casino (301 East Fremont Street; 702-388-2400), the tallest building in Nevada at 34 stories. Here you'll find the ultimate in lucky charms, like a crystal ball containing 10,000 four-leaf clovers and one of Secretariat's horseshoes. The exhibits tell the origin of some common and obscure superstitions and good-luck symbols, such as two-tailed lizards and medicine bags.

Across the street is the **El Portal Theater** (310 East Fremont Street), the city's first modern movie house, which was built in 1928. The once-elegant facility is now used as a souvenir shop, although the original marquee still stands.

At the opposite end of the gambling spectrum from the upscale casinos that cater to high rollers is the **Gold Spike Hotel & Casino** (400 East Ogden Avenue; 702-384-8444), which offers the best gambling deal in town. All blackjack tables have a $1 minimum, most slot and video poker machines take nickels and you can still play the penny slots here.

Children take center stage at the **Rainbow Company** (821 Las Vegas Boulevard North; 702-229-6553; admission). Sponsored by the city of Las Vegas, this troupe consists of 35 members between the ages of 7 and 17. The company stages a full season of family-oriented productions, including classics such as *Sleeping Beauty* and awareness-raising productions such as *Apologies*, a drama about teen suicide.

The **Lied Discovery Children's Museum** (833 Las Vegas Boulevard North; 702-382-5437; admission) hasn't a single "Do Not Touch" sign in the building; instead, children are invited to interact with the 130 exhibits. The experience is more than fun and games; exhibits challenge kids' physical and mental abilities while demonstrating principles of art, science and the humanities. One exhibit gives you a chance to guide a model space shuttle into orbit; another tests your ability to shoot baskets—while sitting in a wheelchair. Your reaction time is measured with a drag-race light; whispers are transmitted across the building by way of parabolic "dishes"; and make-believe supermarkets and banks teach children how to shop and—equally important—how to pay for things.

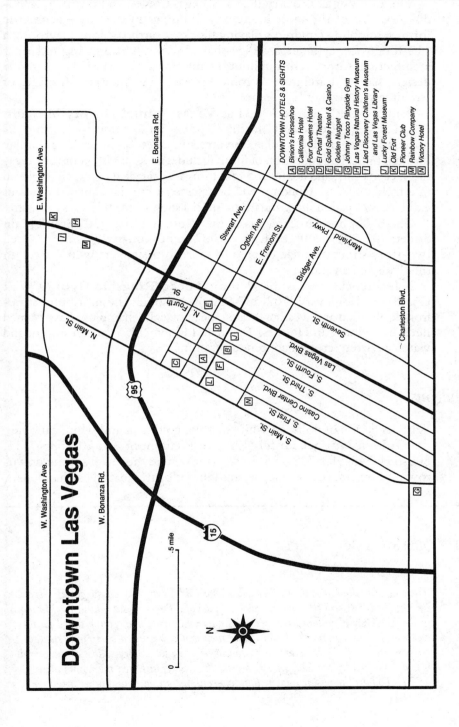

Downtown Las Vegas

DOWNTOWN HOTELS & SIGHTS

A Binion's Horseshoe
B California Hotel
C Four Queens Hotel
D El Portal Theater
E Gold Spike Hotel & Casino
F Golden Nugget
G Johnny Tocco Ringside Gym
H Las Vegas Natural History Museum
I Lied Discovery Children's Museum
    and Las Vegas Library
J Lucky Forest Museum
K Old Fort
L Pioneer Club
M Rainbow Company
N Victory Hotel

The **Las Vegas Library** (833 Las Vegas Boulevard North; 702-382-3493) is one of the most interesting buildings in the city—geometric forms resembling children's playing blocks, a birthday cone playroom, a 112-foot tower cylinder, a wedge-shaped administration wing and other architectural surprises throughout the interior are combined in a unique design that won architect Antoine Predock the American Institute of Architects' Award of Excellence.

Another kids' favorite is the **Las Vegas Natural History Museum** (900 Las Vegas Boulevard North; 702-384-3466; admission). From dinosaurs to present-day wildlife, the museum takes its visitors on a journey through time. The collection of fossils includes skeletons of prehistoric creatures, cave bears, and a skull and foot from a *Tyrannosaurus rex*, all displayed in a lifelike setting. Children will be fascinated by the animated dinosaur exhibits, 300-gallon shark aquarium, special shows and children's museum.

The oldest hotel in Las Vegas is the **Victory Hotel** (307 South Main Street; 702-384-0260), built in 1910. The mission-style, white-washed two-story structure once catered to railroad passengers who relaxed in the shade of its veranda.

A few blocks west is the **Johnny Tocco Ringside Gym** (9 West Charleston Boulevard; 702-387-9320). Although the moribund storefront looks tired and weather-beaten, heavyweight champions have trained here, including Ali, Holmes, Tyson and Holyfield. You can stop in and watch a current crop of contenders training.

Lodging

With its facade of polished white marble, gold trim and white canopies, the **Golden Nugget Hotel** (129 East Fremont Street; 702-385-7111, 800-634-3454, fax 702-386-8362) stands out as the jewel among downtown hostelries. Inside, the elegant lobby features leaf-glass chandeliers,

---

THE OLD MORMON FORT

*The oldest building in southern Nevada is **The Old Fort** (908 Las Vegas Boulevard North; 702-386-6510), which was once part of a larger presidio built by Mormons in 1855. They abandoned it three years later when Brigham Young called for the return of his missionaries to Utah. Since then it has been used as a ranch shed, a guest room for an 1895 resort and a concrete-testing laboratory. Most of the presidio was demolished by the Elks in 1963, and the city repurchased the remnant in 1971. Today, the restored adobe building contains antiques and other artifacts.*

The Las Vegas Stars, Triple A affiliate of the San Diego Padres, step up to bat at the Cashman Field Complex (850 Las Vegas Boulevard North; 702-386-7100).

white marble floors and columns, etched-glass panels, gold and brass accessories, and red Oriental rugs. The white-marble-and-gold-trim motif is carried throughout the casino, restaurants and common areas. The 1900 guest rooms are among the most luxurious in town and feature cream-colored carpets and wall covering, light-wood tables, club chairs and tropical print bedspreads and draperies. Hotel amenities include four fine restaurants, a celebrity showroom and an outdoor pool surrounded by mature palm trees. Moderate to deluxe.

The first thing you notice about **Binion's Horseshoe** (128 East Fremont Street; 702-382-1600, 800-622-6468, fax 702-384-1574, though please confirm reservations by voice) is the noisy, elbow-to-elbow casino. The emphasis here is on gambling, Wild West style. Not unexpectedly, the hotel's decor reflects an Old West theme with dark wood panels, etched-glass chandeliers and antique furnishings. Of the 380 guest rooms, 80 are part of the original hotel; all of these offer Victorian wallpaper and brass or painted-iron beds and quilted spreads. The 300 tower rooms, which were annexed from the defunct Mint Hotel, are more modern in decor, featuring plush carpeting, velvet headboards and white-enameled furniture. The hotel's steak house is one of the best in town, and the rooftop restaurant has sweeping views of the city. Budget to moderate.

The 650-room **California Hotel** (12 Ogden Avenue; 702-385-1222, 800-634-6255, fax 702-388-2660) has catered to the Hawaiian tourist market since it was built in 1975. About 90 percent of the clientele is from the Islands, so hotel staff wear aloha shirts, the restaurants serve Asian specialties and the bars offer tropical drinks. The main casino floor, which is decorated with crystal chandeliers, etched glass and Italian marble, features two restaurants, two bars and a 24-hour coffee shop. The mezzanine level has a Waikiki-style bar, sports book (betting area) and cluster of shops. The rooms are decorated with peach-and-blue upholstery and drapes, rust carpeting and light wood paneling and trim. The California added about 400 guest rooms when it purchased the Main Street Station, located directly across Main Street. The rose rooms, which are used for overflow from the main hotel, are clean but somewhat motel-like with faux-wood furnishings and faded carpeting. The hotel plans to reopen Main Street Station's casino and other public areas in late 1994 or early 1995. Budget.

Reflecting a New Orleans motif, the **Four Queens Hotel** (202 Fremont Street; 702-385-4011, 800-634-6045, fax 702-387-5122) is the grand old dame of downtown. The lobby decor suggests the French

Quarter with its carved wood registration desk, brass trim, and hurricane-lamp chandeliers. The 720 bright and cheerful rooms feature plush tan carpets, dark polished wood furniture, brocade wallpaper and Victorian four-poster beds. Hotel amenities include three restaurants, two bars and a lounge for the hotel's famous Monday night jazz concerts. For seniors 55 and older, the Four Queens Club 55 entitles members to discounts on rooms (seven days a week), meals, drinks and services. Members are also invited to special parties, bingo sessions and other events. Budget.

Jackie Gaughan's Plaza Hotel (1 Main Street; 702-386-2110, 800-634-6575, fax 702-382-8281) is the only caravansary in town with a built-in train depot and Greyhound bus station. Rail and bus travelers can step off the platform into the hotel's casino. The 1037 moderately priced rooms are open and airy and feature plush green carpeting, walnut veneer, and colorful patterned draperies and bedspreads. Make sure you ask for a room that faces Fremont Street rather than the railroad yard behind the hotel. The complex has three restaurants, including one serving excellent Chinese-Thai cuisine and another with a front-row view of Glitter Gulch's neon pyrotechnics. Other amenities include a celebrity showroom, a pool, a jogging track and the only tennis courts in the downtown area.

Every day is St. Patrick's Day at the 34-story **Fitzgerald's Hotel** (301 Fremont Street; 702-388-2400, 800-274-5825, fax 702-388-2181), the tallest building in the state of Nevada. Commonly referred to as the "Fitz," the 650-room hotel has a playful "Luck of the Irish" theme: Shamrocks, leprechauns and four-leaf clovers are used throughout, along with emerald-green carpeting and wall covering in public areas and green uniforms for the staff. The budget-priced rooms have dark green carpeting, but the wall coverings and furnishings are more subdued in light

---

DOWNTOWN'S FIRSTBORN

Built in 1941, the El Cortez (600 East Fremont Street; 702-385-5200, 800-634-6703) is the oldest hotel-casino in town. The southwest wing retains the original adobe brick building, tiled roof and neon marquee, which once stood three blocks from the nearest paved street. Since then, a 14-story, 200-room tower has been added, but the original walk-up rooms with wooden floors and tile baths remain. The hotel was once owned by Benjamin "Bugsy" Siegel, who sold it when he needed to raise cash for his "Fabulous" Flamingo Hotel on the Strip. Today, El Cortez caters mostly to budget travelers, seniors and slot players. The tower rooms, modest with modern furnishings, are budget-priced. Two restaurants, which often have long lines, serve large portions at bargain prices.

Built in 1923, the Hitching Post Wedding Chapel (226 Las Vegas Boulevard South; 702-387-5080) is the city's oldest.

---

pastels and earth tones. The large casino dominates the hotel's ground level, with restaurants and bar on the mezzanine.

The **Lady Luck Hotel** (206 North Third Street; 702-477-3000, 800-523-9582, fax 702-477-3002) is favored by tour groups because of its 796 budget-priced rooms and bargain restaurants. The hotel also has one of the brightest casinos in town. The contemporary guest rooms are also bright and open and feature pastel color schemes and light-wood furnishings. In addition to three restaurants and an all-you-can-eat buffet, the hotel offers a heated pool and cabaret lounge entertainment.

One of the best-kept secrets downtown is the **Las Vegas Club** (18 East Fremont Street; 702-385-1664, 800-634-6532, fax 702-387-6071). Despite its glittery neon and mirrored exterior, the hotel has a friendly, small-town atmosphere. The lobby is separate from the casino, with potted plants and comfortable chairs for relaxing. The hall leading to the casino is decorated with sports memorabilia such as autographed photos, baseballs, bats and gloves, vintage programs and ticket stubs. The mirrored ceiling creates an open feeling—even when it's packed, the casino never feels cramped and noisy. The 224 budget-priced rooms are modern affairs with Southwestern color schemes, white wood furniture and ceramic lamps. The hotel has a good steak house and an excellent coffee shop, which usually draws a line of people for breakfast and lunch sittings.

Restaurants

The aroma of mesquite-broiled seafood greets visitors to the **Pasta Pirate** (12 Ogden Avenue; 702-385-1222) in the California Hotel. Patterned after a dockside fish factory, the intimate room features open ventilator ducts, a brick floor, tin walls, fishnets and neon signs. The budget-to-moderate-priced specials include steamed clams, Australian sea bass and snow crab legs. Ask about the fresh catch of the day. The hotel's **Redwood Bar & Grill** features a cozy lodge atmosphere accented by decorative wood paneling, copper fixtures, country English furniture and a fieldstone fireplace. The deluxe-priced cuisine includes steak Diane, chicken with apricot sauce, roast prime rib and an 18-ounce porterhouse steak special.

Salvadoreño (720 North Main Street; 702-385-3600) serves authentic Salvadoran cuisine in a hole-in-the-wall eatery. Although the jukebox is sometimes loud enough to wake the dead, and the walls are covered with maps and posters of chaotic El Salvador, the cuisine is both politically correct and fiscally prudent. Seating is of the early dinette school of design, and *plátanos* (fried bananas in milk) and *pastelles de gallina* (chicken and vegetable pies) are budget-priced. Other hearty entrées are *carne guisada* (beef stew with carrots, potatoes, rice and refried beans) and *pollo encebollado* (deep-fried chicken with onions and bell peppers). The thick, homemade corn tortillas are of the I-dare-you-to-eat-just-one variety. Budget.

Hearty eaters will like **Binion's Steakhouse** (128 East Fremont Street; 702-382-1600) in Binion's Horseshoe Hotel. Brocade-covered booths and oil paintings highlight the restaurant's Old West theme. Be prepared for generous portions of prime rib, New York steak, filet mignon or a 20-ounce porterhouse steak. Fish and chicken dishes are also offered. Moderate. For gourmet dining with a view of the city, take the hotel's exterior glass elevator to the **Skye Room**, where the specialty of the house is veal Oscar. Other deluxe to ultra-deluxe entrées include roast Long Island duckling and rack of lamb. Night owls will find Las Vegas' all-time food bargain in Binion's 24-hour **coffee shop**: a complete New York steak dinner for two bucks, served from 10 p.m. to 5:30 a.m.

If you think the best restaurants are found in the most expensive hotels, come to **Andre's** (401 South Sixth Street; 702-385-5016). Here, in a converted wood-frame house on a downtown side street, you'll find classic French cuisine in several intimate dining rooms, all dimly lit, discreet and furnished with country antiques. As you would expect, the service is impeccable. Appetizers include smoked baby coho salmon with dill sauce; smoked trout with *rémoulade* sauce; three pâtés with black currant sauce; and snails *en croûte maison* or bourguignonne. Main entrées include frogs' legs, imported Dover sole, stuffed Australian lobster tail, and stuffed pork tenderloin with apples and walnuts. The dessert cart adds the perfect touch: almond chocolate cake, fruit tarts or fresh berries. There's also an extensive wine cellar. Deluxe to ultra-deluxe.

FOOD ON THE RUN

In addition to the hot dog stands and soft-pretzel vendors, there are a few good inexpensive places to grab a quick bite. **Kung Fu** *(110 North Third Street; 702-384-9734) serves a variety of Thai and Chinese specialties in generous portions.* **Your Place or Mine** *(621 Carson Avenue; 702-386-6060) is a great spot for breakfast or lunch; the avocado, green pepper and fruit salads and wholesome sandwiches will satisfy the most famished shopper. Be sure to try the homemade date-nut bread.* **Fritter's** *(316 Bridger Avenue; 702-384-3115) also serves only breakfast and lunch, specializing in bagels and croissant sandwiches, along with ice cream and frozen yogurt.*

The Center Stage Restaurant (Jackie Gaughan's Plaza Hotel, 1 Main Street; 702-386-2513) provides the best view of Glitter Gulch's neon light show.

Some of the better deals in the city are at the Lady Luck Hotel (206 North Third Street; 702-477-3000). The **Prime Rib Room** features a prime rib dinner and all-you-can-eat salad bar at budget prices. Other specials in the garden-style, rattan-accented dining room include the bountiful breakfast and lunch buffets. Budget-priced Chinese cuisine and rare Asian art are featured in the **Emperor's Room**. Mainstays include Mandarin garlic chicken, shrimp and scallops in a nest and Peking duck. After dining, be sure to check out the *Soldiers of Xian* replicas. Plush burgundy velour will ensconce diners in the intimate **Burgundy Room**, where they can view art by Salvador Dali and sculptures by Max Le Verrier. The house specialty is Maine lobster, chosen live from the tank at the entrance. Other deluxe-priced entrées include fresh swordfish, salmon and seafood kabobs, and Black Angus beef selections. The seafood served over angel-hair pasta is a delight.

Posh and cozy best describe **Lillie Langtry's** (129 East Fremont Street; 702-385-7111) in the Golden Nugget Hotel. Draped booths, Venetian-glass chandeliers and a domed ceiling help create one of the nicest rooms downtown. Traditional Cantonese favorites such as stir-fried lobster, Mongolian beef and Kung Pao chicken are the mainstays on the deluxe-to-ultra-deluxe-priced menu. For Italian specialties visit **Stefano's**, a cheerful room accented by colorful murals, hand-blown glass chandeliers and tiles from Salerno. Deluxe entrées include linguine with clams, scampi *fra diavolo* and veal piccata, or create a meal with appetizers such as fresh mussels, calamari *alla Luciana* and steamed clams.

Another classy downtown restaurant is **Hugo's Cellar** (202 East Fremont Street; 702-385-4011) at the Four Queens Hotel. A fresh rose handed to each female guest sets the tone for dining in this intimate, brick-and-brass-accented room. Entrées include steaks, veal, lamb, duck, chicken and seafood. A waiter prepares your salad tableside from a well-stocked cart. A compote tray of chocolate-dipped fruits precedes the pastry cart, which tempts you with sweet treats. Moderate to deluxe.

For authentic and inexpensive Mexican food visit **El Sombrero** (807 South Main Street; 702-382-9234). From the outside, this tiny cantina looks like a Tijuana jail, complete with bars on the windows. It doesn't improve much on the inside—six booths, six tables, a loud Mexican jukebox and a garish wall mural. But the food is good and plentiful: *menudo, chile colorado, natillas* and dinner specials—shrimp on tomatoes, scrambled eggs with Mexican sausage, and diced beef with red chili sauce. Selections on the breakfast and lunch menus are among the best bargains in the city.

For traditional dishes with a Pacific Rim influence, try the **Second Street Grill** (200 East Fremont Street; 702-385-3232) in Sam Boyd's Fremont Hotel. The spacious dining room has a neo-Roman flourish with faux-marble columns, indirect lighting, and white wood furniture with dark upholstery and tablecloths. In addition to seafood, veal, beef and poultry entrées, you can sample innovative specialty dishes such as deep-fried *lumpia* with basil-peanut dip, Mongolian hot seafood pot, wok-charred salmon and king-crab-leg hash. Moderate.

A favorite with locals for decades, **Chicago Joe's** (820 South Fourth Street; 702-382-5246) is a delightful restaurant in a converted home near the downtown courthouse. The dining areas, separated by the bar, are small but not cramped. Specialties include snails and pasta, lobster, veal, eggplant parmigiana, lasagna, cheese ravioli, linguine with calamari, fresh steamed or baked clams and meatball sandwiches. Moderate.

Shopping

The Las Vegas neighborhood known as Glitter Gulch suffered a commercial decline during the 1980s, mainly because of the shift in tourism to the Strip's megaresorts and the growth of retail centers in the suburbs. But the new Fremont Street Experience is expected to revitalize downtown when it's completed in mid to late 1995. In order to help keep pace with the high-tech attractions at the Strip resorts, downtown hotel owners in mid-1994 began construction of a massive canopy that will eventually cover Fremont Street from Main Street to Las Vegas Boulevard. When completed, the canopy—called *The Fremont Street Experience*—will provide laser light, pyrotechnic and special effects shows for walkers below, who will find Fremont Street converted to a walking mall.

In the meantime, the area's shopping consists mostly of souvenir and T-shirt shops, drugstores, check-cashing outlets, pawnshops and fast-food eateries. There are a few gems, however, hidden downtown.

LAS VEGAS GOES '50s

For Las Vegas' version of "Happy Days," pop in a Buddy Holly tape and drive to **Wimpy's** *(2437 Las Vegas Boulevard North; 702-642-5710). This drive-in (not drive-through) has been around since poodle skirts and saddle shoes. The teens back in the '50s used to gather here and at the Blue Onion on East Charleston. Well, the Blue Onion is gone, but Wimpy's remains. Pull up to the service phone and order a burger, corn dog, turkey sandwich, chili dog, banana split or milk shake. Budget.*

Hawaii sends more tourists to Las Vegas than any other state except California.

One of them is the **Desert Indian Shop** (108 North Third Street; 702-384-4977), notable for its imaginative collection of Navajo, Zuni and Hopi jewelry and crafts. The turquoise-inlaid bolos and rings and etched silver bracelets are particularly beautiful. If you're lucky, you might even meet some of the artists who come here from Arizona and New Mexico to sell their handiwork. Also on sale are artifacts of the Old West.

Another store specializing in Indian art and crafts is **Trader Bill's** (324 Fremont Street; 702-383-1010), which also sells a complete line of authentic moccasins, baskets, rugs and handmade pottery.

Just a few blocks south of Fremont Street you'll find the city's largest selection of turquoise jewelry at **Turquoise Chief** (1402 Las Vegas Boulevard South; 702-383-6069). This shop also handles Native American sand paintings, dolls, bolos and hand-carved fetishes.

A fun place to visit is **Sunglass City** (506 Fremont Street; 702-388-0622), with its huge assortment of designer sunglasses—everything from Ray-Ban and Revo to Porsche and Serengeti. Even more fun than picking out a pair is haggling over the price. You can save considerably over what you would pay in a mall boutique if you're persistent. The store also stocks thousands of men's and women's watches, from 14K gold Rolexes to $1.99 plastic models.

If you have a sharp eye for a bargain, especially in jewelry, consider one of the local pawnshops. Gamblers frequently turn to them for quick cash, so you can often find an inexpensive VCR, guitar or gold ring. On my last visit to **Bobby's Jewelry & Loan** (626 Las Vegas Boulevard South; 702-382-2486), I found a smoke sapphire man's ring and tourmaline woman's ring, both selling for one-third of their value. Other places to check are **Ace Loan Company** (215 North Third Street; 702-384-5771), **Stoney's Loan & Jewelry** (126 South First Street; 702-384-2686) and **The Hock Shop** (808 Las Vegas Boulevard South; 702-384-3042).

If you need a change in your luck, or love life, there's **Bell, Book & Candle** (1725 East Charleston Boulevard; 702-384-6807), which sells potions, charms, talismans, crystal balls and other "magick" supplies (*magick* because the emphasis here is on sorcery and witchcraft, rather than New Age occult and metaphysics). The store also stocks rare candles, books and tapes, conducts classes in witchcraft, and has a black cat patrolling the display cases.

Instead of stuffing coins into a slot machine (the casinos will hate me for this), why not buy one and take it home with you? They are legal in about 40 states (the dealers have updated lists), and local merchants usually guarantee their machines and ship them to your home. Most of the reconditioned electronic slot machines start at around $900. Video poker machines are slightly higher. If you shop and haggle you may save on the price. The mechanically operated antique slot machines are more costly. A vintage "War Eagle" or a "Bursting Cherry" can cost between $2500 and $3000. The genuine antiques—100 years and older—can command prices in five figures.

Some of the better places to purchase gambling equipment are in or near downtown. One of the largest collections of slot machines—as well as other gambling supplies—is at **Gamblers General Store** (800 South Main Street; 702-382-9903). Here you can select from two dozen reconditioned and vintage slot machines. Also on hand are full-size blackjack, craps and roulette tables—complete with green-felt layouts—priced from $1200 to $5000. Or, if you need a folding poker table for your friendly Saturday-night get-togethers, you can buy one for about $250.

The General Store also stocks every type of gambling paraphernalia imaginable. In addition to hundreds of gambling books and videos, you can buy playing cards, dice sets, customized poker chips, coin changers, green visor shades, raffle drums, bingo cages and boards, a dealer apron (one size fits all), croupier sticks and felt layouts for every type of casino game. There are even dice-inlaid toilet seats so you'll never forget where your money went in Las Vegas.

The House of Antique Slots (1243 Las Vegas Boulevard South; 702-382-1520) has a museum-like collection of older gambling devices, as well as antique vending machines, furniture and wall art. Other dealers worth checking are **Ancient Slots & Antiques** (3127 Industrial Road; 702-796-7779); **A-1 Casino Slots** (2206 Paradise Road; 702-

---

A MOST UNUSUAL TRADING POST

Ray's Beaver Bag (727 Las Vegas Boulevard South; 702-386-8746) is probably the strangest, and most interesting, store in town. Advertised as a pre-1840 black-powder gun shop, the store is more like a Yukon trading post. Of course, it does stock a complete line of black-powder muzzle loaders—all reproductions—and accessories. But there's so much more: hunting knives and tomahawks, cast-iron cookware, coonskin caps, snake-tanning kits, beeswax from Maine, handmade moccasins, leather pouches and bags, and authentic Indian porcupine-quill jewelry. Even if you don't intend to go trapping or fur trading, you'll want to look at the racks of pioneer and western clothing. There are cotton frontier dresses, dusters, capotes made from Hudson Bay blankets, a full-length bearskin coat and the original calvary coat worn by actor Gary Cole in the film Son of Morning Star.

735-3935), which also sells vintage jukeboxes and coke machines; **J&T Inc.** (2603 South Highland Avenue; 702-732-4712), specializing in antique slot machines; and **Slot Machines for Sale** (3021 Business Lane; 702-736-5900), which also carries blackjack, keno and video poker machines, as well as vintage vending machines.

For books on the history, restoration or collecting of slot machines, stop by **Mead Publishing** (1515 South Commerce Street; 702-387-8750). You'll also find a variety of books on pinball machines, jukeboxes and other coin-operated collectibles, as well as gambling-related publications.

If words like "psychedelic" and "love-in" recall good memories, you'll want to visit **Vintage Madness** (918 South Fourth Street; 702-386-3910). This funky little store—a converted house—is vintage 1960s, overflowing with racks of bell-bottoms, flower-power skirts, tie-dyed T-shirts, Jackie Kennedy–style dresses, Nehru jackets, Madras shirts, Cuban-heeled shoes, costume jewelry and much more. To enhance your shopping pleasure, rock music from the 60s plays constantly, and the interior is a colorful psychedelic explosion.

For more of the retro look, **Flashback** (1460 East Charleston Boulevard; 702-598-0633) will suit you. It is crammed with men's and women's clothes, shoes and accessories—even underwear—from the 1940s through the 1970s, along with a small collection of vintage radios, and a massive professional hairdryer from a 50s beauty shop—perfect for inflating your bouffant hairdo. Some of the memorable blasts from the past might include a 60s bandstand tuxedo with satin piping, lamb broadtail jackets with matching pillbox hats and silk ties from the 40s. For a 70s look, try platform shoes and boots, some with rhinestones embedded in the heels. Don't overlook the glass display cases in the back; they hold such treasures as 60s "cat" eyeglass frames and rhinestone junk jewelry.

Other shops where you might find a slinky evening gown, fox stole, sequined party dress, satin nightgown or any other type of vintage clothing—from the avant garde to the whimsical—include **Deja Vu** (2046 East Charleston Boulevard; 702-382-1165); **Re-Finery** (518 Park Paseo; 702-384-7340); **Designing Woman** (600 South Sixth Street; 702-385-0888); and **Valentino's Zootsuit Collection** (1111 Las Vegas Boulevard South; 702-383-9555), which has a fabulous selection of men's ties from the 1920s to the 1940s.

ANTIQUES GUILD

Little-known to most tourists, as well as many Las Vegas residents, are the antique and collectible shops on East Charleston Boulevard, just a couple of miles southeast of the downtown area. There are about two dozen, and most belong to an informal guild that promotes their stores.

Hub Cap Annie's (1602 East Charleston Boulevard; 702-387-1148) claims to have the world's largest collection of hub caps. Where she got 'em—or why—is a mystery.

Many of them retain the charm of the converted homes they occupy. Their treasures range from Victorian jewelry and antique German clocks to vintage pipe organs and retro-chic clothing. East Charleston may not have the panache of say, Los Angeles' Melrose Avenue, but shoppers won't be intimidated by overbearing salespeople or outlandish prices.

Silver Horse Antiques (1651 East Charleston Boulevard; 702-385-2700) sells all categories of antiques and collectibles, from ebony dresser sets, cast-iron skillets, glassware, china, old bottles and cruets to oak sideboards and dressers—with prices ranging from a few dollars for an old glass-stoppered bottle to a thousand for a dining table. An unusual feature of the store is the functioning, one-chair (vintage, of course) barber shop, complete with wall cases displaying straight razors, shaving mugs and brushes.

Under the same roof in the back room is the **Sunshine Clock Shop** (702-363-1312), featuring a collection that includes a genuine Calumet wall clock, German-made and Tiffany grandfather clocks, mantle clocks like your grandmother owned and black iron clocks from the 1930s. Ray Emery, one of eight certified clock-makers in the United States, collects clocks from around the country to display here, and can restore or repair yours.

Located in a cavernous two-story warehouse, **Red Rooster Antiques** (307 West Charleston Avenue; 702-382-5253) offers the country look in collectibles, furniture and handcrafted gifts. Wander through the many rooms and you'll discover glass milk bottles, canning jars, hand-embroidered linens and old kitchen tools like hand-cranked nut grinders and orange presses. Among the furniture, you'll find dressers, hall trees, cupboards, sideboards, a weathered trunk and—perhaps—a horse-collar mirror. There's even a niche for old rusted farm implements and livestock harnesses.

The **Gypsy Caravan Mall** (624 South Maryland Parkway; 702-384-1870) is a collection of about 20 dealers who've set up shop in a converted grocery store. Here you'll find everything from vintage furniture such as a French recamier, Chinese silk chests and English spool cabinets to antique metal toys and lunch boxes to Victorian jewelry and glassware.

For upscale antiquers, **Showcase Antiques** (1632 East Charleston Boulevard; 702-384-1117) tends toward the well-designed or the unusual in furniture and china, with an accent on the Asian. In this clean airy shop, with Oriental rugs underfoot, you'll find such items as an elegant small desk that has hidden compartments and folds into a chest on legs; a fringed silk grand-piano shawl with superlative Asian embroidery; a fine rush-seat, ladder-back bench; a small foldaway dining table with cane-seat chairs; a Frank Lloyd Wright–style lamp; and a sleek mahogany hall table and matching beveled mirror. Be sure to look in the back rooms where the owner has collected antique organs with pipes and foot pedals.

Antique Square (2014–2026 East Charleston Boulevard) is home to a dozen stores. One of the best in this serpentine mall is **Nicolas & Osvaldo** (702-386-0238), where several rooms and a long hall lined with cabinets show off a large range of antiques. A mix of periods, styles and tastes is reflected in the crystal, china, decorative teacups, clocks, chandeliers and silver tea sets. One cabinet is filled with tiny sterling silver pieces: salt and pepper shakers, spoons, thimbles, tea strainers, pickle forks, cream pitchers, baby spoons, coasters and napkin rings. And bronze art deco table lamps, statuettes, busts and statues dot the shop's landscape. If metal statuary doesn't appeal, try the palace urn from the Meissen region of Germany, the Civil War battle flag, or the 17th-century rosewood desk ornately carved with fire-breathing dragons.

American collectibles are the specialty at **Yana's Junke** (Antique Square; 702-388-0051). Displayed are items such as a hand-cranked ice cream maker, a pierced-tin cabinet, Ball canning jars, and Coca-Cola ice chests.

Gagliano's Antiques (702-366-8561) offers gold and silver coins, Asian and primitive artifacts, early Americana and a few big game trophies. On display are coins, old costume jewelry and real jewelry. Old tools decorate the walls. The shop also contains a collection of tin boxes, coffee grinders and butter churns, some 100 to 200 years old, including a glass Dazey churn with wooden paddles.

Treasures waiting to be found at **Granny's Nook** (702-598-1983) might include a pineapple-decorated poster bed, an upholstered bench, marble-topped and tiled washstands, an oak desk with red inlaid leather and a pair of converted carriage lamps. Other possibilities include handmade quilts and embroidered linens, a cupid photo in a double-heart-shaped frame and a white Denmark telephone from the 1930s. Among the plates and decorative ceramics you'll find fiesta ware, blue willow and a humorous yellow ceramic camel cookie jar.

If you enjoy sifting through boxes of classy junk, come to **Devere's Curiosity Shop** (702-366-8555), where you may unearth letter-openers, Asian carvings, hat pins and postcards.

Nicholas Antonio Antiques (702-385-7772) has an unending selection of swords, knives and daggers, as well as such attractions as a 12-inch square carved ivory box, a three-inch-high Chinese ivory horseman, ivory-headed walking sticks, armies of two-inch lead soldiers, a collection of silver pocketknives and a shoebox of old postcards.

Your pocketbook may not be able to stand it, but most of the items at **Buzz & Co. Fine Antiques** (702-384-2034) are breathtaking. There's a 19th-century French d'or bronze chandelier; an inlaid leather-topped brass-trimmed cherry desk; and a pair of Italian frosted green glass horses weighing 60 pounds each—originally made for royalty and signed by the artist. Any shopper would be dazzled by the Tiffany dragonfly lamp, the Italian majolica vase from the late 19th century or the bronze mermaid hoisting a real shell overhead that holds not a pearl but a light bulb.

A Little Bit of Heaven (702-383-9599) sprawls over several large rooms and offers such items as a white porcelain Christmas creche, panels of stained glass, a collection of china animal salt and pepper shakers and a set of yellow Federal glass dishes. You may also find a collection of tiny clocks, Hummels or *Wizard of Oz* plates, as well as bed and armoire sets.

A few blocks east of Antique Square, **Yesteryear Mart** (1626 East Charleston Boulevard; 702-384-6946) shows off exquisite art glass pieces, bowls, lamps and a fine jewelry collection, as well as some furniture.

Maudie's Antique Cottage (3310 East Charleston Boulevard; 702-457-4379) is a converted house fronted by a white picket fence. Inside, you'll find Victorian-flavored American antiques along with gifts, new and antique dolls and teddy bears. All of the furniture here has been refinished, from marble-topped hall tables and washstands to pine and oak Hoosiers. The floor and ceiling lamps are antiques but the shop also carries reproductions. Doll collectors can find Maud Humphreys, Bessie Pease Gutmans, Madame Alexanders and Jennys, a 1930s bisque Kewpie-like doll and a Victorian baby doll. Fiesta ware, Jewel-T dinnerware and dancing animal pitchers are among the other collectibles.

Although not among the shops on East Charleston Boulevard, **Losee Road Antiques** (2270 Losee Road; 702-649-3800) is a 5000-square-foot emporium that recently joined the guild and merits attention. About 20 dealers share space under the roof of this converted factory. You'll find

---

NEW TO YOU

Sugarplums (2022 East Charleston Boulevard; 702-385-6059) is a treasure chest of collectibles, featuring fancy crystal and china, decorative wall plates, dolls, porcelain figurines, evening bags from the 1920s and 1930s, and late-1800s silverware and perfume bottles. Although the furniture in this exquisite shop is for sale, the owner uses it to display miniatures such as saltcellars with tiny spoons, thimbles, deco rings and Victorian cameos.

In 1988 a perfume and scent bottle society was formed at the shop with 18 people from across the nation; in three years' time it had grown to an international membership of 950. Here you'll see everything from massive 24-ounce perfume bottles down to the tiniest scent bottle and art-glass atomizers. You may also discover such treasures as the 1800–1830s French crystal and gold-plated scent box containing six bottles and funnels.

Hoosier cabinets, desks, secretaries, quilts, glassware, clocks, early televisions and radios, primitives, farm equipment and collectibles.

Nightlife

For an old-fashioned jam session try the **Fremont Street Reggae and
Blues Club** (400 East Fremont Street; 702-594-4640), a storefront nightclub decorated in cold black, silver and grays but often packed to the
rafters with rollicking revelers. The nightspot is a hangout for members
of the Las Vegas Blues Society and popular reggae groups such as Fully &
Betta, Black Uhuru and Pete Thoennes, open seven nights a week. Cover.

A few blocks from the courthouse, **Down Under Grill & Pub** (300
South Fourth Street; 702-382-6162) attracts more attorneys than an industrial accident. But don't despair, they're here to enjoy the atmosphere, not to take depositions. Despite the name, the only connection to
Australia is a picture of a kangaroo. But the dart games are fun, the deli
food is tasty, the booths are private and the fish tanks are soothing.

If you're an anglophile looking for a quiet drink and some conversation with transplanted Brits, go to the **Mad Dogs and Englishmen
Pub** (515 South Las Vegas Boulevard; 702-382-5075). The retreat offers darts, 19 specialty beers and ales and a young, hip mix of patrons.

Melinda: The First Lady of Magic and Her Folies Revue at the **Lady Luck
Hotel** (206 North Third Street; 702-477-3000) is downtown's only
full-scale production show. In addition to Melinda Saxe's parlor-room
tricks, which often use animals such as camels and exotic birds, the show
features chorus-line dancers and a world-class juggler. Nudity in the late
show; cover charge.

The **French Quarter Lounge** (202 East Fremont Street; 702-385-
4011) at the Four Queens Hotel resembles a New Orleans courtyard, complete with ivy trellises and a mural of a Southern mansion. Musicians from
pop and Cajun to country-and-western begin in the afternoon. The award-
winning Monday Night Jazz session has been a tradition since 1982. Shows
lean toward the big band era, although national and international guest artists
are often featured. No cover, but there's a two-drink minimum.

The **Cabaret Showroom** (129 East Fremont Street; 702-385-7111)
in the Golden Nugget Hotel is the only downtown hotel to offer headliner
entertainment. More intimate than the Strip theaters, the Cabaret features
stars such as Don Rickles, Lou Rawls and Melissa Manchester. Cover.

For a jolt of alternative and underground rock, visit the **Huntridge
Performing Arts Theatre** (1208 East Charleston Boulevard; 702-477-
0242), a converted movie house built in the 1940s that now hosts dance
parties and concerts featuring mostly local bands, with occasional headliners such as Motorhead and Area 51.

FOUR

Greater Las Vegas

Most visitors are surprised, if not shocked, to learn there's a *city* beyond the bright lights of the Strip resorts and Glitter Gulch casinos. But not far from the pulsating delirium of the gambling halls and showroom extravaganzas is a modern, exuberant city of 850,000 citizens, with its own uncommon sights and unique attractions waiting to be discovered.

On the surface, the Greater Las Vegas area appears to be like any other Southwestern city, complete with schools and libraries, baseball diamonds and swimming pools, shopping malls and inner-city neighborhoods, haute cuisine and history, art museums and classical music. Look closer and you'll discover this city's slice of life is speckled; it has more texture and depth than most communities.

Perhaps it's the influence of the glamorous resort industry or the city's frontier heritage that creates a sense of freedom, fantasy, luxury and mobility, and makes this a municipal kaleidoscope unlike anywhere else in the country.

Why bother venturing beyond the Strip and downtown tourist centers? There are a hundred reasons, any of which would justify the effort. See the mildly exotic animals of Nevada's only public zoological park; visit the restored buildings of a Wild West ghost town at the Heritage Museum; discover Korean calligraphy, bonsai pots and hand-carved fishbone in the city's rapidly growing Asian commercial center; sample innovative cuisine from Southern deep-fried chicken to Middle Eastern delicacies; twirl around a country-and-western dancefloor ablaze with color or skim across a crystalline ice skating rink; shop for handmade crafts and jewelry from regional Native Americans; ponder avant garde art displays of bullet-riddled highway signs and exhibits of neon sculp-

The Liberace Museum glitters and glows as the area's third-most popular tourist attraction, behind Hoover Dam and Lake Mead.

ture; attend Saturday evening concerts in the park or Sunday afternoon football games; gape at 300 varieties of desert succulents, marvel at the inner workings of a gourmet chocolate factory or buy a lock-picking kit, can of Mace or submachine gun (after you've had a chance to fire it).

Exploring Greater Las Vegas is a great way to detox from a busy convention or a marathon gambling session, but most of all it's a way to experience the city Tom Wolfe once called the "Versailles of America."

If you find tinsel titillating, a must-see is the **Liberace Museum** (1775 East Tropicana Avenue in the Liberace Plaza; 702-798-5595; admission). Dedicated to the flamboyant entertainer, the museum features Liberace's sequined, jeweled and rhinestoned costumes, feathered capes and million-dollar furs. Also in the collection are stage jewelry, including a piano-shaped ring with 260 diamonds, ivory keys and black jade in a white-and-yellow 18-K gold setting, 15 rare and antique pianos and five cars—highlighted by a custom Rolls Royce decorated with thousands of mirror tiles. There is also a reproduction of Liberace's office and bedroom from his Spanish-style hacienda in Palm Springs, displaying his miniature piano collection, personal music arrangements, a rare Moser crystal collection from Czechoslovakia, a variety of musical instruments and an ornately inlaid Louis XV desk originally owned by Czar Nicholas II of Russia.

For pop art, **Debora Spanover Fine Art** (1775 East Tropicana Avenue in the Liberace Plaza; 702-739-0072) specializes in originals, limited editions and animation art. People-pleasing artists represented include Erté, Alvar, Andy Warhol, Roy Lichtenstein and Peter Max.

On the campus of the University of Nevada, Las Vegas (UNLV) is the **Marjorie Barrick Museum of Natural History** (702-739-3381), featuring exhibits of live desert reptiles, mammals and insects. A special display houses the endangered desert tortoise. The adjoining arboretum has a collection of indigenous plants as well as a demonstration garden. There are also exhibits dealing with archaeology and anthropology, Mojave desert fossils and a large skeleton of an ichthyosaur, a whale-sized sea lizard that is Nevada's state fossil.

The **Donna Beam Gallery** (702-895-3893), also on the UNLV campus, holds exhibits by students and faculty of the university's Department of Art. In addition, the UNLV-based Nevada Institute for Contemporary Art presents the work of guest artists here, such as Luis Jimenez's sculpture and drawings. A recent exhibition included photos on the demise of rivers in the Southwest due to damming.

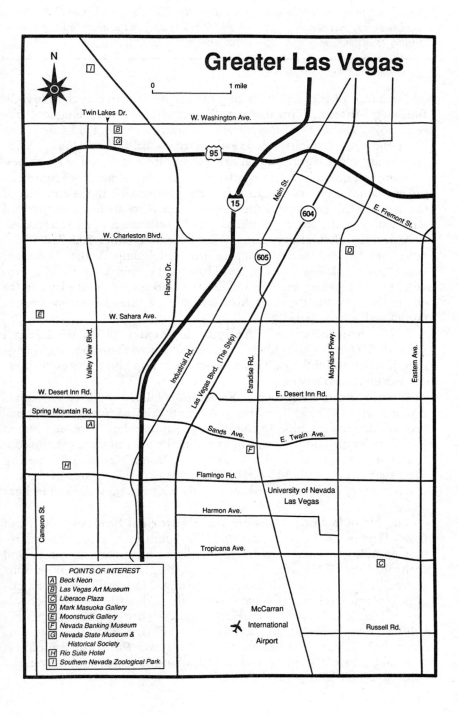

N

Greater Las Vegas

0   1 mile

Twin Lakes Dr.

W. Washington Ave.

95

15

Main St.

604

E. Fremont St.

W. Charleston Blvd.

Rancho Dr.

605

W. Sahara Ave.

Valley View Blvd.

Industrial Rd.

Las Vegas Blvd. (The Strip)

Paradise Rd.

Maryland Pkwy.

Eastern Ave.

W. Desert Inn Rd.

E. Desert Inn Rd.

Spring Mountain Rd.

Sands Ave.

E. Twain Ave.

Flamingo Rd.

University of Nevada
Las Vegas

Cameron St.

Harmon Ave.

Tropicana Ave.

POINTS OF INTEREST
A Beck Neon
B Las Vegas Art Museum
C Liberace Plaza
D Mark Masuoka Gallery
E Moonstruck Gallery
F Nevada Banking Museum
G Nevada State Museum &
   Historical Society
H Rio Suite Hotel
I Southern Nevada Zoological Park

McCarran
International
Airport

Russell Rd.

Raising awareness about the hearing impaired, the Sign Design Theatre (9 Cactus Garden Drive, Henderson; 702-454-7446) brings deaf and hearing children together to perform more than 200 shows annually.

A century of the state's banking history is contained at the **Nevada Banking Museum** (First Interstate Tower, 3800 Howard Hughes Parkway; 702-791-6373). Displays trace the history of 200 banks that have come and gone. Exhibits include early currency, passbooks, letterhead, liberty bonds, silver ingots, gambling tokens, coins and old teller machines.

Although not known as a citadel of the arts, Las Vegas has a burgeoning arts community whose artists find their inspiration in the austerity of the desert or the gaudiness of the Strip. Because there are few preconceived standards or traditions to uphold, the artistic climate is open and fertile.

Moonstruck Gallery (6368 West Sahara Avenue; 702-364-0531) represents an imaginative group of artists including Robert Bateman, Bev Doolittle, James Gurney, and Howard Terpning, whose Western, wildlife and aviation originals and limited editions are on display and for sale in this storefront gallery. Also available are fine glass sculpture, ceramics and custom jewelry.

Stroll across the street to **Antigua de Mexico** (6374 West Sahara Avenue; 702-253-0101) for Mexican handcrafted furniture, wall hangings, jewelry and folk art. This well-stocked shop also features Japanese acrylics by Kei Amatsu.

Western artists are shown at **Kneeland Gallery** (4750 West Sahara Avenue; 702-870-5933), where you'll find original, watercolors, pen-and-ink drawings, sculpture and jewelry. Among the artists represented are Veloy Vigil, Thom Ross, Michael King Prime and Gregg Robinson.

For quintessential Las Vegas art go to **Beck Neon** (3889 Spring Mountain Road; 702-362-0616), the city's first gallery and studio devoted entirely to neon art. Pieces include wall art and sculpture in light and glass.

The **Nevada State Museum and Historical Society** (700 Twin Lakes Drive, Las Vegas; 702-486-5205; admission), a 35,000-square-foot complex, displays and interprets the history, natural history and anthropology of Nevada. Three permanent galleries contain exhibits on regional history (mining, nuclear testing, Hoover Dam and ranching), biological science (flora and fauna of the desert), and the archeology of southern Nevada. Three other galleries are devoted to rotating exhibits. There are also an auditorium and library, bookstore and museum shop. Located on the grounds of **Lorenzi Park**, the museum is surrounded by native plants and animals of southern Nevada, as well as a small, five-acre lake.

Across the lake is the **Las Vegas Art Museum** (3333 West Washington Boulevard; 702-647-4300). Built in 1935 from wooden railroad ties, the museum's three galleries have rotating exhibits of local artists' work. A reception–open house for exhibiting artists is held the first Sunday of the month. There's also a permanent collection of 20th-century Western art.

Offbeat works of prominent Nevada artists and upcoming talent are showcased at the **Mark Masuoka Gallery** (1149 South Maryland Parkway; 702-366-0377). Artists featured include John Buck, Misha Gordin, Jun Kaneko and Hiroki Morinoue. Exhibitions vary from oil, gold leaf and aluminum leaf on canvas to photographs of desert shooting sites.

The only public zoo in the state, the **Southern Nevada Zoological Park** (1775 North Rancho Drive; 702-648-5955; admission) has a small but interesting collection of rare and exotic animals, Western wildlife, botanical displays and a petting zoo. Included are a Bengal tiger, an Asian spotted leopard, an African lion, African green monkeys and a cougar who was nursed back to health after being transported here from northern Nevada by the highway patrol. The friendly staff explains the history behind each exhibit.

Most of the city's neon landmarks were created by the **Young Electric Sign Company** (5119 Cameron Street; 702-876-8080), the oldest neon sign company in southern Nevada. A visit to the company's boneyard of old signs is worth the trip. Neon relics include the old Silver Slipper and original Golden Nugget signs.

Horse lovers should consider **Horseman's Park** (5800 East Flamingo Road; 702-455-7508), a complete equestrian center that includes lighted rodeo and show arenas. The park hosts major rodeos, horse shows and other equestrian events throughout the year.

CULTURE IN LAS VEGAS?

Although Las Vegas doesn't threaten Stratford-on-Avon as a cultural citadel, the city has a lively and expanding arts community. It is home to dozens of resident arts groups and galleries, a nationally respected dance theater, a symphony orchestra, an opera company, community theaters, chamber music ensembles and museums. Some of the biggest names in classical music, from Itzhak Perlman to Leontyne Price, have toured Las Vegas as part of the university's Charles Vanda Master Series. International dance troupes and ensembles have been guests of the Southern Nevada Community Concert Association. To find out what's happening in town, check the Friday edition of the Las Vegas Review-Journal. *Or call the city's 24-hour **Arts Hotline** (702-385-4444, ext. 2172).*

Next door is **Dog Fancier's Park**, a 12-acre facility dedicated to dog shows and training classes. Call the Clark County Parks and Recreation Department at (702) 455-7508 for a schedule of events for either park.

A great place to spend a couple of hours is the **Ethel M Chocolate Factory & Cactus Garden** (2 Cactus Garden Drive, Henderson; 702-458-8864). The *M* stands for *Mars*, as in Forrest Mars—the creator of Mars Bars, Milky Ways, 3 Musketeers, Snickers and M&Ms. Mars, one of the world's wealthiest men, lives in Las Vegas. Ethel M Chocolates were named for the candy magnate's mother and are now produced exclusively in Las Vegas, where the factory is open daily for free tours. Most of the activity takes place weekday mornings; from behind glass windows, when you can watch gourmet chocolates being created, then sample some of the butter creams, truffles, caramels or nut clusters.

If you define a good read as the Burpee seed catalogue, and names like Vaux-le-Vicomte, Stowe and Sissinghurts make your green thumb tingle, then walk next door. The Ethel M Cactus Garden is a 2.5-acre outdoor preserve rich with more than 350 species of cacti, succulents and desert plants such as ocotillo, Clokeys cholla, aloe vera and prickly pear. The garden was designed and landscaped by Gary Lyons, curator of the Desert Garden of the Huntington Library and Botanical Gardens in California. Just be sure to heed the sign: "Please be careful. Cactus bite."

If the chocolates haven't given you a sugar high, drive over to the **Kidd Marshmallow Factory** (8203 Gibson Road, Henderson; 702-564-5400), where you can watch marshmallows being made and sample the results.

The colorful history of the Las Vegas region is recorded at the **Clark County Heritage Museum** (1830 South Boulder Highway, Henderson; 702-455-7955; admission). There's a permanent time-line exhibit, where visitors can explore a prehistoric gypsum cave, learn about minerals in a reconstructed mine, cruise down the Colorado River by steam-

---

HERITAGE STREET

*Step back in time as you tour **Heritage Street** (1830 South Boulder Highway, Henderson; 702-455-7955; admission), a collection of historic buildings and houses from various periods in southern Nevada's history that have been relocated to the grounds of the Clark County Heritage Museum, renovated and furnished with period artifacts. Visit a 1900s newspaper print shop complete with working press and copies of early newspapers; a resurrected ghost town featuring weather-beaten structures and vintage vehicles from the 1880s era; and a railroad depot, 1905 Union Pacific steam engine, boxcar and caboose.*

boat, or visit an early Vegas tent house. The exhibit also includes a display of original gambling equipment and memorabilia. The gift shop sells educational toys, Native American arts and crafts, minerals, books, publications and gifts that relate to Nevada or the Southwest.

Lodging

An increasingly popular phenomenon in Las Vegas is the neighborhood hotel-casino, sometimes built on the outskirts of town and usually remote from established tourist centers. The idea behind these resorts was to provide a place where residents could gamble and otherwise entertain themselves in a less tourist-oriented environment. As it turned out, these hotels have become attractive to visitors because of their friendly atmosphere, budget rates and unique amenities.

A Brazilian carnival is the theme at **Rio Suite Hotel** (3200 West Flamingo Road; 702-252-7777, 800-888-1808, fax 702-253-6090), an upbeat, fast-paced resort. About two miles west of the Strip, the hotel is easily identified by its brightly lit sign resembling a geyser erupting neon streams of water. In the registration area, guests are greeted by brass parrots, colorful ribbons of neon, nautilus shells on the ceiling and plush carpeting that suggests a floor of confetti and streamers. The 860 suites feature rich earth tones accented by tropical-print spreads and curtains, smoked-glass tables, velour and rattan furnishings in the sitting area, floor-to-ceiling windows for panoramic city views, refrigerators, electronic safes and drip coffeemakers. Hotel amenities include three restaurants, a New York–style bar-and-grill and a pool area with a sandy beach, waterfalls and palm trees. Moderate.

The most popular neighborhood hotel is the **Gold Coast Hotel** (4000 West Flamingo Road; 702-367-7111, 800-331-5334, fax 702-367-8419). The complex has a Spanish flair, with a white adobe exterior and red tile roof. The registration area features tiled floors, an arched entry, carved wood doors and stained-glass windows. The 750 rooms are large and bright, with plush blue carpet, light adobe walls with wood trim, and Southwestern-style curtains and spreads. The list of hotel amenities has something for everyone: four restaurants, five bars, two large casinos, a 72-lane bowling alley, a country-and-western dance hall and a cabaret lounge for other live bands. There's more: The pool is surrounded by landscaping, waterfalls and a tropical bar; the two movie theaters are the only ones in town to screen foreign and offbeat art films; and the tiny shopping arcade has a wine-and-spirits shop with more than 200 collectible miniatures. Moderate.

Originally built in the mid-1970s as a motor court and bingo parlor, the **Palace Station** (2411 West Sahara Avenue; 702-367-2411, 800-634-3101) has blossomed into a modern resort hotel. The bingo room is still one of the busiest in town, but the hotel now boasts five excellent restaurants, a piano bar, live entertainment, a new 22-story tower and a huge casino that caters to die-hard slot and video poker fanatics. The 600-room tower has a marbled lobby accented with chrome and polished brass, and decorated with restored and antique slot machines from the 1920s and 1930s. The rooms are decorated in warm colors contrasted with bold print bedspreads and feature carved wood furniture, overstuffed easy chairs, built-in dressing tables, floor-to-ceiling windows and brass wall and ceiling lamps; moderate. The 400 older rooms in the original section of the hotel are clean and pleasant with earth-tone color schemes. Budget to moderate.

Surrounded by open desert and mountains, the **Santa Fe Hotel** (4949 North Rancho Drive; 702-658-4900, 800-872-6823, fax 702-658-4919) is the newest of the neighborhood resorts. Because of its remote location, the farthest from the action, guests enjoy a more relaxed pace, and facilities are seldom crowded. As you'd expect from the name, the low-profile hotel has a Southwestern flavor, with white stucco walls and a red tile roof. The rooms are colored with cool pastels accented by Navajo-pattern prints and white wood furniture. The hotel has two restaurants, a lounge with Dixieland or jazz musicians, a bowling alley and an ice skating rink that doubles as an ice hockey arena. Budget.

If you want a taste of the Old West, circle the wagons and head for **Sam's Town Hotel** (5111 Boulder Highway; 702-456-7777, 800-634-6371, fax 702-454-8014). Starting with the Western movie-set exterior, everything here emphasizes the spirit of the Old West: There are a gambling hall, ten saloons and five restaurants offering up home-style chuck. Other amenities include a Western dance hall, bowling alley, horseshoe-shaped swimming pool, ice-cream parlor and two-story Western emporium that's the largest in Nevada. The 200 garden-style guest rooms are motel-modern, featuring modest decor in soft earth tones. Budget.

Restaurants

EASTSIDE   For a taste of North Africa, try the **Red Sea Restaurant** (2226 Paradise Road; 702-893-1740), which specializes in traditional Ethiopian cuisine. The dining area is small and cozy, like a living room, with overstuffed chairs—actually large cushions—and wooden basket tables that look like TV trays. The furnishings reflect the Ethiopian eating ritual: family members eat in a parlor setting rather than at a table. Most of the dishes consist of spicy stews of chicken, beef, spinach, eggs, greens, chickpeas and yogurt, all served on a communal *injera*, a large rubbery pancake made from teff, a grain from the Horn of Africa. Instead of utensils, pieces of the bread are broken off and used to scoop up the tasty stews and condiments. Accompany your meal with *mes*, a

---

Every day is Thanksgiving at the Country Inn (2425 East Desert Inn Road; 702-731-5035), where the specialty is a complete turkey dinner with all the fixings.

---

flavorful honey mead wine, or *sewa*, a dark barley beer. You should also try the Ethiopian coffee, which is sugared and cardamon-spiced and served ceremoniously in a traditional clay urn. Budget to moderate.

For a hearty and budget-priced meal check out the **Bootlegger** (5025 South Eastern Avenue; 702-736-4939). This family-run café is famous for its pasta selections: eggplant and broccoli parmigiana, baked rigatoni, lasagna, baked *mostaccioli* and baked meat ravioli. There's also a wide variety of seafood, beef, veal and chicken dinners. The house specialty is seafood *diavolo* made cioppino-style with jumbo shrimp, clams and calamari in marinara sauce, served over a bed of linguine.

Besides traditional Moroccan cuisine, **Marrakech** (3900 Paradise Road; 702-737-5611) offers the ambience of the North African desert. First you're seated at low, brass-inlaid tables with decorated pillows for reclining. Waiters dressed in traditional caftans and slippers perform the sacred hand-washing ritual. (The not-so-sacred belly dancers arrive later.) Then the deluxe-priced, seven-course dinner starts with Itarira soup and Moroccan salad. Pastilla—phyllo dough over a mixture of ground chicken, almonds and scrambled eggs—is next. But the real eating is just beginning: Flaming lamb brochette is followed by roast chicken or lamb shank and honey-covered *chabakia*.

The owners of **Jerome's** (4503 Paradise Road; 702-792-3772) wanted to bring a bit of San Francisco to Las Vegas. The food selections come close to hitting the Bay city's mark and include fresh sourdough bread, lamb Sausalito, Russian oysters and mussel saffron soup topped with puff pastry. Also featured are grilled sea scallops, blackened swordfish and grilled yellowfin tuna, as well as chicken, veal, beef and pasta dishes. Two extensive wine lists include a large selection of Napa Valley chardonnays and cabernet sauvignons and imported "cellar selections" such as a Mondavi/Rothschild Opus One and Chateau Margaux Bordeaux Pavillon Rouge. Moderate to deluxe.

For budget-priced Mexican food try **Garcia's** (1030 East Flamingo Road; 702-731-0628). This colorful restaurant, accented with Mexican tile and gigantic, rhinestone-studded sombreros, specializes in sizzling fajitas served on a table-top brazier. Also recommended are the chimichangas, tostadas, enchiladas and Mexican pizza—a flour tortilla covered with cheese and seasoned beef, ranchero sauce, diced tomatoes and a spicy Mexican garnish.

The most popular spot for outdoor dining is **Café Michelle** (1350 East Flamingo Road; 735-8686), except during July and August, when you can sauté mushrooms on the sidewalk. Dining alfresco in a shopping center may not compare to the Champs-Élysées, but think of all the francs you're saving. Besides, you might spot a celebrity while you dine on fresh fish, veal, pastas, crêpes, braised calf sweetbreads *financière*, asparagus and spinach omelettes and frittatas. Moderate.

The city's well-heeled "now" people congregate at **The Tillerman** (2245 East Flamingo Road; 702-731-4036). But you don't need a cellular phone to enjoy this bistro's skylight, central atrium or balcony seating. Famous for its seafood specials, the kitchen offers a catch of the day that could include Pacific salmon, swordfish, Chilean grouper, Norwegian salmon, shark or fresh tuna. Prime rib, New York strip and beef brochette are also popular entrées on the deluxe-priced menu. More than 200 labels are stocked in the wine cellar.

Innovative southern Italian food is the specialty at **Cipriani** (2790 East Flamingo Road; 702-367-6711). Don't let the silly lighthouse and beached lifeboat outside fool you. Inside, the dining room is posh with crystal chandeliers, French doors and salmon-colored drapes. Signature dishes include fettucine with caviar and salmon, veal Montebianco, chicken *frascati* and scampi imperiale. The five-course special dinner features osso bucco, seafood, veal or chicken. Moderate to deluxe.

The antipasto salad bar is the specialty at the **Vineyard** (3630 South Maryland Parkway; 702-731-1606), a grocery-style restaurant with fauxbrick walls, hanging plants, dark wood furniture, checkered tablecloths and a "pushcart" canopy over the buffet bar. Italian specialties include chicken Vesuvio, osso bucco, veal and homemade pasta. Budget to moderate.

The city's only strictly kosher restaurant, **Jerusalem Restaurant & Deli** (1305 Vegas Valley Drive; 702-735-2878) serves solid mainstream dishes in portions that would warm any Jewish mother's heart. The dinner feast includes soup or salad, stuffed cabbage, meatballs, kebab and baked chicken served with rice and vegetables. Other entrées are *suniyeh,* chicken schnitzel and beef Carmel—hummus topped with chopped beef and pine nuts. For lunch there are salami and pastrami sand-

---

THE ONLY GAME IN TOWN

*For more adventuresome game than you'll ever find in a casino, visit **Anthony's** (3620 East Flamingo Road; 702-454-0000). This lively restaurant, decorated with brass fixtures and etched glass, has the widest selection of fresh game in the city. Specialties include lion with port sauce, camel steak in Bordeaux sauce, buffalo steak in bordelaise sauce and alligator steak. Less exotic selections include orange roughy, broiled swordfish steak and quail stuffed with mushrooms. Deluxe.*

wiches, falafel, kebabs, tuna and potato salads and potato and vegetable latkes. Moderate.

The **Celebrity Deli** (4055 South Maryland Parkway; 702-733-7827) is a lively Bronx-style café, with tile floors, formica-topped dinette tables and wooden chairs, all surrounded by chilly pastels of pink and lavender. The budget-priced menu features traditional deli favorites such as corned beef, pastrami, turkey and salami, with dinner entrées such as smoked fish, stuffed cabbage, brisket of beef and Romanian steak. Among the fresh baked goods are bagels, knishes, kugels and danishes.

The chef at **Wo Fat** (3700 East Desert Inn Road; 702-451-6656) brought more than the name of the famous Honolulu restaurant to Las Vegas. He also brought many dishes that made the Chinatown restaurant so popular there. You can sample such Island chicken dishes as cold chicken in onion sauce, mushroom boneless chicken and pot-roast chicken. From the sea, there are lobster with black bean sauce, abalone with black mushrooms, shrimp with tomatoes and green peppers and clams with black bean sauce. Budget to moderate.

A scaled-down version of Benihana, **Geisha Steakhouse** (3751 East Desert Inn Road; 702-451-9814) serves complete Japanese dinners at six hibachi tables. Begin with beef and mushroom soup and then watch your chef orchestrate dinner on the hot table. Entrée choices are sesame chicken, thin New York steak, samurai New York steak, shogun filet mignon, scallops, shrimp and lobster—all served with hibachi shrimp, vegetables, fried rice and a glass of plum wine. Moderate.

Macayo Vegas (1741 East Charleston Boulevard; 702-382-5605) has been serving traditional Mexican dishes since 1960. The dining room is accented with Southwestern art and furnishings while the cuisine has a southern Mexican flavor. Entrées include chicken Maximilian, crab enchilada and shrimp à la Vera Cruz. Traditional fajitas, tamales, chimichangas and chile rellenos are also expertly prepared. Budget.

Another culinary landmark is **Fong's** (2021 East Charleston Boulevard; 702-382-1644), which originally opened in 1933 as the Silver Café. The big neon pagoda, Chinese-red booths and Buddha rock shrine bring the Far East to the Wild West. Traditional Chinese fare includes *moo goo gai pan*, almond duck, Chinese sausage with vegetables and abalone Cantonese. Tropical drinks such as the Scorpion, Zombie and Fong's Special are generous and potent. Budget to moderate.

RESTAURANT ROW   A two-mile stretch of East Tropicana Boulevard is home to a score of restaurants.

From the outside, **Rafters** (1350 East Tropicana Boulevard; 702-739-9463) looks like the Santa Barbara Mission, but inside the decor is distinctively San Francisco. So is the seafood, purchased in the San Francisco Bay Area and flown to Las Vegas. The blackboard specials vary with the season, but you can expect salmon, petrale sole, swordfish and sea bass, as well as other Pacific fish and shellfish. Oysters Rockefeller, topped with cayenne and Pernod, is the most popular appetizer. Vegetarians can choose pasta or tofu parmigiana. Two of the best desserts are the peaches in beaujolais with zabaglione sauce and Anjou pears poached in zinfandel and swimming in heavy cream. Deluxe.

Just a few steps from the Liberace Museum, **Carluccio's Tivoli Gardens** (1775 East Tropicana Boulevard; 702-795-3236) is a family-owned Italian restaurant serving generous portions. Inviting appetizers such as mussels, shrimp scampi, crab-stuffed shrimp, calamari and clams served steamed or baked on the half shell are the best offerings. House specialties include chicken florentine, shrimp *fra diavolo*, *zuppa de* clams, linguine with red or white clam sauce and seafood diablo. Prices range from budget to moderate.

China First (1801 East Tropicana Boulevard; 702-736-2828) is a friendly neighborhood restaurant that does a flavorful rendition of all the classics. A crisp-tablecloth setting is the backdrop for traditional Chinese dishes. Try the shrimp with vegetables in a lobster sauce or stir-fried with cashews and vegetables, pepper beef, ruby beef, lemon chicken and sweet-and-sour pork. The delicate shrimp puffs, lettuce chicken and mu shu pork are tasty appetizers. Desserts of glazed bananas or fried pudding are satisfying finales. Moderate.

At the **Sicilian Café** (3510 East Tropicana Boulevard; 702-456-1300) you can sample a taste of Sicily or learn to speak the language. The owners are three generations of Sicilians who serve up such specialties as chicken braciola, shrimp veneziani, caponatina, clams, mussels, cioppino, fettuccine con prosciutto, linguine pescatore and a variety of other pasta dishes. Choose from the informal, deli-style dining area with its

---

OLDIE BUT GOODIE

*The oldest restaurant in Las Vegas, the **Green Shack** (2504 East Fremont Street; 702-383-0007) is a little diner with a wagon-wheel front. When it originally opened as the Colorado in 1929, Jimmie Jones and her mother, Effie, sold fried chicken from the window of their two-room house. A railroad barracks was later converted and used as a dining room. The main part of today's dining room is that same barracks. The restaurant is clean and homey—handmade crafts and memorabilia from the early days adorn the dining room. A bar and cocktail lounge have been added, and a one-man band plays on weekends in the glow of the year-round Christmas tree. Moderate.*

For a fiesta complete with strolling mariachis and the largest margaritas in Las Vegas, drop in to Ricardo's (2380 East Tropicana Boulevard; 702-798-4515).

---

wooden café chairs and checkered tablecloths, or the formal dining room with deep green carpeting and upholstered booths. Moderate.

For hickory-smoked ribs, it's **Tommy's Barbecue** (3430 East Tropicana Boulevard; 702-435-7780). In this modest, wood-paneled dining room you can feast on moderately priced ribs, beef links, barbecued sirloin and chicken—all prepared in smoke ovens. Other entrées include steaks—filet mignon to porterhouse—and veal. The place is also famous for its onion rings and desserts. Try the strawberry amaretto, Oreo or cherry cheesecake, or the pecan pie.

WESTSIDE   Hidden in a shopping center, **Bamboo Garden** (4850 West Flamingo Road; 702-871-3262) is one of the best Chinese restaurants in Las Vegas. Because of its obscure location, it's seldom crowded. Owner Jack Tong, formerly of Caesars Palace, has put together an imaginative menu that features hot braised pineapple fish, sizzling fish Shanghai-style stir-fried with vegetables, chicken sautéed in honey sauce, firecracker beef made with a spicy hot pepper sauce and Hunan eggplant. You can also enjoy Mongolian lamb and oceania—seafood served in a nest. Moderate.

One of the few restaurants with a view of the entire Strip is **The 2nd Story** (4485 South Jones Boulevard; 702-368-2257). The panorama begins with a ride on an exterior elevator and ends with a table on the rooftop patio, which features a ceiling that opens and closes, depending on the weather. From here the Strip hotels look like sparkling diamonds on a black velvet cloth. Nightly specials range from orange roughy with fresh peach sauce and chicken breast stuffed with scallops to baby rack of lamb in honey mustard and smoked salmon with sour cream. Moderate.

Ferraro's (5900 West Flamingo Road; 702-364-5300) is a favorite hangout of Jerry Lewis' when he's in town. George Kirby, Paul Anka and a host of hotel executives also regularly feast on the southern Italian cuisine. This bistro is also a hit with locals, who make an entire meal of the appetizers, such as the artichoke stuffed with bread crumbs, garlic, romano cheese and black olives in light wine sauce, or the deep-fried squid in spicy tomato and onion sauce. Moderate.

For an authentic Chinese dining experience, head for the **Chinese Garden** (5485 West Sahara Avenue; 702-876-5432). Built pagoda-style with gardens in front, this elegant restaurant features a step-down dining room surrounded by private booths and a quiet cocktail lounge with a piano bar. Expect fresh, properly cooked food without MSG. Pick out your own live Maine lobster or crab from the fish tank. They are served Cantonese style, cooked in black bean garlic sauce with scallions and ginger. The flounder served on a bed of scallions and bean sprouts is a local favorite. The royal Peking duck is served tableside on a steamed biscuit with scallions. Traditional fare such as sweet-and-sour pork, *moo goo gai pan,* almond chicken, pineapple chicken and lychees for dessert are also available. Moderate.

If you enjoy dining alfresco, come to **Café Nicolle** (4760 West Sahara Avenue; 702-870-7675), where the outdoor tables are accented by palm trees and flower boxes, and misted with a fine spray during the hotter summer days. Inside, it's New York modern, with black-and-gray lucite tables accented with brass fixtures and red upholstery. Appetizers include French escargots *bourguignonne*, mushrooms stuffed with crabmeat and Italian prosciutto and melon. Entrées, served with either caesar or garden salad, include filet mignon with béarnaise sauce, lamb chops à la Greque with oregano, chicken française and veal piccata or scallopini. Moderate.

Great breakfasts are served at **The Egg and I** (4533 West Sahara Avenue; 702-364-9686), where customers line up early on weekend mornings. The wait is seldom long, and it's tempered by complimentary coffee or tea. Egg specialties include a variety of omelettes, huevos rancheros, eggs benedict and a vegetarian version with sliced tomatoes, avocado and two poached eggs, smothered in hollandaise sauce. All are served with ranch potatoes and a choice of toast or English muffin. Other favorites are the frittatas, open-faced omelettes served in the skillet, Belgian waffles served with blueberries or strawberries and French toast. The plate-sized pancakes are wonderful, especially the apple-and-cinnamon ones served with an applesauce syrup. A nice touch is the pitcher of ice water garnished with lemon slices and pot of hot coffee on the table. Budget.

A Southern-style mansion sets the scene for **Philip's Supper House** (4545 West Sahara Avenue; 702-873-5222). With three dining rooms, bay windows, upholstered walls and a cozy bar, it is a favorite with Vegas residents. The deluxe-priced menu features oysters Rockefeller, steamed clams, oysters on the half shell, scampi and artichoke hearts française. Among the popular entrées are lamb chops, steaks, veal and an enticing selection of seafood: blackened whitefish, scalone (a combination of scallops and abalone), halibut picante, scallops, swordfish steak, salmon, trout, sand dabs and Alaskan king crab legs. The dinner salads are of the knife-and-fork variety, and the hot bread is always fresh.

Osaka (4205 West Sahara Avenue; 702-876-4988) offers three ways to dine on Japanese cuisine: the sushi bar, the main dining room and the tatami room, where you remove your shoes and sit on the floor at low tables. Sushi offerings include inari cone, octopus, cucumber roll, flying fish eggs and a California roll of crab, shrimp, avocado and cucumber. Ask for low-sodium tamari sauce instead of soy sauce if you're health-conscious. Some of the exotic seafood selections are broiled eels teriyaki, sashimi, *yakisakana* and breaded oysters—all accompanied by soup, rice and tea. Moderate.

Authentic Vietnamese food is served at **Saigon** (4251 West Sahara Avenue; 702-362-9978), a small, storefront café with dinette-style seating. The food can be incendiary, so insist on full disclosure from your waiter. Signature specials are squid with traditional hot sauce, sautéed shrimp with vegetables and hot sautéed beef with lemongrass. Although Vietnam is not famous for desserts, do try the sweet yellow bean and coconut pudding. Moderate.

Living up to its name, **Harrington's Classic Steak Company** (4760 West Sahara Avenue; 702-878-7374) features a supper-club-style dining room with stained, dark wood panels, white-brocade-upholstered booths, hardwood tables with Windsor chairs and a grand piano. The specialty is hickory-broiled, aged Midwestern steaks, but you can also feast on fresh seafood, veal Oscar and game hens. The wines range from a Fetzer Chardonnay to a 1970 Mouton-Rothschild. Deluxe to ultra-deluxe.

Don't judge **The Venetian** (3713 West Sahara Avenue; 702-876-4190) by the ghastly, studio-set mural on its facade. It is a longtime favorite of Vegas residents. Since the mid-1950s, this family-run restaurant has served savory dishes such as neck bones à la Venetian—pork bones and meat marinated in wine, vinegar, capers and pepperoncini, then simmered until tender. Veal (milanese, scallopini, parmigiana, française and marsala) and chicken (cacciatore, angelo, marsala and al dentino) are the dinner mainstays, along with fresh seafood. Moderate.

If northern Italian is your desire, check out **Romeo's** (2800 West Sahara Avenue; 702-873-5400), an upscale, ivy-clad Italian restaurant in a mission-style building surrounded by trees, a lit fountain and a pond. Inside, it's "Tavern on the Green": deep teal carpet throughout, high-

---

A TASTE OF THE MIDDLE EAST

*One of the best finds in town is the **Middle Eastern Bazaar** (4147 South Maryland Parkway; 702-731-6030), situated in a nondescript shopping plaza near the university. Sticklers for grand decor and sophisticated service should look elsewhere. Here you place your order at the back of the grocery store, take a seat at one of the seven tables and wait. If you like Middle Eastern cuisine, the wait is worth it. Vegetarian specialties include baba ghanoush, baked eggplant, grape leaves, hummus and tabbouleh. Meaty offerings include kibbe, kabob sandwich (the house specialty) and gyros salad. Several varieties of Middle Eastern coffees are available—as well as Moroccan and chamomile teas. Complete your feast with the homemade rose water, saffron and pistachio ice cream and a cup of sweet Turkish coffee. Budget.*

backed upholstered chairs, double tablecloths and a brass-and-hardwood piano bar. Two of the best appetizers on the menu are the New Zealand green lip mussels and the little neck clams. The antipasto table overflows with buffalo mozzarella, carpaccio, roasted red peppers, calamari and marinated zucchini. Among the tasty entrées are cognac-flambéed veal, fettuccine with Norwegian king salmon and shallots, and filet mignon flavored with marsala. Deluxe.

For a California-style breakfast or lunch visit the **Coffee Pub** (2800 West Sahara Avenue; 702-367-1913), a stylish little bistro with mosaic-topped tables and patio dining. The menu is basically California With-It: sandwiches named for the Golden State's in-spots, spinach salad, quiche, crab soufflé roll, and soup and salad combinations. The natural shakes are made with fresh fruit juices and sorbet. Save room for dessert, because the carrot cake, chocolate mousse and homemade muffins are out of this world. The white chocolate cheesecake, especially with a cup of Kenya coffee, is sinful. Breakfast specials include omelettes, quiches, croissants, fresh fruit and muffins, bagels and Belgian waffles. Budget.

If you like fire and spice, **India King** (2202 West Charleston Boulevard in the Rancho Shopping Plaza; 702-385-7977) serves some of the finest Indian food this side of New Delhi. The extensive menu was created by executive chef Hans Raj Kapotra of the Hotel Oberoi Intercontinental in New Delhi. Begin with an appetizer of *chooza pakora* or vegetable samosa. The *roti* (barbecue bread) also makes a good begin-

---

COFFEEHOUSES STIR UP MEMORIES OF THE SIXTIES

In keeping with the retro-chic craze that has swept the fashion industry, Las Vegas has sprouted a number of coffeehouses that specialize in fresh-brewed espresso, cappuccino, caffe latte and café au lait. In some you'll even find quiet music, poetry readings and intelligent conversation. Among the better ones are the Java Hut (3860 West Sahara Avenue; 702-248-4844), which serves specialty coffees and gourmet pastries, along with live entertainment, poetry readings and storytelling; Cucina Espresso, Inc. (3900 Paradise Road; 702-792-9045), where you can sit outdoors and relax with a cup of gourmet coffee sandwiches and pastry; and the Coffee Bar in Basset Book Store (2323 South Decatur Boulevard; 702-258-0999), which features rich coffee blends, tasty pastries and weekly lectures delivered by local authors. Others worth visiting include Jitter's Gourmet Coffee (2457 East Tropicana Boulevard; 702-898-0056); Miss Italia Coffee Bar (2243 Rampart Boulevard; 702-228-3225); and Café Espresso Roma (4440 South Maryland Parkway; 702-369-1540), which attracts a noisy college crowd, except on Thursdays, which is reserved for poetry readings.

If you suffer from slot machine elbow, try Shiatsu Acupressure of Nevada (953 East Sahara Avenue in Commercial Center; 702-733-1978).

ning. Tandoori offerings, cooked in a charcoal clay oven, include chicken, boneless leg of lamb and minced lamb blended with spices and herbs. The curry dishes are incendiary but won't put you in an altered state. If you should find your temperature rising, cool down with a bottle of Golden Eagle Lager beer, India's number-one beer. Don't leave without trying one of the cold desserts, such as homemade Indian ice cream or rice pudding with almonds and pistachios. Moderate.

Hungry for a hearty, ranch-style breakfast? The **Omelet House** (2150 West Charleston Boulevard; 702-384-6868), a longtime favorite of the nearby medical center crowd, is a rustic eatery with wooden booths and tables. Voted the city's best breakfast house, it specializes in—can you guess—omelettes, a whopping 32 at last count. Unique varieties include one filled with ham, pineapple, coconut and cheese and another with crab stuffed with broccoli and smothered with cheddar cheese. All are accompanied by a heaping order of breakfast spuds. Although not as famous as the omelettes, the hamburgers are among the best in town. The homemade chili, vegetable soup, and ham and beans are also popular on the budget-priced menu.

Fine dining in a supermarket center? The **Aristocrat** (850 South Rancho Drive; 702-870-1977) is a storefront bistro with linen tablecloths, fresh flowers and a gourmet menu. Appetizers include mussels in mustard vinaigrette sauce, marinated salmon and bay scallops, crêpes filled with seafood and escargots in Roquefort. Nightly specials may include osso bucco, sautéed pheasant with port wine over wild rice, duck à l'orange over wild rice, chicken Oscar, thresher shark and saddle of rabbit. The chocolate mousse on a bed of raspberry sauce is a cruel joke for dieters. Moderate to deluxe.

If you crave more sweet treats, walk across the asphalt to **Rancho Bakery** (850 South Rancho Drive; 702-870-6449), rated among the city's best for pastries and fresh-baked bread, including the popular braided challah and rye breads, which sell out early in the day. Also very popular are the cheese and prune danish, black-and-white cookies and sugar-free turnovers, which you can take with you or enjoy with a cup of steaming espresso. Budget.

Bring an appetite to **Bob Taylor's Ranch House** (6250 Rio Vista Road; 702-645-1399), an Old West steak house, complete with tack and cowboy memorabilia on the walls. This place is famous for its steaks—thick, aged New York, filet mignon, T-bone, porterhouse—all cooked on a mesquite grill. If you have an unabashed appetite, there's a 28-

ounce Diamond Jim Brady cut (it should be Diamond John Candy cut). The slab takes a half hour to cook (medium rare) and who knows how long to eat. The menu also offers seafood and chicken dishes. Deluxe.

Shopping

Constructed in 1962, **Commercial Center** (953 East Sahara Avenue) is one of the oldest retail shopping centers in the city. Built like a U-shaped fort with parking in the center, it is a cluster of about 30 specialty shops and restaurants, flanked by Sahara and Karen avenues, about a mile east of the Strip.

Although the Center is home to several clothing boutiques, an art supply store, an athletic club and two pool halls, it is best known for its Asian shops and restaurants. Here you can slurp noodles, shop for a kimono or find the perfect bonsai pot.

Two markets, **Oriental Foods** (702-735-2788) and **Asian Market** (702-734-7653), are filled with Japanese and Chinese foodstuffs, from black-seaweed-wrapped crackers to dried cuttlefish. These are excellent places to buy fresh fish, exotic mushrooms and herbs. You'll also find shelves of inexpensive porcelain tea and sake sets, bowls, chopsticks, fans, magazines and videos.

For a wider variety, consider **David Ming Oriental Art Goods** (702-737-0277), a fabulous source of bamboo and rattan furniture, hand-carved fishbone, ivory, jade, rose quartz, amethyst and lapis figures. There are also rice-paper scrolls, hand-painted screens and silk kimonos.

Nearby is the **Korean Art & Gift Shop** (Commercial Center; 702-734-2700), specializing in the calligraphy and ceramic art of Changpo. Considered a national hero in his native Korea, Changpo is a master of the ancient art of calligraphy. His work, which appears on scrolls and vases, captures the artistic spirit of the 5000-year-old tradition. Also avail-

---

AN EYE TOWARD THE OCCULT

*If your soul needs healing, and whose doesn't, consider the **Psychic Eye Book Shop** (953 East Sahara Avenue in Commercial Center; 702-369-6622). Here you can buy herbs, crystals and amulets, find occult and astrology books and receive a psychic reading. Before you laugh, let me say I used to believe psychics were lucky prognosticators with a gift of gab and an ear for fad. But that was before I had my fortune told by Patrice. Her predictions were uncanny; it was like sitting in the front seat with Mother Teresa. Patrice is good, but you must call for an appointment.*

The ultimate gambler's bookstore is Gambler's Book Club (630 South 11th Street; 702-382-7555), a Las Vegas institution since its opening in 1964. Check out the compulsive gambling section.

able are watercolor drawings of Korean landscapes, ceramics, Korean cosmetics, kimonos and silk jackets.

For serious or novice philatelists, **Evans Stamps** (Commercial Center; 702-731-5543) has a collection from around the world. Here you can buy single-issue stamps or complete collections.

Just a few blocks south on Maryland Parkway is the **Boulevard Mall** (3528 South Maryland Parkway; 702-735-8268), the state's largest enclosed shopping center. Anchored by such department stores as Sears, J.C. Penney, Dillard's and Broadway Southwest, the mall has 140 stores that cater mostly to mid-range shoppers. The wide variety of merchandise offered includes clothing, shoes, greeting cards, books, jewelry, gifts, pet supplies, pharmaceuticals, and high-tech toys and gadgets. You can catch a movie at the mall's three-screen theater and refuel at the fast-food court. The valet parking is free, and you can have your car washed while you shop (not free).

Used bookstores are always a unique adventure. Poring over titles, it's hard to know what treasures you'll uncover. **Amber Unicorn** (2202 West Charleston Boulevard; 702-384-5838) is a bibliophile's dream. Here you can browse through thousands of well-organized used and antiquarian books, while sipping a cup of coffee or tea. Especially interesting is the collection of local history and lore.

There's something introspective—as well as adventurous—about browsing through a bookstore. You're intensely alone, until you stumble upon the right selection and are transported to a new and exciting world.

If you want some light reading for lounging around the pool or for the flight home, go to **Readmore Books & Magazines** (2560 South Maryland Parkway; 702-732-4453). Besides paperback books, the store carries the largest collection of magazines in town—thousands of titles, from *Alaska Men* and *Columbia Journalism Review* to *UFO* and *Tour America*.

Two other excellent used bookstores are **Albion Book Company** (2466 East Desert Inn Road; 702-792-9554), which specializes in Americana, military history and first editions, and **Book Stop III** (1440 East Charleston Boulevard; 702-386-4858), which stocks out-of-print and rare editions.

If you're looking for an out-of-town newspaper, the largest selection is at **Tower Records** (4110 South Maryland Parkway; 702-731-0800).

If your reading interest is the occult, there's the **Psychic Institute** (4800 South Maryland Parkway; 702-798-8448), right across the street from the university. In addition to books on astrology, yoga, tarot cards, psychic healing and other metaphysical subjects, you can purchase crystals, amulets and pyramid generators or have a psychic reading or aura portrait done here. Another fascinating shop is **Bertae Specialties** (2401 West Charleston Boulevard; 702-878-5113), specializing in inspirational, self-help, metaphysical, Christianity and meditation materials. You can also take a class in dowsing, hypnosis or ESP.

In addition to the city's antique guild, there's a **Collectible Record Dealers Alliance**, made up of several record shops specializing in rare records, tapes and sheet music. One of the oldest in town is the **Music Room** (1406 Las Vegas Boulevard South; 702-387-3366), which has a great jazz collection—record albums and sheet music—that includes Fats Waller, the Dorseys, Stan Getz, Gene Krupa and the complete Glenn Miller catalog. It also offers a good selection of opera, classical and Broadway tunes, and has antique radios, phonographs and posters for sale.

On the wall of **The Last Record Store** (555 East Sahara Avenue; 702-796-8001) is a sign that reads: Get a Life—Get a Turntable. Good advice, considering the store has the largest collection of used record albums in the city. Well represented are rare rock from the '50s, '60s and '70s, as well as jazz, Broadway and movie soundtracks.

If you've ever wondered what happened to all those 45-rpm singles, go to **J-Mars Records** (2620 South Maryland Parkway, 702-796-6366). Here you'll find the largest selection of 45s in the city—from early pop and rock to classical. There's a huge collection of Beatles music—albums and tapes—as well as posters, buttons and other memorabilia.

The music at **The Underground** (1164 East Twain Avenue; 702-733-7025) is not yet vintage but might be collectible. Specializing in alternative rock, imports and college radio, the store has a curious selection of albums, tapes and discs, from African Head Charge and the Young Black Teenagers to Bad Brains and the Butthole Surfers. You can also find a T-shirt or poster to go with your offbeat album.

AGENT 007 SHOPPED HERE

*When I first walked into the **Spy Factory** (2228 Paradise Road; 702-893-0779), I thought it was a novelty store. After all, those couldn't be real smoke grenades, stun guns or lock-picking kits. But they were real, as are the electronic surveillance devices and wiretaps, bullet-proof vests and cans of mace. Some of the wares that might actually be useful include a wallet that beeps when you leave your credit card behind, rearview sunglasses, a safe disguised as a box of Quaker Oats, a radar detector and a video camera the size of a pack of cigarettes. Counterespionage, anyone?*

Nightlife

At **Carollo's** (2301 East Sunset Road; 702-361-3712), dark wood paneling and oil paintings of the New England countryside make a strange backdrop for live rock music, but it works. The dancefloor is packed on the weekend; the Wednesday night talent contests and Thursday ladies' nights are also popular.

Although it sounds inconceivable, heavy metal *lite* is the fare at **Hurricane** (1650 East Tropicana Avenue; 702-798-3883), where the punkish crowd wears purposely ripped jeans, and tattoo their noses rather than pierce them. This makes for a more civilized venture onto the huge, step-down dancefloor, where you can bang heads to the twangy strains of loud local bands. There's also a weekly talent contest in which "Tomorrow's Stars Today" assault your eardrums. Cover.

Sneakers (2250 East Tropicana Avenue; 702-798-0272) is all a sports bar should be: laid-back and friendly, raucous at times, with everything from golf clubs (wood shafts!) and hockey sticks on the wall to two satellite dishes on the roof. And, with ten big screens for optimal viewing and the best burgers in town, this is couch-potato heaven. Another thing: After the games have ended, they turn up the music and have a block party in front of the place.

Leave your silk tie and crocodile purse at the hotel when you come to **Ferdinand's** (5006 South Maryland Parkway; 702-798-6962), a throwback to old Las Vegas. The building is ghastly gray brick with a torn canopy over the entrance, but it's better on the inside, where longtime customers sit on drooping couches around the pool table, listen to country-and-western on the jukebox or watch movies on the large screen. The regulars look like extras from "Green Acres," but it's a fun place. Luaus, pool, video-poker tourneys and all-you-can-eat rib parties are held regularly. And there's an entire wall devoted to jazz memorabilia, a reminder of the days when Carl Fontana played here.

Most of the city's major concerts, operas, plays and dance productions are presented at the University of Nevada, Las Vegas (UNLV) **Performing Arts Center** (4505 South Maryland Parkway; 702-739-3535). At the heart of UNLV's modern facility is the 1900-seat **Artemus Ham Concert Hall**, whose acoustics were once praised by violinist Isaac Stern as warm and vibrant. Also part of the Center are the 530-seat Judy Baley Theatre and the more intimate 235-seat **Black Box Theatre**.

You can't miss the trendy **Hard Rock Café** (4475 Paradise Road; 702-733-8400) at the corner of Paradise and Harmon—there's a 77-foot-high guitar out front. Inside, it's rock-and-roll memorabilia, signed photos and lots of college students. The bar is lively, and the food is excellent.

Strip entertainers and visiting celebrities who like to be seen come to **Café Michelle** (1350 East Flamingo Road; 702-732-8687) for an after-show drink in the quiet, intimate lounge portion of this popular café. The piano bar and the outdoor patio are popular during the week. There's jazz on the weekends.

Schizophrenics will love **Goodtimes** (1775 East Tropicana Avenue; 702-736-9494), the city's only split personality nightclub. On one side you've got a friendly, neighborhood "Cheers"-style cocktail lounge with wood paneling, fireplace, piano bar and friendly service. But just down the hall you've got a maniacal disco with neon lights, a 3000-watt sound system and a stainless steel dancefloor. The deejay plays mostly techno-industrial rock, but during occasional lapses he'll feature sweet-sounding Motown and Beatles tunes from the '60s. The club lives up to its name on Thursday nights, when Trash Disco is the theme and people squeeze into their bellbottoms and faux-silk shirts and disco duck to the Bee Gees and Donna Summer. Cover.

Despite its chain-store heritage, **TGI Friday's** (1800 East Flamingo Road; 702-732-9905) is one of the city's three best singles bars. Despite the nonstop trading of phone numbers, the atmosphere is casual, not desperate, and the emphasis is on fun. There's an extensive menu and a nice dining area.

If you already have a date, go to **Favorites** (4110 South Maryland Parkway; 702-796-1776), a friendly little affair with tiny wooden café tables and a huge oak bar. The dollar draft beer is appealing, but the feature attraction is the variety of live music, ranging from an 18-piece jazz band jamming on Thursday nights to frequent razings by out-of-town punk groups. When the music dies down, take a turn at the pool table, but beware the redhead who goes by the alias Sandy.

For a bit of Ireland, try **Paddy's Pub** (4160 South Pecos Road; 702-435-1684). The colonial yellow building with white pillars belies the quaint Irish pub inside. Guinness, Harp and Bass are on tap; Shamrock, Schnapps and Bushmill Irish whiskey are among the bar offerings. Irish stew, corned beef and cabbage, fish and chips, and a lively game of darts round out the Dublin-like experience.

ACADEMIA ACTION

*Located across from the university campus, the atmosphere at **Big Al and Eddie's** (4632 South Maryland Parkway; 702-736-7808) is quiet and restrained. Perhaps that's why it's an early-evening meeting place for university professors, who gather to discuss cognitive dissonance, Max Planck's Theory and other light topics. A nice place for a quiet drink and conversation.*

You can fire a live submachine gun, 9 mm Uzi or other automatic weapon (fee required) at The Gun Store (2900 East Tropicana Avenue; 702-454-1110).

Arthur Murray would have had a field day at **Pepper's Lounge** (2929 East Desert Inn Road; 702-731-3234). Live entertainment varies from contemporary rock and big band to Latin salsa and easy listening. But the dancers—almost exclusively a local crowd—seem like they know what they're doing.

A popular singles hangout, **Elephant Bar** (2797 Maryland Parkway; 702-737-1586) has a safari ambiance. A cascading waterfall greets visitors to the lounge, decorated with faux palm trees, revolving ceiling fans and rattan furniture. Not exactly Nairobi, but the tropical drinks are strong enough to make it an upbeat watering hole frequented by young corporate types.

The most popular country spot in town, the **Silver Dollar Saloon** (2501 East Charleston Boulevard; 702-382-6921) features a large dancefloor, and a stage with live music nightly. During the day you can sit at the ample horseshoe-shaped bar or play pool and listen to Shenandoah, Eddie Raven and the Judds on the jukebox.

Die-hard rock fans will love the **Shark Club** (3765 East Harmon Avenue; 702-795-7525), which caters to a youngish crowd that hip-hops to techno pop, alternative and Top-40 dance tunes. Surrounding the ample dancefloor are walls of video screens that play reverberating rock videos interspersed with weird cartoons. Ladies are admitted free on Tuesday and Thursday nights, and on Wednesdays there's an all-acoustic jam session. Cover.

The cow skulls and branding irons are the tip-off: **Rockabilly's** (4660 Boulder Highway; 702-458-0096) is a western saloon and dance hall. But most of the cowboys are of the suburban variety; they prefer driving Broncos to riding them. Good food is served 'round the clock, and if you don't know how to two-step, there are free dance lessons every night.

For a taste of Gilley's of Las Vegas come to the country-flavored **Western Dance Hall** (5111 Boulder Highway; 702-456-7777) at Sam's Town Hotel. Surrounded by buffalo heads, branding irons and Remington-style prints, you can line dance or clog your way into oblivion. There are also dance lessons for city folk not up to speed on the latest steps.

Cowboy hospitality is the fare at **Partners** (8560 Las Vegas Boulevard South; 702-361-8599). Down-home country music with a band called (what else?) Hoss gets the place whooping and hollering. Attire is mostly tight jeans, boots and Peterbilt caps, but the place is friendly and the beer is cold.

A popular hangout with the college crowd is the **Sports Pub** (4440 South Maryland Parkway; 702-796-8870), across the street from the

UNLV campus. The walls, tables and booths scream Rebel red, and the dancefloor is usually packed with undulating undergrads bebopping to live local bands. Mix in drink specials and atavistic hormones and you have a collegiate hot spot.

Not exactly Rick's Place, but **Play It Again Sam** (4120 Spring Mountain Road; 702-876-1550) features candlelit tables in solarium booths that surround the low-key lounge. Live blues and jazz attract celebrity regulars such as Walter Matthau and David Brenner, who dine on the fajitas.

For an entertainment smorgasbord, try the Gold Coast Hotel (4000 West Flamingo Road; 702-367-7111). The **East Lounge** features musical entertainment, usually Dixieland or honky-tonk bands; the **West Lounge** is more audience-interactive with stand-up comedians, singers and other acts. Both have comfy red-leather club chairs and wooden tables, with small dancefloors in front of the elevated stages. The hotel's **Dance Hall & Saloon** is a huge, barnlike room with wood-grain walls, a high red ceiling and wrought-iron chandeliers. The music varies from rock to country. Every Tuesday is big band night when fox-trotters take over the large oval dancefloor.

A throwback to Vegas of the '60s is the **Copacabana Showroom** (3700 West Flamingo Road; 702-252-7777) at the Rio Suites Hotel, where you'll find a genuine supper club that combines food and fun with its Latin-theme revue, *Conga!* Seating is at booths and tables on three concentric tiers that surround the step-down stage, where singers and dancers perform, some with plastic vegetables on their heads. Enhancing the experience are videos of tropical rain forests, exotic beaches and distant ports of call, which are displayed on 12 video walls surrounding the round theater. The menu selections of salmon, chicken and prime rib are tasty, and don't be surprised when your waitress emerges from the Conga line carrying your order above her head. Cover.

THE LAST OF THE ROADHOUSES

*For the feel of a genuine roadhouse, try **The Still** (9495 Las Vegas Boulevard South, Las Vegas; 702-361-7012), eight miles south of Tropicana Boulevard on the old Los Angeles Highway. Drive south on the Strip past the old McCarran Field terminal and aged motels waiting for guests who never arrive, and keep driving until the Strip skyline is just a blur in your rearview mirror. You'll recognize The Still by its peaked, corrugated tin roof and brick walls. Inside, there's cedar paneling, parquet floors, a copper-clad still and an upstairs banquet room designed as a jail. The music is usually easy listening rock from the '50s and '60s, but it could be jazz or rhythm-and-blues.*

A waterfront bar in the desert? That would be the **Sand Dollar Lounge** (3355 Spring Mountain Road; 702-871-6651). Fishnets and mooring poles create a nautical ambience at this popular lounge tucked into an undistinguished business complex. Despite the atmosphere, there are no clambakes or fish fries, only the popular resident Boogieman Blues Band.

A shrine to rock-and-roll, **Tommy Rockers** (3550 South Decatur Boulevard; 702-368-7625) doubles as a nightclub and restaurant. The walls are plastered with photos, rare album covers, sheet music, 45-rpm records and other memorabilia. Drinks are also rock-oriented. Try the Proud Mary, a straightforward bloody Mary that's just hot enough so you won't stop breathing, or the Moody Blues Blast from the Past, a crazy concoction of rums, liqueurs and fruit juices. Tommy and his band play nightly, and he encourages the crowd to get rowdy and have fun.

Spago it ain't, but **Hob Nob** (3340 South Highland Avenue; 702-734-2426) is a watering hole for local musicians who want to hang out with their own. A rotating roster of jazz artists, mixed in with some '50s and '60s rock, keeps the place hopping.

A converted warehouse behind the Mirage is now the **Palladium** (3665 Industrial Road; 702-733-6366), a funky Western dance hall, complete with covered wagons, howling coyotes, orange neon saguaros and pioneer props ranging from milk cans to frying pans. The club features tri-level seating around a dancefloor where multi-colored lights flash to the twang of a steel guitar. With two bars, a shooters bar and a score of bartenders and waitresses, you won't wait long for your drinks. Dance lessons include traditional line dancing, as well as a Vegas-style Electric Slide or Tush Push. Cover.

The trendy **Bugsy's** (6145 West Sahara Avenue; 702-876-9322) is decorated with plate glass, neon tubes, brass railings and open steel beams that pyramid to a skylight and atrium windows. But there's plenty of room for fun and games with mezzanine seating around the game pits and pool tables. An unpretentious bar draws a mostly local crowd.

A popular spot with local hotel and casino workers is the **Loading Dock Lounge** (2411 West Sahara Avenue; 702-367-2411) at the Palace Station Hotel. The bands begin playing in the afternoon, usually rock or rhythm-and-blues, but the dancing doesn't begin until midevening.

A mecca for Raider football fans, **Hawkins Sports Lounge** (717 North Rancho Drive; 702-647-3550) is short on ambience and long on memories from Frank Hawkins' football days with the team. The place is packed when his old team takes the field. Hawkins, a running back turned politician, still greets customers and shares wild stories of his years in Oakland.

Overlooking the ice rink at the Santa Fe Hotel, the **Ice Lounge** (4949 North Rancho Drive; 702-658-4900) has a good-sized dancefloor, plush club chairs and a raised stage for the nightly Dixieland or rock bands.

Parks

A visit to a community park can make you forget that southern Nevada is part of the arid Mojave Desert. Greenbelts, shade trees, picnic grounds, fully developed recreational areas and lakes at selected sites spell pastoral relief from a noisy, crowded casino.

Joggers will like the tree-lined, 1000-yard track at **Jaycee Park** (St. Louis and Eastern avenues; 702-386-6297). Located three miles east of the Strip, you can also toss a few horseshoes or try the new bocce courts.

Picnickers can spread their blankets on the lush grass by a lake at the 30-acre **Freedom Park** (Mojave Road and East Washington Boulevard; 702-386-6297). Volleyball courts, a jogging track, a fitness center and a playground are here to jump-start your gambling-weary body.

A few parks offer unique facilities and host special events. One of these is **Angel Park** (Westcliff and Durango drives; 702-255-9515), which provides a relaxing stopover on the drive to Red Rock Canyon. Facilities include a jogging track, tennis courts, physical fitness equipment and a picnic area with barbecue grills. Kids can enjoy a playground and cool off at the spray fountain.

Cyclists will love the 20-acre motocross track at **Nellis Meadows** (4949 East Cheyenne Avenue; 702-455-4384), which is surrounded by greenbelts and playgrounds. BMX bicycle races are held throughout the year.

The Sporting Life

GOLF

Las Vegas is a golfer's dream. In addition to the championship-quality Strip courses, try the Arnold Palmer–designed **Angel Park Golf Course** (100 South Rampart Boulevard; 702-254-4653), **Canyon Gate Country Club** (2001 Canyon Gate Drive; 702-363-0303), **Desert Rose Golf Course** (5483 Clubhouse Drive; 702-431-4653), **Los Prados Coun-**

CONCERTS IN THE PARK

Summer evenings are a good time to relax and enjoy a free concert in the park. At Jaycee Park (St. Louis and Eastern avenues; 702-386-6297) you can listen to bluegrass and country-and-western bands every Sunday evening in August, or tap your toes to the strains of a big band every Sunday afternoon in June. Jazz by local, national or international musicians is featured Saturday evenings in June at Paradise Park (4770 Harrison Avenue; 702-455-4384).

try Club (5150 Los Prados Circle; 702-645-5696), the Jay Morrish–designed **Painted Desert Country Club** (5555 Painted Mirage Way; 702-645-2568), **Spanish Trail Country Club** (5050 Spanish Trail Lane; 702-364-0357), **TPC at Summerlin Golf Club** (1700 Village Center Circles; 702-256-0222) and **Sunrise Golf Club** (5000 East Flamingo Road; 702-456-3160).

If you're sightseeing in Henderson, try the **Black Mountain Country Club** (500 Greenway Road; 702-565-7933) or the **Legacy Golf Club** (130 Par Excellence Drive; 702-897-2187).

TENNIS

Public parks with tennis courts include **Jaycee Park** (St. Louis and Eastern avenues; 702-386-6297), **Angel Park** (Westcliff and Durango drives; 702-255-9515) and **Sunset Park** (2575 East Sunset Road; 702-455-8200). Health clubs with courts open to the public are **Studio 96 Tennis & Health Club** (3896 Swenson Avenue; 702-735-8153) and **Twin Lakes Racquet Club** (3075 West Washington Boulevard; 702-647-3434).

ICE SKATING/ROLLER SKATING

Yes, you can ice skate in Las Vegas. The **Santa Fe Hotel and Casino** (4949 North Rancho Drive; 702-658-4991) has an ice rink that doubles as an NHL regulation-size hockey arena.

For roller skating try the **Crystal Palace** (4740 South Decatur Boulevard, 702-253-9832; 3901 North Rancho Drive, 702-645-4892; 4680 Boulder Highway, 702-458-0177).

JOGGING

Joggers usually require nothing more than a pair of running shoes and an uncrowded sidewalk. But if you prefer running on grass to pounding the pavement, try the athletic fields at the **University of Nevada, Las Vegas** (4505 South Maryland Parkway; 702-739-3150), or any of the city and county parks. You'll find paved jogging tracks as well as fitness courts at **Angel Park** (Westcliff and Durango drives; 702-255-9515) and **Jaycee Park** (St. Louis and Eastern avenues; 702-386-6297).

BICYCLING

Cyclists will find Valhalla at the 20-acre cycling track at **Nellis Meadows** (4949 East Cheyenne Avenue; 702-455-4384), a park surrounded by greenbelts and playgrounds. There are also bike paths through tree-shaded groves and small fishing lakes at **Floyd Lamb State Park** (9200 Tule Springs Road; 702-486-5413).

FIVE

Casinos and Games People Play

Casinos

There's never been anything subtle about a Las Vegas casino. When Monte Carlo debuted as a casino resort in 1879, Sarah Bernhardt recited a symbolic poem at the *Place du Casino*. For the introduction of Las Vegas as a modern gambling resort in 1946, the Flamingo Hotel hired Abbott and Costello.

While Las Vegas casinos remain an outrageous sanctuary of fantasy, luxury and utter madness, they have evolved from rooms of green-felt craps and blackjack tables to incredible electronic arcades. The Vegas World Hotel & Casino, for instance, has one roulette wheel, four craps tables, 22 blackjack tables—and 2000 slot and video poker machines. The result is a sort of high-tech fairyland with electrified sights and sounds that relentlessly beckon visitors to defy the odds in the hope that, for one magical moment, time will stand still and the lightning bolt of fortune will strike them.

Slot machines, along with video poker and keno, are now the most popular casino games, with blackjack running a strong second. The introduction in 1984 of the $1 slot machine, which makes more money for the casino in one evening than a $1 blackjack table, marked the beginning of the trend toward more machines.

The impact of electronic gambling devices is especially noticeable in the downtown casinos, where more than 70 percent of the floor space is devoted to slot, keno and poker machines.

On the Strip, machines account for about 55 percent of casino space, but the figure is growing. As the Strip resorts expand, they are following the downtown casinos' lead and devoting more space to electronic games.

Also growing are the number of casinos that offer sports betting. In 1980 there were fewer than a dozen places to wager on sports, but today nearly every casino has some form of sports book, from the theater-like megabooks with banks of video screens at the Las Vegas Hilton and Caesars Palace to walk-up betting windows at the Santa Fe and El Cortez.

All Las Vegas casinos deal in the same basic commodity: a chance to beat the odds. In addition to the hundreds, if not thousands, of slot, video poker and keno machines, casinos may offer craps, blackjack, baccarat, roulette, live keno and the wheel of fortune (Big Six). Some also have bingo parlors and poker rooms.

Generally, the downtown casinos have lower table minimums than the Strip casinos. Blackjack tables with $1 minimum bets are common downtown, as are 50-cent craps tables and nickel (and even penny) slot machines. On the Strip, you'll rarely find a blackjack table with less than a $5 minimum bet. And you usually have to hunt for a nickel slot machine, then wait in line when you find it.

Following are some of the best or most interesting casinos.

STRIP AREA CASINOS

At the south end of the Strip, the **Hacienda Hotel** (3950 Las Vegas Boulevard South; 702-739-8911) features a casino newly remodeled with brick, tile and Spanish decor, and graced by a waterfall at the entrance. The effect gives the seldom-crowded casino an open, easygoing atmosphere, punctuated by the occasional clank of coins in a slot bucket.

The 100,000-square-foot, Egyptian-theme casino at **Luxor** (3900 Las Vegas Boulevard South; 702-262-4000) features deep red carpet, sandstone walls decorated with colorful Egyptian murals, bas-relief sculptures of ancient kings and queens, and a 3000-foot river around its perimeter. In addition to 2500 state-of-the-art slot machines, 87 table games, a keno lounge and a poker room, there's a bright and airy sports book with

---

THE EYE IN THE SKY

Every casino in Las Vegas has an electronic surveillance system that monitors and records activity in the casino. The number of television cameras hidden in the ceiling may be as few as four at a small place like the Bourbon Street Casino or as many as 50 at the Las Vegas Hilton. The video cams are connected to VCRs, which tape every game in the house. The tape recordings, which are saved for three days, are used as a check against cheats, thieves and dishonest employees. They are also used to settle complaints from customers and disputes between gamblers.

Casinos prefer to pay a hundred $1000 jackpots rather than one $100,000 jackpot, because they have a better chance of recovering their losses from the smaller winners, who usually continue to play in hopes of winning again.

light-wood furniture and a built-in TV monitor at each seat. Cocktail service is quick and friendly and, miraculously, each waitress has black Cleopatra-like hair.

Frenzied best describes the **Excalibur** casino (3850 Las Vegas Boulevard South; 702-597-7777), a 100,000-square-foot red-on-red monstrosity that often sounds like a tin-can factory in an earthquake. At least the race and sports book is away from the 2600 slot machines, so horse players can study their *Daily Racing Form* in peace.

A refreshing change from the traditional red-on-red motif can be found at the **Tropicana Hotel** (3801 Las Vegas Boulevard South; 702-739-2222), where the casino is decorated in tropical flower prints and lush green carpets. It has a poker room, sports book and poolside video poker machines. You can even play blackjack in the pool at the swim-up blackjack tables, which have a special, waterproof layout and money driers.

The world's largest casino at the **MGM Grand** (3799 Las Vegas Boulevard South; 702-891-1111) sprawls over 171,000 square feet—larger than the field at Yankee Stadium. Although touted as having four theme areas—Emerald City, Hollywood, Monte Carlo and Sports—they all blend together in a collage of rainbow-colored carpeting, floral wall coverings, marquee-style lighting and eerie faux trees reminiscent of Sleepy Hollow. Because of the casino's size, the sound from 3500 slot machines is surprisingly muffled, and the separate poker, baccarat, keno and sports betting areas provide relief from the angst of spinning reels and dropping coins.

The remodeled casino at the **Aladdin Hotel** (3667 Las Vegas Boulevard South; 702-736-0111) is one of the most elegant on the Strip, with gold fixtures and chandeliers set off against red ceilings and walls. The 75,000-square-foot casino features a race and sports book and tables for nonsmokers.

The step-down casino at **Bally's** (3645 Las Vegas Boulevard South; 702-739-4111) is the size of a football field, but the tables and machines are well spaced so players never feel cramped. And the seating in the sports and race book gives all an unobstructed view of the large-screen TVs.

Although usually crowded, the **Barbary Coast** (3595 Las Vegas Boulevard South; 702-737-7111) has a friendly atmosphere. The setting is turn-of-the-century San Francisco, with Victorian chandeliers, carved oak and a stained-glass mural depicting, appropriately, *The Garden of Earthly Delights*. Slot and video poker machines and the race and sports book attract the most players.

In keeping with its Miami modern heritage the **Flamingo Hilton** (3555 Las Vegas Boulevard South; 702-733-3111) features tropical pink, magenta and tangerine neon accents in a rambling, bustling casino, which is usually overflowing with tour groups and international travelers booked through Hilton's far-reaching reservation system. In addition to the normal mix of table games and slot machines, the Flamingo features sic bo, an Asian dice game where players try to pick the numbers or combination of numbers on three rolled dice. The most fascinating part of the game is the colorful Chinese table layout, which looks like a Hong Kong test pattern gone berserk.

No casino attracts more tourists than **Caesars Palace** (3570 Las Vegas Boulevard South; 702-731-7110). Here you'll find three rambling casinos that feature high, blackened ceilings, gold-and-neon slot pavilions and Monte Carlo–style baccarat parlors—not to mention the wandering gladiators and Roman goddesses who will pose with you for snapshots. Whether you're a serious gambler or novice, Caesars has a game for you, from $10,000-a-hand baccarat to nickel slots. The state-of-the-art race and sports book is among the best in town.

Next door, the **Mirage** (3400 Las Vegas Boulevard South; 702-791-7111) is challenging Caesars Palace as the home of the high roller. The top five floors of the hotel contain penthouse suites dedicated to big-spending gamblers. Downstairs, the casino decor suggests a Polynesian village, with its colorful tropical prints and canopies over the gaming areas. A separate casino behind a gold door is reserved for players who are willing to play blackjack at a minimum of $1000 a hand. (On average, that's about $50,000 an hour.) The race and sports book features an adjoining tropical bar with TV carousels for easy viewing.

Appropriately, booty and plunder decorate the buccaneer-theme casino at **Treasure Island** (3300 Las Vegas Boulevard South; 702-894-7111), where you'll find treasure chests overflowing with doubloons and jewels, black carpet inlaid with more images of pirate loot, and 17th-century art carved into the rich gold-and-white ceilings. Slot machines and gaming tables are tightly grouped, but players don't seem to mind the close quarters, as the casino is always packed.

The Asian-theme casino at the **Imperial Palace** (3535 Las Vegas Boulevard South; 702-731-3311) is tastefully done in bamboo and rattan furnishings under a dragon-motif ceiling. Most of the action, however, is up the escalator at the race and sports book, where you'll find frequent betting promotions, such as more favorable point spreads and lower vigorish. The casino's football handicapping contest is among the city's most popular, and there's even a drive-up window for placing bets on the run.

Beginning gamblers will like **Harrah's** (3475 Las Vegas Boulevard South; 702-369-5000). The dealers are friendly and helpful, and the

The only smoke-free casino in Las Vegas is the Silver City Casino (3001 Las Vegas Boulevard South; 702-732-4152), which also has a smoke-free restaurant.

casino offers lessons in playing the table games. There are 2000 slot and video poker machines, and a third-floor bingo parlor where you can buy a card for as little as 20 cents. A strolling Dixieland band adds to the New Orleans riverboat motif.

One of the classiest casinos in Las Vegas, the **Sheraton Desert Inn** (3145 Las Vegas Boulevard South; 702-733-4444) has a small select clientele of high rollers, who gamble beneath 30 circular brass chandeliers that look like Saturn's rings. The limits on the table games start higher than at other casinos, but the race and sports book attracts a lot of medium-level players.

Single-deck blackjack is the star attraction at the **Frontier Hotel** (3120 Las Vegas Boulevard South; 702-794-8200). This fact is announced on the marquee that once advertised Siegfried & Roy. Since the magicians left in 1988, the Frontier's owners have focused on serious gambling: blackjack, liberal craps betting and an elaborate race and sports book.

The expanded **Stardust Hotel** (3000 Las Vegas Boulevard South; 702-732-6111) has nearly 2000 slot machines, five roulette wheels, six craps tables, 50 blackjack tables—and plenty of room in which to maneuver. The popular race and sports book is the first to set the betting lines during football season, and its sports handicappers' library is filled with information for horse players and sports bettors.

The casino at the **Riviera Hotel** (2901 Las Vegas Boulevard South; 702-734-5110) is spread out over 125,000 square feet and decorated with plush carpeting, marble floors, brass columns and touches of pink neon. Gamblers will find 90 table games, 1600 slot machines, two keno parlors and a race and sports book. The Riviera's slot promotions are among the Strip's most aggressive, with daily free pull contests, $40 of slot play for $20 and a separate section for nickel slot players.

Times Square on New Year's Eve best describes **Circus Circus** (2880 Las Vegas Boulevard South; 702-734-0410), where throngs of slot players congregate. A haven for low rollers, the casino under the big top features low-minimum table games, but how a blackjack player can decide to hit or stand while a trapeze artist in spangled tights flies overhead is beyond me.

If you want to learn how to play baccarat, come to the **Sahara** (2535 Las Vegas Boulevard South; 702-737-2111), where lessons are given daily in the game James Bond made famous. The casino is also one of the brightest and roomiest in town, with slot and video poker machines on one side and table games, guarded by statues of sultans, on the other.

Daily slot tournaments (entry fees under $20) and a free drawing for a "shower of cash" keep the casino hopping.

One of the best-designed casinos is at the **Las Vegas Hilton** (3000 Paradise Road; 702-732-5111). The step-down casino is in the middle of the hotel, with the registration area, restaurants and shopping arcades surrounding it. Table games are at the center of the casino, flanked by slot machines and a keno lounge. Because of the upscale clientele, table limits have higher minimums, and most of the slots are of the $1 variety. Tuxedo-clad change personnel dispense $100 and $500 slot tokens in a canopied slot gazebo.

DOWNTOWN CASINOS

Despite its downtown location, the **Golden Nugget** (129 East Fremont Street; 702-385-7111) looks like a Strip casino: plush carpeting in tropical colors and white marble walls accented by brass and gold trim. The hotel even has a floor of ultraluxurious suites for high rollers. But the casino caters to all gamblers, so $1 blackjack tables and nickel slots are plentiful.

If you're serious about blackjack, come to the **Las Vegas Club** (18 East Fremont Street; 702-385-1664), where liberal rules allow you to double down on any two, three or four cards; split and re-split any pair; surrender your original hand for half your bet; and win on six cards totaling less than 21. There are just a handful of tables, but the open and airy casino is seldom crowded. The sports book is one of the most popular with local bettors, and during football season it's a madhouse on game day.

If you like fast action, **Binion's Horseshoe** (128 East Fremont Street; 702-382-1600) is for you. Day or night, the casino is usually packed. Every seat at the blackjack tables is filled, dice shooters crowd two deep around the craps tables and slot players feverishly work the row upon row of machines as if possessed. You can place any size wager here— there is no betting limit, and you can have your picture taken with $1 million in cash. The World Series of Poker, a three-week event held every April, attracts the world's most-skilled hold 'em and seven card stud players who compete for a $1 million first prize.

Don't expect a sun-kissed, Golden State theme at the **California Hotel** (12 East Ogden Avenue; 702-385-1222). The motif here is South Pacific Paradise because of the Hawaiian tourists who make the California their number-one destination. Dealers wear aloha shirts and muumuus to make the clientele feel at home, and the restaurants feature Island specialties. The modern casino is accented with crystal chandeliers, etched glass and Italian marble, and contains lots of nickel slot and video poker machines, as well as $2 blackjack tables.

Legalized gambling is offered 24 hours a day in Las Vegas. The minimum age to gamble is 21—casinos can refuse to pay jackpots or other winnings to minors.

If you've got pull, try the world's largest slot machine (certified by Guinness) at the **Four Queens** (202 East Fremont Street; 702-385-4011). Appropriately dubbed the "Queens Machine," the one-armed beast is 9 feet high and 18 feet long, and accommodates six players who sit in chairs, shovel dollar coins into the slot and pray all eight reels line up with queens. If their prayers are answered, the jackpot pays $300,000. More-prudent gamblers can get free craps or poker lessons in the chandeliered casino.

Video poker is the name of the game at the **El Cortez** (600 East Fremont Street; 702-385-5200), which already has more of the popular machines than any other downtown hotel and keeps adding them—not a single nook or cranny is wasted. Because there are so many nickel poker and keno machines, the action in the split-level casino is sometimes intense. But be patient and you'll find a comfortable spot to join the fray.

A throwback to the old sawdust joints is the **Gold Spike** (400 East Ogden Avenue; 702-384-8444). There's nothing fancy here, no crystal chandeliers or marble floors, just an old, western-style casino with friendly, unpretentious dealers and plenty of $1 blackjack tables, nickel (and penny) slots, 40-cent keno, 10-cent roulette—and a lousy coffee shop.

GREATER LAS VEGAS CASINOS

Locals flock to the **Gold Coast** (4000 West Flamingo Road; 702-367-7111), which is as much a community center as a gambling hall. If you get tired of shooting dice or playing the slots, you can bowl a line or two, catch a movie in the twin-screen theater, learn the Texas two-step, or simply relax in the ice-cream parlor and watch hotel guests struggle with their luggage. Unless you're a bingo player, avoid the mezzanine level, where hundreds of very serious bingo fanatics gather ten times a day for sessions that resemble after-Christmas sales.

If you want to gamble in a friendlier, less frenzied environment, try the **Palace Station** (2411 West Sahara Avenue; 702-367-2411). Expansion has resulted in a bright and roomy 100,000-square-foot casino. The added section contains almost exclusively slots, video poker and keno machines, which attract throngs of local players. Also popular with locals are the huge bingo parlor and the race and sports book.

There's a carnival atmosphere at the calypso-theme **Rio Suites Hotel** (3700 West Flamingo Road; 702-252-7777) with its confetti colors, thatched huts and faux coconut palms. In addition to the foliage, you'll find the usual casino games and machines, plus a bright and spacious sports book and Jackpot Jungle, a slot and video poker arcade equipped with TV monitors for viewing old movies and hotel information while gambling.

The friendliest dealers, change persons and cocktail waitresses in town are at the **Santa Fe** (4949 North Rancho Drive; 702-658-4900). The staff's attitude is probably a reflection of the relaxed atmosphere in the warm, spacious, Southwestern-style casino. Or maybe it's because the management hosts picnics and barbecues in the parking lot. Whatever the reason, the Santa Fe is the most comfortable place in Las Vegas to gamble your money away.

Despite its Dodge City ambience, **Sam's Town** (5111 West Boulder Highway; 702-456-7777) is a complete and sophisticated gambling casino. There are 2000 slot machines in all shapes and sizes in the two-floor casino, plus 36 blackjack tables, four craps tables and a European-style roulette wheel (no double zero), a rarity in the United States. The ten-table poker room offers lessons in Texas Hold 'Em and Seven Card Stud, and the bingo parlor hosts 11 sessions beginning at 7:45 a.m., with a free continental breakfast midmorning and full breakfast at the 2:45 a.m. session.

Games People Play

WINNERS AND LOSERS

One thing every professional gambler understands is that winning is a hit-and-run proposition. The professional also understands that the casino enjoys an advantage in every game and that the longer you expose yourself to it, the greater your chances of losing.

The house advantage (or edge) is the result of a combination of things: the odds or percentages inherent in the game, rules designed to favor the casino, payoffs at less than actual odds or predetermined payoffs, such as those in slot machines.

The casinos' edge may be small—as in baccarat and sports betting—or enormous—as in keno and the wheel of fortune. But it's an edge that generates $5 billion a year in gambling profits for the casinos.

So, if the casino has an advantage in every game, why gamble at all? Because gambling can be fun and exciting. In rare instances, it can even be profitable.

The casino's advantage occurs over the long run, over a large number of events, bets or games. But dramatic fluctuations in winning and losing percentages can and do occur over a short time span. The winning gambler knows how to take advantage of the short winning streaks that invariably occur.

Everyone understands the axiom of quitting while you're ahead, but few have the willpower to do so. And it's understandable. It's difficult to leave the blackjack or craps table in the middle of the evening, even though you've doubled your initial bankroll. You may not want to leave your friends or the partylike atmosphere. Or you may simply believe your winning streak will continue and you'll win more.

It's also difficult to stop playing a slot or video poker machine, especially after you've hit some pretty substantial jackpots. There's excitement in watching the machine light up and in hearing the coins pour into the metal tray.

The most worn-out story in Las Vegas is the one about the gambler who hit a winning streak, lost it all, then lost more money trying to get even. This occurs every hour of every day. To be successful, you must understand that no matter how well the cards are falling, no matter how hot the dice, no matter how loose the slot machines, the trend will eventually reverse itself. And when it does, you must have the willpower not only to recognize the change in fortune, but to react to it by altering or stopping play.

Most visitors come to Las Vegas with the intention of making their bankroll last as long as possible. They do this by finding a game in which they lose at a slow pace. If that's entertainment, fine. But why not play the game, and if you get lucky and win a jackpot or two, take a break from the casino. Do some shopping or sightseeing, or get a magazine and relax by the pool. You might find that coming home with your mad money intact actually made the trip more fun.

THE HOUSE ADVANTAGE

Gambling experts like to express the house advantage as a percentage. In some cases, the percentage is a result of mathematical computations and accurately reflects the likelihood of winning or losing. In other cases, it's an educated guess based on computer studies.

THE ORIGIN OF THE SLOT MACHINE

Although slot machines are practically synonymous with Las Vegas, they first appeared in San Francisco's waterfront saloons during the 1890s. They were mostly upright, rotary-wheel pin games until Charles Fey, a Bavarian immigrant, invented a cast-iron, tabletop device in 1895 that had three wheels, each with ten symbols on it, usually of playing card suits. When a saloon patron lined up three symbols, he was paid off in free drinks. Eventually, the gamblers demanded and got payoffs in coins. The first machines were called Liberty Bells and are the backbone of today's slot machine.

For instance, baccarat is assigned a house advantage of about 1.36 percent when the gambler bets on the player hand, with zero percent representing an even or 50-50 chance of the player winning, and 100 percent representing absolutely no chance of winning.

The percentage is interpreted as follows: The player will theoretically lose 1.36 cents for every dollar bet during the course of play. In a short period, the player may win despite the casino's edge, but in the long run the house advantage will prevail.

Using a simple coin flip as an example, there is no advantage to either heads or tails. Mathematically, each has an equal chance of landing. But if you flip the coin 100 times, you might find heads landing 58 times and tails 42. Over the 100 tosses, you might also discover heads landing five times in a row or tails landing six out of eight times.

Although the house percentage may not be practical in predicting the outcome of a game of chance, it is useful as a guide in deciding which games give you the best opportunity of winning. Keno, for instance, has a house advantage of more than 25 percent, while the most popular craps bets have a house advantage of only 1.4 percent. Obviously, your chances of winning at craps are significantly greater than at keno. But people continue to play keno with its poor chance of winning because it offers the possibility of lottery-like jackpots.

Blackjack

Blackjack, or 21, is the casinos' most popular table game. The rules are simple to learn, and, if you follow sound basic strategy, you can greatly reduce the casino's edge and possibly swing it in your favor.

The game is played with one or more decks of 52 cards. Cards are valued at face value, except for aces, which are valued at either one or 11 points. Face cards—jacks, queens and kings—are valued at 10 points.

The object of the game is to beat the dealer. A player does this by having a higher-valued hand than the dealer, while not busting by exceeding 21 points. If either the player or dealer busts, the other wins automatically. A major advantage for the dealer is that the player must play his hand first. Even if a player busts and the dealer subsequently busts as well, the player loses. Ties are a standoff or push, and neither wins.

If either the player or dealer is dealt an ace and a 10-valued card, he has a blackjack. A blackjack is an immediate winner and pays the player at 3-2 odds. Other winning hands are paid at 1-1 or even money. If the dealer is dealt a blackjack, the player immediately loses. If both the dealer and player are dealt blackjacks, it is a standoff.

The play begins with the dealer distributing two cards to each player and two to himself, dealt one at a time with the first card going to the player. One of the dealer's cards is exposed to help the player decide whether to hit (take another card) or stand (play the ones he has). In addition to standing pat, the player may double down his hand or split pairs.

By doubling down, the player doubles his initial bet and accepts one additional card to complete his hand.

By splitting pairs, the player also doubles his bet, but separates his two identical cards into two separate hands, to which he draws additional cards. Each hand is played separately, taking hits as needed. The only exception is that a player who splits aces is only allowed to take one additional card for each ace. If that additional card is another ace, however, the player can split again.

Doubling down and splitting are powerful techniques to increase your chances of winning.

THE RULES

1. The player can double down on his first two cards. Some casinos allow doubling down only if the player's two-card total is 10 or 11. This is a disadvantage to the player, and he should find a casino where doubling is not so restricted.

2. The player can split any pair.

3. After splitting pairs, the player may not double down, except at a few casinos.

4. The dealer must stand on hands totaling 17 or higher. Some casinos, notably in downtown Las Vegas, require their dealers to hit a soft 17. A soft hand is one that contains an ace. Again, this is to the player's disadvantage; it's better to play against a dealer who will not hit a soft 17.

5. Insurance pays 2-1. When the dealer's up-card is an ace, he will offer the player a chance to insure himself against the dealer's possible blackjack. The player can risk half his original bet and win 2-1 should the dealer hold a blackjack (the net result, if the dealer holds a blackjack, is the player breaks even). This is usually a bad bet, even when the player holds a blackjack of his own, because the casino is offering 2-1 for an event that should pay 9-4. Unless a player is an expert and counts cards, he or she should not take the insurance.

BASIC STRATEGY

The basic winning strategy for blackjack, based on computer-generated studies, is given below. It tells the player when to hit, stand, double down or split pairs, depending on the dealer's up-card. A summary of the strategy, in the form of a chart for easy reference, follows.

SPLITTING PAIRS: Always split aces and 8-8. Never split 5-5 or 10-10. Split 4-4 against the dealer's 5 or 6. Split 9-9 against the dealer's 2, 3, 4, 5, 6, 8 or 9. Split 7-7 against the dealer's 2, 3, 4, 5, 6 or 7. Split 6-6 against the dealer's 2, 3, 4, 5 or 6. Split 2-2 and 3-3 against the dealer's 4, 5, 6 or 7.

DOUBLING DOWN: Double down on 11, no matter what the dealer shows. Double down on 10 when the dealer shows anything except a 10 (dealer's 10 also includes face cards) or ace. Double down on 9 when the dealer shows 2, 3, 4, 5 or 6. Double down on soft 17 (Ace-6) if the dealer shows 2, 3, 4, 5 or 6. Double down on soft 18 (Ace-7) if the dealer shows 3, 4, 5 or 6. Double down on soft 13, 14, 15 or 16 against the dealer's 4, 5 or 6.

HIT OR STAND: With a hard hand (no aces) against the dealer's 7 or higher, the player should hit until he reaches at least 17. With a hard hand against the dealer's 4, 5 or 6, stand on a 12 or higher; if against the dealer's 2 or 3, hit a 12.

With a soft hand, hit all totals of 17 or lower. Against the dealer's 9 or 10, hit a soft 18.

COUNTING CARDS

Once you've mastered the basic blackjack strategy, the house advantage is probably less than 1 percent. But, remember, there's always the element of chance when the cards are dealt; don't expect the winning and losing hands to balance automatically. Still, using the basic strategy will give you confidence that all of your moves are the proper ones.

In addition to using the basic strategy, you can enhance your chances by learning to count cards and vary the size of your bets.

Counting cards is the method used by every professional blackjack player. Most nonprofessionals are horrified at the idea of having to memorize every card that is played at the table. But this isn't necessary.

One of the simplest and most effective methods of counting cards involves keeping track of the balance between high cards (aces, 10s and face cards) and low-valued cards (2, 3, 4, 5 and 6).

This is important because, when the deck is rich in high cards, it is favorable to the player. When there are more low cards that haven't been played, it is favorable to the dealer.

Once you are able to determine how the cards are balanced in the unplayed deck, you can vary your bets accordingly: You will bet larger amounts when there are a lot of high cards remaining, and you will bet the minimum when there are mostly low cards to be played.

To keep a running count of the cards remaining in the deck, assign a value of 1 to the low cards (2, 3, 4, 5 and 6), and a value of -1 to the high cards (10s, face cards and aces). Ignore the 7s, 8s and 9s. Since there are

BLACKJACK BASIC STRATEGY

		DEALER'S UP-CARD									
	YOUR HAND	2	3	4	5	6	7	8	9	10	ACE
SOFT HANDS	soft 19+	S	S	S	S	S	S	S	S	S	S
	soft 18	S	Db	Db	Db	Db	S	S	H	H	H
	soft 17	Db	Db	Db	Db	Db	H	H	H	H	H
	soft 16	H	H	Db	Db	Db	H	H	H	H	H
	soft 15	H	H	Db	Db	Db	H	H	H	H	H
	soft 14	H	H	Db	Db	Db	H	H	H	H	H
	soft 13	H	H	Db	Db	Db	H	H	H	H	H
HARD HANDS	hard 17+	S	S	S	S	S	S	S	S	S	S
	hard 16	S	S	S	S	S	H	H	H	H	H
	hard 15	S	S	S	S	S	H	H	H	H	H
	hard 14	S	S	S	S	S	H	H	H	H	H
	hard 13	S	S	S	S	S	H	H	H	H	H
	hard 12	H	H	S	S	S	H	H	H	H	H
	11	Db	Db	Db	Db	Db	Db	Db	Db	Db	Db
	10	Db	Db	Db	Db	Db	Db	Db	Db	H	H
	9	Db	Db	Db	Db	Db	H	H	H	H	H
	8 or less	H	H	H	H	H	H	H	H	H	H
SPLITTING PAIRS	ace-ace	Sp	Sp	Sp	Sp	Sp	Sp	Sp	Sp	Sp	Sp
	10-10	S	S	S	S	S	S	S	S	S	S
	9-9	Sp	Sp	Sp	Sp	Sp	S	Sp	Sp	S	S
	8-8	Sp	Sp	Sp	Sp	Sp	Sp	Sp	Sp	Sp	Sp
	7-7	Sp	Sp	Sp	Sp	Sp	Sp	H	H	H	H
	6-6	Sp	Sp	Sp	Sp	Sp	H	H	H	H	H
	5-5	Db	Db	Db	Db	Db	Db	Db	Db	H	H
	4-4	H	H	H	Sp	Sp	H	H	H	H	H
	3-3	H	H	Sp	Sp	Sp	Sp	H	H	H	H
	2-2	H	H	Sp	Sp	Sp	Sp	H	H	H	H

H=Hit   S=Stand   Sp=Split Pairs   Db=Double Down

equal numbers of low cards and high cards in the deck (or in several decks) the initial count will be zero.

Once play has begun, you add and subtract the values of the cards that have been used. This may sound complicated, but it really isn't. For instance, if your first hand contained 3, K, 7, and the dealer had an Ace, 6, 5, 10, the running count remains zero. The 3 and K cancel each other in one hand, as do the Ace-10 and 5-6. Therefore the deck is still neutral.

But, if the next hand contained 10, J and 7, 8, 10, the running count is now -3 (the J and two 10s each have a value of -1; the 7 and 8 are neutral).

A running count of -3 tells you the deck is slightly unfavorable to the player; therefore you make a minimum bet at this point. You will wait for the deck to swing to the positive side, a running count of at least +2, indicating a greater number of high cards remaining to be played.

Generally, the running count won't vary too far from zero. It will bounce back and forth from +5 to -5. But the higher the positive number, the more the odds are in your favor.

MULTIPLE ACTION BLACKJACK

Developed and introduced by the Four Queens Hotel, multiple action blackjack is a fast-paced variation of standard 21. Players pit one hand of blackjack against the dealer's three hands. The game's popularity is rapidly spreading because of the chance to win three bets with one good hand. Casinos like the game because they can book more bets in a shorter period of time.

The game follows traditional blackjack rules, except the player makes up to three bets for their two-card hands, and the dealer plays separate hands against the player's one. It sounds confusing but is surprisingly simple.

Play begins with the player making up to three bets and getting two cards. The dealer takes an up card but no hole card. The player makes his decisions—hit, stand, split or double down—based on the dealer's up card. If he busts, he loses all his bets.

After the player stands, the dealer gives himself a hole card and plays that hand according to normal hit/stand rules. The difference in this game is that the dealer's result affects only the player's first bet. After winning, losing or tying that hand, the dealer discards all but his original up card. He then takes a new hole card and plays the hand again, this time against the player's second bet. The process is repeated if the player had placed three bets.

Although the game has the lure of winning large bets, it also entices players to misplay hands. Because of the possibility of busting and losing three bets, players are tempted to stand with "stiff" totals (12–16) versus the dealer's high card (7-ace). But the fact that you're playing three bets against three different hole cards doesn't alter proper strategy (as outlined in previous sections). Basic strategy is the same whether you make decisions one at a time or three at a time as you do in Multiple Action Blackjack.

Craps

Craps is one of the fastest moving and most exciting games in the casino. And, because of its low house percentage against the player, it provides a chance to win large sums of money in relatively short periods of play.

It is also one of the least understood games, mainly because of the complicated table layout. The game, however, is very simple. A player or shooter rolls a pair of dice that determines the outcome of his and other players' bets.

The shooter's first roll of the dice is called the come-out roll. If he rolls a 7 or 11, he, and those who bet with him, win. If he throws a 2, 3 or 12, that is craps, and he and the other players who bet with him lose.

If the dice turn up a 4, 5, 6, 8, 9 or 10, that number becomes the shooter's established point, and he must continue rolling the dice until he makes the number again in order to win. If the shooter rolls a 7 before his point, he sevens out and loses.

Although the object of the game is very simple, craps is complicated by the myriad of bets available to the players. Most of those bets are heavily weighted in favor of the casino, and should be avoided.

THE BETS

PASS LINE: By playing the Pass Line, you're betting with the shooter. An immediate 7 or 11 on the come-out roll wins; a 2, 3 or 12 loses. If a point is established (4, 5, 6, 8, 9 or 10), it must be repeated before a 7 is thrown in order to win. The Pass Line bet pays even money and, with a house advantage of 1.41 percent, is one of the best bets at the table.

SHAVED DICE?

To prevent some numbers from appearing more frequently than others, dice are manufactured to a tolerance of 0.00002 inch (two ten-thousandths), or about 1/17 the thickness of a human hair. Originally made from bone and ivory, dice used in modern casinos are fashioned from cellulose nitrate and cellulose acetate. The largest manufacturer of dice is **Paulson Dice & Card** *(2121 Industrial Road; 702-384-2425), which produces about 25,000 pairs a month.*

DON'T PASS: The Don't Pass bettor bets against the shooter. He therefore wins his bet if the come-out roll is a 2 or 3 (at most casinos a 12 is a push), and loses if the shooter throws a 7 or 11. If the shooter establishes a point, a 7 must be thrown before the point is rolled again in order to win. This even-money bet has approximately the same house advantage of winning as the Pass bet.

COME & DON'T COME BETS: These bets are identical to the Pass and Don't Pass bets, except that they can be placed only after a point has been established. That is, an immediate 7 or 11 is a winner; a 2, 3 or 12 loses, and any other number becomes an established point for the Come bettor. The reverse is true for the Don't Come bettor. In addition, you can place as many consecutive Come/Don't Come bets as you like, while you are limited to one Pass/Don't Pass bet. The advantage of these bets is that they allow players to increase their chances of winning during any given roll of the dice. They offer the same odds as the Pass/Don't Pass bets.

PLACE BETS: A bet on any or all of the Place numbers (4, 5, 6, 8, 9 or 10) is a bet that the number or numbers will be thrown before a 7. The 4 and 10 pay at 9-5 odds; the 5 and 9 at 7-5 odds; and the 6 and 8 at 7-6 odds. Placing the 6 and 8 is a fairly good bet because the house edge is 1.52 percent. However, placing the 5 and 9 and the 4 and 10 are less attractive because the house edge jumps to 4 percent and 6.73 percent, respectively.

THE FIELD: This is a one-roll bet that any number in the Field—2, 3, 4, 9, 10, 11 or 12—will be rolled. If any other number—5, 6, 7 or 8—is thrown, the bet is lost. The house advantage on this bet is nearly 6 percent, too great to recommend it.

BIG 6 AND BIG 8: A bet on either the 6 or the 8, or both, can be made at any time, and either must appear before a 7 is thrown in order to win. Because the bet only pays even money, instead of its true odds of 6-5, the house enjoys an advantage of 9.09 percent.

PROPOSITION BETS: These bets, which include the Hard Ways and One-Roll Bets in the center of the layout, are all poor betting propositions. Because the house advantage varies from 10 percent to 17 percent, they should never be made.

FREE ODDS: Although there's nothing on the table to indicate the existence of this bet, it is one of the most advantageous to the player. It is available to all Pass/Don't Pass and Come/Don't Come bettors after a point has been established. Once the shooter establishes a point, a player can make a bet equal to his previous bet and receive true odds (instead of even money) if the point is made. This amounts to 2-1 on the 4 and 10; 3-2 on the 5 and 9; and 6-5 on the 6 and 8. If the casino offers double odds, the player can double his previous bet. It's always to the player's advantage to make the free odds bet, especially at double odds, because it gives you the chance to win more money at correct odds when the shooter is on a hot roll. With single odds, the house edge is reduced to 0.8 percent; with double odds it's reduced further, to 0.6 percent.

BASIC STRATEGY

As with other casino games, the goal in craps is to capitalize on the relatively short cycle of streaks that invariably occur. These are marked by prolonged passes of the dice by a given shooter. That is, the shooter continues to roll, oftentimes for many minutes, without sevening out.

You can take advantage of these hot streaks by playing the Pass Line, backing that bet with Free Odds bets, and placing multiple Come bets, also with Free Odds.

Professional gamblers disagree on the number of Come bets to place. The most aggressive players make Come bets on every roll until all the point numbers are covered. This gives them the opportunity to win many bets in a short period of time, provided the dice stay hot and the shooter continues to roll without hitting a 7.

But that method is too risky. A sound strategy calls for placing a maximum of two Come bets, which, coupled with the original Pass Line bets, give the player three numbers always working for him. When one of the points is made and his bet is paid off, the player places another Come bet to keep three numbers working.

TO RECAP:

1. Bet the Pass Line and back up the bet with a Free Odds bet.

2. Make two additional Come bets, also taking the Free Odds bets.

3. Stop betting after three points have been established.

4. If one of the Come bets is won, immediately place another Come bet. Similarly, if the original Pass Line bet is won, make another Pass Line bet.

This system lets the player capitalize during a shooter's hot streak while minimizing his losses when the dice eventually turn cold.

Roulette

Roulette has never gained the popularity here that it has in Europe. The game is played at a relatively slow pace, and the house advantage of 5.26 percent makes it the most difficult table game to beat.

Another drawback to roulette is the American-style wheel, which has 36 numbers plus 0 and 00. In Europe, roulette wheels have just a single 0.

However, if you're a die-hard roulette player, you'll find a European-style wheel in two Las Vegas casinos, **Sam's Town** (5111 Boulder Highway; 702-456-7777) and the **Nevada Hotel** (235 South Main Street; 702-385-7311).

The game is simple to play; a roulette dealer spins the wheel and waits for the ivory ball to land on a number. Bettors have the option of trying to guess on which number out of the possible 38 the ball will land, or they can bet on a combination of numbers or on whether the number will be red or black.

The various roulette bets and their payoffs are listed below:

Red or black	1 to 1
Odd or even	1 to 1
Numbers 1-18 or 19-36	1 to 1
Any one number	35 to 1
Groups of 12 numbers	2 to 1
Groups of 6 numbers	5 to 1
Groups of 4 numbers	8 to 1
Groups of 3 numbers	11 to 1
Groups of 2 numbers	17 to 1
Group of 0, 00, 1, 2 and 3	6 to 1

BASIC STRATEGY

Roulette bets can pay handsomely. Pick the right number and your $5 bet, at odds of 35-1, is worth $175. But coming up with a winner takes

---

SO, YOU WANT TO BE A HIGH ROLLER?

Imagine a chartered jet flying to your home town and whisking you off to Las Vegas. A limousine is waiting at the airport to transport you to Caesars Palace, where you're escorted by the front desk manager to your $2000-a-night fantasy suite. Imagine dining in the city's most lavish restaurants and attending the most popular production shows as an invited guest. Imagine all this at no cost to you, except for a promise that you intend to gamble. This is how the hotel's most revered guests, the high rollers, are treated. But that promise to gamble is a costly one. To receive the ultimate in VIP treatment, high rollers are expected to gamble a minimum of $50,000 an hour, or about $750,000 over a three-day, two-night weekend. And some of these whales, as they're often called, bet millions of dollars on a visit. Just like the rest of us, megagamblers sometimes win and sometimes lose. Recently, a businessman from the Far East took one of the casinos for $13.5 million at the baccarat tables. The reverse is not uncommon.

tremendous powers of intuition, or blind luck. Neither lends itself to a sound betting strategy.

Serious players, the few that actually exist, like to bet zones of numbers, that is, groups or columns, rather than a single number, and hope the winning number falls within their zone. The most popular zones are the first, second or third 12 numbers, or a column of 12 numbers.

Also popular, perhaps because of the increased action, is betting red or black. A word of encouragement for color bettors: Lord Jersey once won 17 consecutive maximum bets on black while playing in Monte Carlo, or so the story goes; he retired to the English countryside and never gambled again in his life.

Baccarat

Baccarat is the most glamorous, if not mysterious, game in the casino. The playing tables are usually roped off and the croupiers staffing them are typically dressed in tuxedos.

Because of the Monte Carlo–like aura surrounding the game, most players are intimidated from participating. However, baccarat offers one of the best percentages in the casino, with a house advantage of less than 1.4 percent on bank and player bets.

THE PLAY

The object of the game is surprisingly simple. Baccarat is played with multiple decks of standard playing cards. Two hands composed of two cards each are dealt—one for the player and one for the bank. Players can bet on either hand.

The winning hand is determined by the point totals of the respective hands. All 10s and face cards are valued at zero. The rest of the cards retain their face value (the ace counts as one).

If the two–card total exceeds 10 points, you simply count the last digit of the number as your score. For instance, if a hand contains a 6 and 8 for a total of 14, the hand is valued at 4. The winning hand, either the bank or the player, has a higher total value than the other.

THE RULES

The rules determining whether additional cards are drawn are complicated, but it is not necessary for the player to memorize them. The croupier will decide if and when a draw is necessary; the player is never required to make that decision. They are included here so the player will understand the reasons behind the croupier's action.

1. If either hand has a value of 8 or 9 (these scores are called naturals), no further cards are dealt. The higher of the two hands is declared the winner. Should both hands have the same value, a tie is declared and neither wins.

2. If neither hand is a natural, a set of complicated rules comes into play. These are illustrated in the accompanying chart, but again, the croupier will make the decisions on drawing cards. Basically, the player's hand will take a third card if its value is from zero to 5. It must stand on 6 or 7. The bank's hand must draw if its value is from zero to 2. When the bank has a value of 3 or more, draw is determined by the printed rules. Below are the rules for drawing:

PLAYER'S HAND:		
First 2 cards		
1-2-3-4-5-10	Draws a card	
6-7	Stands	
8-9	Natural—Stands	
BANK'S HAND:		
First 2 cards	Draws when player's third card is:	No draw when third card is:
1-2-10	Draws a card	
3	1-2-3-4-5-6-7-9-10	8
4	2-3-4-5-6-7	1-8-9-10
5	4-5-6-7	1-2-3-8-9-10
6	6-7	1-2-3-4-5-8-9-10
7	Stands	Stands
8-9	Natural—Stands	Natural—Stands

3. A bet on the player's hand pays even money. But, because the bank hand has a slightly higher percentage of winning (50.7 percent), winning bets on the bank hand are subject to a 5 percent commission paid to the casino. (In practice, the bank bets are paid at even money, and the accumulated commissions are paid to the house at the end of the deal, or when the player leaves the table.)

4. Players can also bet that the hands will end in a tie. This bet pays at odds of 8-1, but it is a poor bet because the house has an advantage of nearly 15 percent.

BASIC STRATEGY

Because players cannot decide when to draw additional cards, there is no skill involved in playing baccarat. It is purely a game of chance. However, streaks do occur, and a winning strategy can take advantage of these cycles.

A sound winning strategy calls for placing bets on the bank hands. This surprises many players because bank bets are subject to the 5 percent commission. However, the bank should win 50.7 percent of the time. And the 5 percent commission is paid only on winnings, and not on losing bets. So, a player has a slightly better advantage by playing the bank.

As with other table games such as blackjack and craps, flat bets will, at the very best, even out over the long run. To be successful at baccarat, you should increase bets after winning hands in order to take advantage of short streaks that often occur. Conversely, never increase losing bets.

A sound betting system for baccarat calls for increasing your bets after a previous win over a cycle of five hands, according to the following schedule:

1. An initial bet of one unit is made.
2. The second bet is three times the original bet.
3. The third bet is four times the original bet.
4. The fourth bet is five times the original bet.
5. The fifth bet is six times the original bet.

After the fifth bet, the cycle reverts to the original bet. Although this system calls for increasing bets in the ratio of 1-3-4-5-6, no bet beyond the second one is ever double the previous bet. This prevents the player from being wiped out by a losing bet.

Keno

Keno has one of the highest house percentages against the player—a minimum of 22 percent—yet the game remains popular. The reason is that it is an inexpensive way to gamble—you can play a keno ticket for as little as 35 cents, or 70 cents in most casinos, and there's a possibility of hitting a huge jackpot.

Anyone who plays keno should think of it as a type of lottery or bingo and not a serious form of gambling. Therefore, money bet on keno should be for fun, without any great expectation of a return.

THE GAME

Keno is played on a blank ticket, which you obtain at the keno parlor or at other locations throughout the hotel-casino. A player selects from 1 to 15 numbers out of a possible 80, and marks them on the ticket. The marks are called spots, and the number of spots determines how much the ticket is worth.

The operator of the game turns on a machine that randomly selects 20 numbered balls out of the possible 80 and calls out the numbers. If the player's numbers match most or all of the numbers selected, he wins a

SAMPLE PAYOFFS FOR 70-CENT KENO

MARK 1 SPOT

Catch	Payoff
1 Pays	2.10

MARK 2 SPOTS

Catch	Payoff
2 Pays	8.50

MARK 3 SPOTS

Catch	Payoff
2 Pays	.70
3 Pays	30.00

MARK 4 SPOTS

Catch	Payoff
2 Pays	.70
3 Pays	2.70
4 Pays	80.00

MARK 5 SPOTS

Catch	Payoff
3 Pays	1.20
4 Pays	15.00
5 Pays	340.00

MARK 6 SPOTS

Catch	Payoff
3 Pays	.60
4 Pays	3.30
5 Pays	60.00
6 Pays	1,100.00

MARK 7 SPOTS

Catch	Payoff
3 Pays	.30
4 Pays	1.20
5 Pays	15.00
6 Pays	230.00
7 Pays	3,500.00

MARK 8 SPOTS

Catch	Payoff
5 Pays	6.00
6 Pays	60.00
7 Pays	1,150.00
8 Pays	12,500.00

MARK 9 SPOTS

Catch	Payoff
4 Pays	.30
5 Pays	2.30
6 Pays	30.00
7 Pays	200.00
8 Pays	2,800.00
9 Pays	12,500.00

MARK 10 SPOTS

Catch	Payoff
5 Pays	1.40
6 Pays	14.00
7 Pays	98.00
8 Pays	700.00
9 Pays	2,660.00
10 Pays	12,500.00

MARK 11 SPOTS

Catch	Payoff
5 Pays	.60
6 Pays	6.00
7 Pays	50.00
8 Pays	250.00
9 Pays	1,200.00
10 Pays	7,500.00
11 Pays	12,500.00

payoff based on how many spots he marked, how many spots he hit or caught, and how much he bet.

Most casinos offer keno at the rate of 70 cents per ticket. Some hotels in downtown Las Vegas offer lower prices, while some Strip resorts have a $1 minimum. The accompanying chart gives sample payoffs for a 70-cent keno ticket.

If a player has a winning ticket, he must present it to the keno operator before the next game begins. Failing to do so voids his winning ticket.

BASIC STRATEGY

The most common keno ticket played is the straight ticket, on which a player marks from 1 to 15 numbers and bets 70 cents or a multiple of 70 cents. Little thinking and planning is necessary to play a straight ticket.

To maximize the chances of winning at keno, serious players should play a way ticket. It is called a way ticket because you place your numbers in groups that give you various combinations or ways of winning. With way tickets you can have more numbers working for you, and you don't have to catch all of them to hit a good payoff.

Basically, a way ticket consists of three or more groups of equal numbers. Each group of numbers is circled, and they are counted in different combinations, which increase the possibility of winning.

For instance, suppose you wanted to play 12 numbers. If you marked the numbers on a straight 70-cent ticket and caught 8 of them, you'd win $150. Now let's see what happens when you mark the same 12 numbers on a way ticket.

Because all way tickets require three or more groups of equal numbers, we will divide the 12 numbers into three groups of four. We could also have divided the 12 into four groups of three or six groups of two. The choice is yours. We do this on the ticket by marking the numbers, as we did on the straight ticket, then circling the three groups.

What we now have is something different from the original 12-spot straight ticket. Counting two groups of numbers at a time, we now have three groups of eight numbers, or the equivalent of three 8-spot tickets.

Because you now have three chances of winning, the cost of the ticket is three times a straight ticket, or $2.10, but the potential payoffs, as you will soon discover, far outweigh the additional cost.

Now if your same eight numbers hit, you are paid on the eight-out-of-eight payoff scale, or a whopping $12,500, instead of the $150 the eight out of 12 ticket would have paid.

This system of betting way tickets may sound complicated, but all casinos that offer the game supply booklets and schedules that can help you mark your tickets.

The largest slot machine jackpot ever won was $9.3 million in May 1992, on a Megabucks machine at Harrah's in Reno.

Video Poker

No other casino game has gained the popularity that video poker has enjoyed over the past few years. In Las Vegas, electronic games—slot machines, video poker and video keno—now occupy more than 50 percent of the casinos' floor space. And most of those machines are video poker machines.

There are several reasons for video poker's popularity. The first is that people can play at their own pace, without pressure from dealers, croupiers or other players. Second, unlike slot machines, video poker involves an element of skill: You must make decisions that determine whether and how much you can win. And, most important, there's always the chance of hitting a lottery-like jackpot.

THE PLAY

The game of video poker is basically five card draw poker. Machines offer several variations to the game, with more being developed every day, but the three that you should concentrate on are: (1) Jacks-or-better draw poker; (2) Jokers Wild poker; and (3) Deuces Wild poker.

Video poker machines may be played with nickels, quarters, 50-cent pieces, or $1 or $5 tokens. Most people play the nickel, quarter or dollar machines.

The play begins after the player inserts coins into the machine. In order to win the highest royal flush jackpot or the progressive jackpot (which continues to grow as coins are played), always play the maximum number of coins, which is usually five.

After the coins are inserted, the machine deals five cards to the player, who must decide which cards, if any, to discard. You play your hand based on the payouts for winning hands, which are listed just above the video screen. Some machines indicate a possible winning hand, such as three-of-a-kind, on the video screen, but don't always rely on the machine to figure your hand for you.

In a game of straight (Jacks or better) draw poker, the chances of getting a royal flush are about 40,000 to 1. Listed below are the odds of receiving a winning hand, before and after the draw.

WINNING HAND	ODDS BEFORE DRAW	ODDS AFTER DRAW
Jacks or better	1 in 7.7	1 in 4.6
Two Pair	1 in 21	1 in 7.7
Three-of-a-kind	1 in 47	1 in 13
Straight	1 in 255	1 in 90
Flush	1 in 525	1 in 92
Full House	1 in 694	1 in 87
Four-of-a-kind	1 in 4170	1 in 423
Straight Flush	1 in 72,200	1 in 9610
Royal Flush	1 in 650,000	1 in 40,100

After deciding which cards to keep, you press the Hold button under those cards, then press the Draw button. (Some machines combine the Deal and Draw buttons into one.) The cards you've discarded will be replaced with new cards and, if you have a winning hand, its payoff will be indicated on the screen. At this point your winnings will drop into the coin bucket, or you'll be given credit for the amount of the winning hand.

A note about credits. Credits allow you to play faster, without having to continually push coins into the slot. But always remember that the credits are yours, and you can collect your coins at any time by pushing the Cash Out or Collect Winnings button. It is not uncommon for players to move to another machine and forget their credits in the old machine.

JACKS-OR-BETTER BASIC STRATEGY

You'll have to decide between the two types of Jacks-or-better machines: Full payout or progressive machines. The full payout pays a fixed amount of coins for a royal flush, usually 4000 coins with the maximum bet. The progressive pays a jackpot that continues to grow until one of its machines hits the royal flush.

The progressive jackpot is higher than the fixed payout, but that is sometimes offset by lower payouts on the other hands, such as full houses and flushes. Always try to play a machine that pays the following jackpots for a one-coin bet:

Royal Flush	800 coins
Straight Flush	50 coins
Four-of-a-kind	25 coins
Full House	9 coins
Flush	6 coins
Straight	4 coins
Three-of-a-kind	3 coins
Two Pair	2 coins
Jacks or better	1 coin

The primary objective at the Jacks-or-better machine is to hit the royal flush. You'll also want to maximize your winnings if you don't hit the royal, which has odds of about 40,000 to one against it. In order to do that, follow this basic strategy:

1. Always draw one card to a royal flush, even if it means breaking a pat high pair (jacks or better), straight or flush. But don't break a pat straight flush for a one-card draw to a royal.

2. Draw two cards to a royal flush, unless you already hold a pat straight flush, straight, flush or three-of-a-kind.

3. Draw one card to a straight flush unless you already hold a pat flush or straight.

4. Draw two cards to a straight flush unless you already hold a pat flush, straight, three-of-a-kind or high pair.

5. If you need one card for either a flush or a straight, draw for the flush.

6. If you need one card for either a flush or a straight and already hold a high pair, keep the high pair.

7. If you need one card for a flush and already hold a low pair (10s or lower), break up the pair and draw for the flush. If you need one card for a straight and already hold a low pair, keep the low pair.

8. Always hold two pair and three-of-a-kind.

9. Always draw to a low pair rather than holding a single high card.

10. Draw five cards when you don't have a single high card that can be paired, and don't have four to a flush or straight.

JOKERS WILD—BASIC STRATEGY

The addition of a joker to the deck results in more winning hands of three-of-a-kind and higher, but fewer high pairs because the even-money payoff is now on Kings-or-better. Also, the overall winning payoff schedule is reduced, and the chances of hitting a natural royal flush are slightly less because of the addition of the 53rd card to the deck.

Nevertheless, Jokers Wild poker is very popular because hands such as straight flushes and four-of-a-kinds are more common, and the mini-jackpot paid on a five-of-a-kind is not out of reach.

Once again, you must decide between the full payout and progressive machines. Whichever you choose, always try to find a machine that pays the following jackpots for a one-coin bet:

Royal Flush (natural)	800 coins
Five-of-a-kind	200 coins
Royal Flush (joker)	100 coins
Straight Flush	50 coins
Four-of-a-kind	20 coins
Full House	7 coins
Flush	5 coins
Straight	3 coins
Three-of-a-kind	2 coins
Two Pair	1 coin
High Pair (Kings or Aces)	1 coin

Because the joker complicates the playing strategy, it will be broken into two parts: hands dealt with a joker and hands dealt without.

HANDS WITH A JOKER:

1. Always draw one card to a royal flush, unless you already hold a pat straight flush or joker royal flush.

2. Draw two cards to a royal flush, unless you already hold a pat straight flush, straight, flush or three-of-a-kind.

3. Draw one card to a straight flush even if you already hold a pat flush or straight.

4. Draw two cards to a straight flush unless you already hold a pat flush, straight or three-of-a-kind.

5. If you need one card for either a flush or a straight, draw for the flush.

6. If you need one card for either a flush or straight and already hold a high pair, keep the high pair.

7. If you're dealt anything less than a high pair, or you can't draw to the hands listed above, hold the joker and draw four cards.

HANDS WITHOUT A JOKER:

1. Always draw one card to a royal flush, even if it means breaking a pat high pair (kings or aces), straight or flush. But don't break a pat straight flush for a one-card draw to a royal.

2. Draw two cards to a royal flush, unless you already hold a pat straight flush, straight, flush or three-of-a-kind.

3. Draw one card to a straight flush even if you already hold a pat flush or straight.

4. Draw two cards to a straight flush unless you already hold a pat flush, straight or three-of-a-kind.

5. If you need one card for either a flush or a straight, draw for the flush.

6. If you need one card for either a flush or straight and already hold a high pair, keep the high pair.

7. If you need one card for a flush or two cards for a straight flush and already hold a low pair (queens or lower), break up the pair and draw. If you need one card for a straight and already hold a low pair, keep the low pair.

8. If you're dealt two pair and one of them is a high pair, keep the high pair. If not, retain both.

9. Always draw to a low pair rather than holding a single high card.

10. Draw five cards when you don't have a single high card that can be paired.

DEUCES WILD—BASIC STRATEGY

Playing Deuces Wild poker can be a lot of fun because of the four wild cards circulating throughout the deck. When the deuces turn up, straight flushes, five-of-a-kinds and even royal flushes become commonplace. But, because hands are easier to make, payoffs are substantially less, and the minimum hand for an even-money return is three-of-a-kind.

The game is popular because there's plenty of action, and the mini-jackpot paid on a hand of Four Deuces occurs quite frequently. Whether you're going to play a full payout or progressive machine, try to find one with the following minimum payouts:

Royal Flush (natural)	800 coins
Four Deuces	200 coins
Royal Flush (deuces)	25 coins
Five-of-a-kind	15 coins
Straight Flush	9 coins
Four-of-a-kind	5 coins
Full House	3 coins
Flush	2 coins
Straight	2 coins
Three-of-a-kind	1 coin

Because the deuces are so important, playing strategy is evaluated according to the number of deuces dealt and the possible hands they may create.

The average slot machine brings in about $280 a day, for an annual total of about $102,000.

HANDS WITH DEUCES:

1. When dealt four deuces, hold all five cards to minimize the chances of losing one in the draw.

2. When dealt three deuces, hold them and draw for the fourth unless you already have a pat royal flush or five-of-a-kind.

3. When dealt two deuces, hold them alone and draw unless you already have a pat four-of-a-kind or better. Also, if you need one card for a royal or straight flush, draw for the one card.

4. When dealt a single deuce, hold any pat hand except break a flush or straight if you have a one-card draw for a royal or straight flush.

HANDS WITHOUT DEUCES:

1. Always draw one card to a royal flush, even if it requires breaking a pat straight flush.

2. Always draw two cards to a royal flush, unless you already hold a pat straight, flush or straight flush.

3. Draw one card to a straight flush unless you already hold a pat flush or straight.

4. Draw two cards to a straight flush unless you already hold a pat flush or straight.

5. If you need one card for either a flush or a straight, draw for the flush.

6. If you need one card for either a flush or straight and already hold any pair, keep the pair.

7. Always hold three-of-a-kind. When dealt two pair, discard one of them and draw.

8. Draw five cards when you don't have a pat hand and you don't have a chance at the hands listed above.

Slot Machines

The mania over slot machines reached a peak in the late 1980s, yet slots remain among the most popular casino games. Because the machines are pure games of chance, there is no strategy involved, but it helps to understand a little about how they work.

Casinos love to promote the so-called payout percentage of their machines. A loose machine is advertised as paying back 97 percent of the coins shoveled into it. Most machines have a statistical payout of around 83 percent to 85 percent. What this means is that over some hypothetical period of time, the machine will return 85 percent of the money plugged into it.

In practice, however, don't expect to sit down at a slot machine and play for an hour with a net loss of 15 percent of your playing money. It's more likely that you'll play for an hour and end up with very little or nothing, or you'll hit a jackpot far exceeding your investment.

THE PLAY

There are basically two types of slot machines: a mechanical model with spinning wheels, and an electronic version that uses a microprocessor to control the action of the wheels. Both require the player to line up certain symbols—cherries, bars, 7s and the like—to win.

It's always important to know what you are betting when playing the slot machine. Study the machine's chart, which tells you how many coins you must play in order to get the maximum payoff. When playing a multiple coin machine, always play the maximum number of coins.

Choose a machine that ensures an adequate amount of playing time. If you can only afford to play 25 cents a game, play a nickel machine and bet a maximum of five coins, rather than a quarter machine playing one coin at a time. Some machines are designed to take pennies (at the Gold Spike and Western Hotel, for instance) or tokens as large as $500 (at Caesars Palace).

The goal of every slot machine player is to hit the machine's jackpot, of course. But equally important is finding a loose machine, that is, one that pays off at a faster rate than it takes in money.

Because jackpots are paid strictly at random, you must be at the right machine at the right time in order to hit one. Our strategy will help you identify loose machines, which may give you the opportunity of hitting a major jackpot.

BASIC STRATEGY

Just like the dice in craps or the cards in blackjack, slot machines can produce a hot or cold streak. They are programmed to return a fixed percentage of coins played, but that percentage occurs over the long run. Players, however, play the slot machine for only a relatively short period of time. So, large fluctuations in the payout percentage—either for or against the player—can and do occur.

It's important to recognize where the machine is in its cycle, that is, what type of streak it is having. To do this, start with a fixed number of coins, say a roll of nickels (200 coins) or a roll of quarters (40 coins). Play the coins, but do not put winnings back into the machine; let them accumulate in the tray. Or, if you're playing a credit machine, play only your starting roll of coins and let the credits accumulate.

After you've played the last of the test coins, count how many are in the tray, or note the credits on the meter. If the machine returned less than 65 percent of the coins you played, move to another machine. For example, if you played a roll of nickels (200 coins), the machine must have returned at least 130 coins to keep you from moving on.

Don't make the mistake of trying to weather the storm. It's possible the machine's cycle will change and the payoffs will increase, but don't waste your money waiting for a winning run.

Conversely, if a machine is paying off, stick to it until it begins to lose. And when it does begin to slip, move on. Don't make the mistake of thinking the machine will once again hit a hot streak. It seldom happens. Remember, the longer you play, the greater your chances of losing.

If you're playing a machine that is paying off, don't reach over and play coins in the adjacent machines. Most casinos stagger their machines placing tight ones next to loose ones. They expect the winnings in one machine to be played into a tighter machine.

Poker

Casinos that offer poker simply provide the tables and dealers, and charge the players an hourly fee or take a percentage of the pot; players gamble against each other. The games usually offered are seven card stud and Texas Hold 'Em.

Unlike video poker, where the goal is to get the highest paying hand, the object in live poker is to beat your opponents. Oftentimes, relatively weak hands, such as a pair of aces, two pair or three of a kind, are sufficient to win the pot. The skill in winning at poker lies in the ability to judge not only the quality of your hand but also those of your opponents.

Although not every poker player is a novice-eating shark, many of the regulars are experts, so beginners should test the waters in low-stakes games or take a few lessons (most casinos offer them free of charge) before taking on the pros. Even after lessons, it's a good idea to watch a game for, say, 20 or 30 minutes, so you understand the method of play.

SEVEN CARD STUD

Most beginners start with seven card stud. It's simple to learn, and the betting sequence provides for substantial pots. Play begins with the dealer giving each player two cards face down, and then one card face up. The player with the lowest card showing makes the first bet. Other players can match the bet, increase the bet or withdraw.

Another card is dealt face up, and the player with the highest hand showing starts this round of betting. This is repeated until four cards have been dealt face up. The seventh and final card is dealt face down to the players who have remained in the game, and the final round of betting begins. During this showdown, players may raise a bet up to three times. When the last bet is covered or called, the dealer calls for the showing of hands and the highest hand wins.

RECOMMENDED STRATEGY

Experts believe the first three cards dealt nearly always determine the outcome of the game. Therefore, playing the first three cards is the most important part of the poker game. If you are dealt none of the combinations described below in the first three cards, drop out.

1. Three-of-a-kind: The odds are about 400 to 1, but it does happen. Play the hand, covering all bets, but don't raise until the sixth card. You want the pot to build, as you have a winning hand in most games.

2. A pair of aces or kings: A good starting point, but watch the table for cards that will improve your hand. If they appear, your chances of winning are reduced. After the fifth card, if betting is heavy and you have not increased the value of your hand, drop out.

3. A pair of queens or jacks: An open pair (one card showing) reduces the value of your hand. Again, if betting is heavy after the fifth card and you have not bettered your hand, drop out.

4. Three cards to a straight flush: A very good start because there are several ways to improve it. Bet or raise during the first round. But after the fifth card, if you have not drawn a card to the straight flush, flush or straight, drop out.

5. Three cards to a flush: With this hand you should complete the flush in one out of six hands. Hold it until the fifth card is dealt. If you have not received another card in your suit, drop out.

6. A low pair (10s or less), three high cards (ace, king, queen or jack), or three cards to a straight: After the fourth card, if you have not increased the hand's value, drop out. You must have good cards to work with. Wait until the next hand; don't bet your whole bankroll on a losing hand.

TEXAS HOLD 'EM

Texas Hold 'Em is considered the game of choice among professional poker players. High-stakes games are played daily in Las Vegas casinos, but the biggest of them all is the $1 million World Series of Poker held every year at Binion's Horseshoe.

The game is very similar to seven card stud, except only two of the seven cards are dealt to the player; the other five are dealt face up, and used collectively by all players.

The play begins with the dealer giving each player two face-down cards. The player to the left of the dealer (moving clockwise) is required to start the betting; the other players will match his or her bet or withdraw. Incidentally, it's not uncommon in these high-stakes games to see players leave early, often after receiving only two or three cards.

The dealer discards or burns the top card from the deck, then deals three cards face up in the center of the table—this is called the flop. Another round of betting is completed. The dealer then burns another card and adds a fourth face-up card to the center. Once again, there's a round of betting.

Finally, a fifth face-up card is dealt to the center. Each player can now determine his or her hand, based on the two face-down cards and the five community cards in the center of the table. A final round of betting occurs, along with a showdown and revealing of hands. Once again, the highest hand wins.

RECOMMENDED STRATEGY

The strategy for Texas Hold 'Em is similar to seven card stud, except it's based on your first two cards. If you're dealt none of the combinations below, drop out.

1. A pair of aces: This is the best starting hand. Hold and bet from the first round.

2. A pair of kings: Another very good hand. Hold and bet from the first round.

3. A pair of queens or jacks: Hold and cover all bets until the fourth up-card is dealt. If you have not increased the value of your hand, drop out.

4. Two high-value cards (ace, king or queen): Hold and cover all bets until the fourth up-card is dealt. If you haven't bettered your hand, drop out.

5. Two high-value cards of the same suit: Hold until the fourth up-card, and if you haven't increased the value of your hand, drop out.

6. A small pair (tens or less): Hold until the fourth up-card. If you haven't increased your hand's value drop out.

Generally, if you haven't received a pair of aces or better—two pair, three of a kind, etc.—after the fourth up-card is dealt, drop out. Seldom is a hand won by less than a pair of aces.

New Poker Games

In an effort to stem the flow of players from "live" table games such as blackjack and craps to user-friendly slot machines and their lottery-like jackpots, casinos have introduced new games that combine the strategy of poker with the chance to win a jackpot. Unlike Hold 'Em and Seven Card Stud, these newer games are often played against the house and offer an escalating jackpot such as those available in video poker.

CARIBBEAN STUD POKER

The most popular of the new games is Caribbean Stud Poker, a longtime staple in cruise ship casinos. The game is played with a standard, 52-card deck on a blackjack-style table. The game's attraction is that it offers three ways for the player to win: beat the dealer with a five-card hand; earn a bonus payoff with a pair or higher; participate in a progressive jackpot that often reaches six figures for an additional $1 ante—and hit a flush or higher.

Players are dealt five cards face down after placing their ante bets—a minimum of $5 in most casinos—and their $1 progressive ante, if they choose to play for the increasing jackpot, the value of which is displayed on an electronic reader board at the table. The dealer receives four cards face down and one card up.

If the player thinks his hand can't beat the dealer's, he may fold and surrender his ante bet. If he thinks he can win, he places a "call bet" equal to double his original ante.

The house has an advantage because the dealer must have an Ace/King or higher to continue play. If he doesn't, the hand is over, and players who remained in the game are paid even money on their original ante, but their call bets are returned unpaid.

If the game continues, and the player's hand beats the dealer's, he's paid even money on his ante, plus a bonus amount on his call bet (see the bonus payout schedule following). And if his winning hand is a flush or higher, and he played in the progressive jackpot, he win's an additional award (see the progressive payout schedule). Of course, if the player's hand fails to beat the dealer's, he loses both ante bets.

BONUS PAYOUT SCHEDULE

One Pair	1 to 1
Two Pairs	2 to 1
Three-of-a-kind	3 to 1
Straight	4 to 1
Flush	5 to 1
Full House	7 to 1
Four-of-a-kind	20 to 1
Straight flush	50 to 1
Royal Flush	100 to 1

PROGRESSIVE JACKPOT PAYOUT

Royal Flush	100 percent
Straight Flush	10 percent
Four-of-a-kind	$100
Full House	$75
Flush	$50

LET IT RIDE POKER

This is an interesting poker variation in that players don't compete against the house or each other. Instead, they simply try to get a good hand by combining three cards dealt to them with the dealer's two "hole" cards. To help their cause, players can take down up to two-thirds of their original bet during play to reduce the risk when chances for a winning hand seem bleak.

Here's how it works: Players make three equal bets and are dealt three cards. Then the dealer receives two cards face down. If the player's not happy with his deal, he can remove one of his bets, or let it ride.

The dealer then turns over one of his cards—which is counted as the player's fourth card—and the player must decide whether to withdraw his second bet or let it ride. In either case, the dealer then turns over his second card, and all the players lay down their cards. The players' hands are determined by combining their three and the dealer's two cards. The minimum winning hand is a pair of tens or better, which pays even money. If the player has a winning hand, he is paid on all his remaining bets (see payoff schedule following).

LET IT RIDE PAYOFF SCHEDULE

Pair of tens or better	1 to 1
Two pair	2 to 1
Three-of-a-kind	3 to 1
Straight	5 to 1
Flush	8 to 1
Full House	11 to 1
Four-of-a-kind	50 to 1
Straight flush	200 to 1
Royal Flush	1000 to 1

PAI GOW POKER

Despite its name, Pai Gow Poker bears little resemblance to its ancient Chinese namesake, which is played with 32 domino-like tiles. Rather, it's a kind of Seven Card Stud in which players arrange their cards into a five-card and two-card hand and try to beat the dealer's similarly-arranged hand.

The game is played with a 52-card deck, and hands are ranked the same as traditional poker. After bets are placed, the dealer deals seven cards face down to the players and himself. Each player arranges his cards into a two-card and five-card hand, making sure the latter outranks the former. If the value of the five-card hand isn't higher than that of the two-card hand, the player automatically loses.

The player wins when both his hands outrank the dealer's. He loses when neither beats the dealer's hands, and it's a tie if he outranks one and not the other.

Because the game frequently ends in a tie with no money changing hands, players find they can play longer with a given bankroll than at blackjack, which actually enjoys a slightly lower house advantage.

Sports Betting

Sports betting is big business in Las Vegas, but it doesn't generate the huge profits the machines and table games bring in. Casinos report that the hold at their sports books is less than 5 percent, which means they keep as profits about 5 percent of all the money wagered. In contrast, the hold for slot machines is more than 60 percent, and it's about 15 percent for table games.

Because sports betting requires more skill than luck, astute gamblers and sports handicappers often find ways to beat the house. To compensate, sports books do everything possible to tilt the percentages in their favor.

The first method is charging a commission on a sports bet. Commonly referred to as the house vigorish, the commission is usually 10 percent. This means that a bettor must risk $110 to win $100 betting on football or basketball games. (If the bettor wins, the original $110 is returned to him.)

Sports books also set up point spreads to make predicting the outcome of a game more difficult. The point spread is the amount of points a favored team must score above the opponent's score in order for a bettor to win his bet, used mainly for football, basketball and hockey betting. For instance, if a football team is favored by seven points, the team must win by eight or more. If it wins by less than seven points, or

Most Las Vegas race books offer Pari-Mutuel waging on horses, which allows players to make unlimited bets at track odds.

loses outright, the bettor loses. If the final score falls on the number, say, 21-14, it is a push and the bet is refunded.

The flip side is that underdogs receive the points and needn't actually win the game for the bettor to win his bet. In the above example, if the underdog either wins the game or loses by up to 6 points, its backers win their bets.

For baseball and hockey bets, the books set odds or a money line. (For hockey, most bettors must contend with a point spread—usually not more than two goals—as well as a money line.)

The money line is a decimal version of betting odds. It is most commonly used in baseball and hockey betting, but it is frequently offered on football bets in lieu of the point spread. Instead of listing a team as a 3-2 favorite, or a 6-7 underdog, the sports books use a plus or minus dollar figure to represent a team's odds of winning.

A team with a negative money line is the perceived favorite, and its payoff is less than the amount risked. Conversely, if a team has a plus money line, it is considered the underdog and pays more than the amount wagered.

For example, if your team has a -1.80 money line, you must risk $1.80 in order to win $1, which, added to your original bet gives you a payoff of $2.80. If your team's money line is +1.80, a win is worth $1.80 for every $1 bet for a like payoff of $2.80, but at a risk of only $1.

If you're a mathematician, you'll have figured out that the plus money line represents odds on the underdog winning, and that the minus money line is the inverse of the odds on the favorite winning. In the above example, the odds on the underdog are 1.80 to 1, and the odds on the favorite are 1 divided by 1.80, or 0.55 to 1.

If this is as confusing to understand as it has been to write, just remember you have to bet the amount of the minus money line to win $1 (or multiples thereof), and that each $1 bet on a plus money line pays off at the amount of the money line.

SIX

Side Trips from Las Vegas

Now that you've seen Siegfried & Roy, stuffed yourself silly on prime **143**
rib and developed a severe case of slot-machine elbow, you might want
a change of pace. Or maybe you've been hammered so hard at the craps
tables that you need a renewal of body and spirit. If so, welcome to
southern Nevada. Beyond the neon pleasure garden of Las Vegas lies a
land of mythic diversity, of scenic and historical treasures free from the
breakneck pace of Las Vegas' nonstop merry-go-round.

Making the change from Lady Luck to Mother Nature is quick and
easy in this part of the country. In every direction, just beyond the city's
neon glow, you'll find some of the most magnificent wilderness in America,
just waiting to be explored by hikers and rock climbers, boaters and
anglers, skiers and birdwatchers, photographers and dreamers.

But discovering nature's wonders doesn't mean renting a Land Ro-
ver, hiring a guide or buttoning up your Patagonias. Most of the destinations listed here are within an hour's drive of Glitter Gulch.

Just a few miles northwest of Las Vegas you'll find the sandstone
escarpments of the Spring Mountains, the pine-fringed creeks and small
springs of Red Rock Canyon, the alpine forestry of Mount Charleston
and the winter ski resorts of Lee Canyon.

Drive northeast and there are small hamlets and farm towns, where
you can belly up to the bar with working cowboys and catch the true
flavor of the American West. Or, if you prefer, you can explore the ruins
of ancient civilizations that lived here long before any white settler set
foot on the continent, or wander among the crimson rock formations of
the Valley of Fire.

In spring, a rainbow of delicate wildflowers colors Red Rock Canyon.

Only 120 miles from Las Vegas, just across the Utah state line, are the magnificent Dixie National Forest and the historic town of St. George, seemingly plucked from the New England countryside, complete with Victorian homes, church spires and emerald green lawns.

South of Las Vegas, the blue-green grandeur of Lake Mead, the charming hamlet of Boulder City, the sparkling riverside resort of Laughlin and the old mining camp of Searchlight create a mosaic waiting to be experienced by those curious enough to venture beyond the dimly lit casinos.

Most of the side trips described in this chapter can be enjoyed in a day or less; some take only a few hours. Others may require more time to explore all an area has to offer. Whatever your intention, you can experience these wonders only if you get away from the slot machines, at least for a little while. Try it, and you'll discover another side to southern Nevada, the *real* side.

Red Rock Canyon Area

Red Rock Canyon is just a 20-minute drive from the Strip, but the distance is better measured in eons—the scene is a majestic mural of nature created over uncounted millennia. The centerpiece of the canyon is a nearly sheer red-and-yellow sandstone escarpment that's more than 13 miles long and almost 3000 feet high. The escarpment is incised with numerous deep canyons formed by snowmelt and rain runoff eroding the rock along cracks in the brittle cliffs. Perennial springs and seasonal streams encourage lush vegetation in relatively cool, shaded places in contrast with the dryness of the desert floor.

To reach this colorful, enchanting wilderness, press your sensible shoe to the accelerator and head west on Charleston Boulevard until you reach this national conservation area. Now that you've left the suburban sprawl and found clean desert air, which is generally ten degrees cooler than that in the city, head to the **Red Rock Visitor's Center** (1000 Scenic Drive; 702-363-1921). Set against the stunning backdrop of the escarpment, the low-profile center blends into the surrounding desert. Inside, a recorded self-guided tour takes you through the geologic and wildlife history of the area, and park rangers are on hand to answer questions. (Nature books—on indigenous flora, fauna and geology—are also for sale here.)

Outside the center, the desert landscape has been carefully set out with representatives of the region's plant life. Leaving the center, you

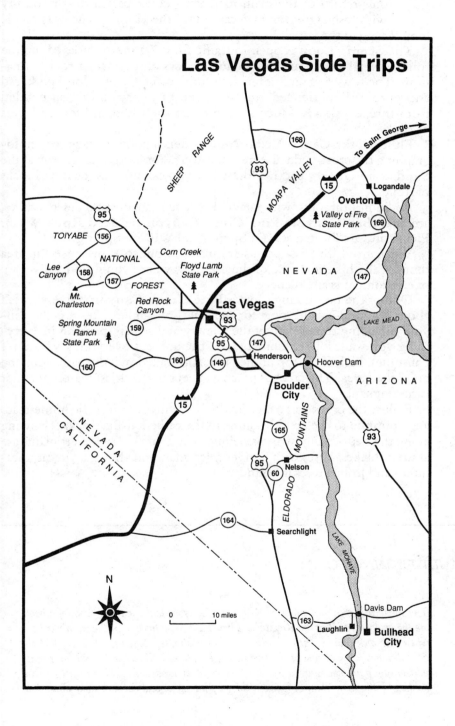

Las Vegas Side Trips

SHEEP RANGE

To Saint George →

168

93

MOAPA VALLEY

15

Logandale

Overton

TOIYABE

95

156

Valley of Fire
State Park

169

Corn Creek

NATIONAL

Floyd Lamb
State Park

NEVADA

147

Lee
Canyon

158

157

FOREST

Mt.
Charleston

Red Rock
Canyon

Las Vegas

93

LAKE MEAD

Spring Mountain
Ranch
State Park

159

95

147

160

160

146

Henderson

Hoover Dam

ARIZONA

15

Boulder
City

NEVADA
CALIFORNIA

MOUNTAINS

165

93

95

60

Nelson

ELDORADO

164

LAKE MOHAVE

Searchlight

N

0   10 miles

163

Davis Dam

Laughlin

Bullhead
City

may either return to the main road for a quick pass through country dotted with Joshua trees and yuccas or take the 13-mile, one-way scenic loop. I suggest the latter.

The **Scenic Loop** is open to traffic from 7 a.m. to dusk. Along the route, several vista points offer choice views of spectacular rock formations. The towering sandstone bluffs form a tapestry of color—pink, red and purple. Experienced climbers, like tiny marionettes suspended from threads, slowly dance their way up the tilted and folded layers of rock.

Either of the **Calico Vista Points** offers a good vantage for photographing the cross-bedded Aztec sandstone. For a closer look, stop at the **Sandstone Quarry** parking lot, where you can walk to the large blocks of stone.

Additional turnouts, with views of wooded canyons and desert washes, are at **Icebox Canyon**, **Pine Creek Canyon** and **Red Rock Wash**. Picnic sites are located at **Red Spring** and **Willow Spring**.

Views from the vista points are magical, but to experience the area thoroughly, hike into one of the canyons, where you'll find a diversity of environments and scenery.

One of the best hiking spots is **Pine Creek Canyon**. Give yourself about one-and-a-half hours for the mild, two-mile hike into the canyon, including time to enjoy the scenery and return (packing in everything you want for refreshment, and packing out everything you don't consume). Park at the top of the bluff, and walk down the path along the creek-bed area. The creek is potable except in the driest season, when it turns stagnant.

Follow the creek past a meadow to the ruins of an historic homestead, and continue to the creek's source in the cathedral-like rocks. Growing along the bed are big, sweet-smelling piñon pines. The desert plants are at their thickest here, with juniper trees, manzanita bushes, yuccas, mesquites and Joshua trees in abundance.

FAULT-FINDING FORAY

*The spectacular rock formations in Red Rock Canyon, laid open like pages of a book, are the geologic result of the **Keystone Thrust Fault**, a fracture in the earth's crust where one rock plate is thrust horizontally over another. Scientists believe that about 65 million years ago two of the earth's crustal plates collided with such force that part of one plate was shoved up and over younger sandstones. This thrust is clearly defined by the sharp contrast between the gray limestone and red sandstone formations.*

The rusted automobiles near Red Rock Canyon's Keystone Fault are believed to have been abandoned by car thieves, who operated there during the '30s and '40s.

If your timing is right, you may glimpse a family of bighorn sheep, a coyote or a kit fox. Birders should bring their field glasses, especially during the spring migration, to catch sight of Scott's, Bullock's and hooded orioles, California thrashers, summer and western tanagers, pine crossbills, golden eagles, white-throated swifts, black-throated gray warblers, blue-gray gnatcatchers, ladder-backed woodpeckers, bushtits, rufous-sided and green-tailed towhees, cactus wrens and black-throated hummingbirds, among other species. For a complete list, pick up a birdwatcher's guide at the visitor's center.

If you'd like a closer view of the region's geologic history, take the **Keystone Thrust** hike, a moderate, three-mile walk beginning at the White Rock Spring turnout. From the lower parking area, follow the dirt road to an abandoned vehicle trail that leads eastward. Follow the trail up the alluvial slope past a prominent hill (called Hogback Ridge) to the right, where you'll find an old car hulk and a well-preserved prehistoric roasting pit. Hike up the ridge for a grand view southward down the Red Rock Valley and along the face of the Sandstone Bluffs.

At the pass, the trail forks; follow the right fork down into a small canyon to view the Keystone Thrust. As you descend, notice the sharp contrast in color between the older gray dolomite on top and the younger red-and-buff sandstone. This piggybacking of older crustal plates on top of younger ones is the distinguishing geologic feature of Red Rock Canyon.

The **Calico Hills** are riddled with natural water catchments called potholes or *tinajas*. After rains, these natural water tanks may be home to small insects, larvae and fairy shrimp. **Icebox Canyon** has a maintained trail for about three-fourths of a mile; the end of the canyon is reached after another half mile of boulder-hopping in the canyon bottom.

You can find shorter hikes along the loop. At the second **Calico Vista**, an easy trail to the bottom of the canyon leads to the Aztec sandstone and, after seasonal rains, to small pools of water. There is also good hiking at **Sandstone Quarry**, where many small canyons offer a delightful escape from casino life.

A few points to keep in mind about hiking in Red Rock Canyon: Avoid dehydration by carrying water with you—most people need a gallon a day while hiking; be wary of flash floods, especially in the late summer months when thunderstorms occur with little warning; all natural and historic features such as plants, animals, rocks and Indian artifacts are protected—you may not disturb, damage or remove them.

After leaving the Scenic Loop, you can turn left on Route 159 (Charleston Boulevard) and head back to the city, or turn right and drive about three miles to **Bonnie Springs Ranch** and **Old Nevada Village** (1 Gunfighter Lane off Highway 160; 702-875-4191; admission). Built in 1843 as a cattle ranch and watering hole for wagon trains going to California, Bonnie Springs Ranch is now a mini amusement park with a petting zoo, duck pond, bird aviary and riding stable. Next door, Old Nevada Village is a full-scale restoration of an old Western town. Although it looks like a movie set, there are no false fronts here—the weathered buildings contain country stores, a saloon, an ice-cream parlor, an opera house, a sheriff's office, a shooting gallery and a silent movie house, and there's a minitrain ride along the outside of the town. Throughout the day, gunfights are staged in the street, along with other Wild West melodramas.

RED ROCK CANYON AREA LODGING AND RESTAURANT

There are no accommodations in the conservation area, and overnight camping is not permitted, but you'll find pleasant, moderately priced rooms at the **Bonnie Springs Motel** (1 Bonnie Springs Ranch Road; 702-875-4400). Most of the 50 guest rooms are decorated in motel-modern mauves and teal; some have jacuzzis. Other amenities include a pool and a restaurant, which features dark wood paneling and pine-topped tables in a dusty, Western-style setting. The restaurant's simple but tasty menu selections include steak, ribs, chicken and fish. Moderate.

RED ROCK CANYON AREA PARKS

For a glimpse of a ranch Howard Hughes once owned, drive three miles east on Route 159 to the turnoff for **Spring Mountain Ranch State Park** (702-875-4141). After paying the $3-per-car entry fee, continue

---

CHILDREN'S DISCOVERY TRAIL

*Kids can learn about the wonders of nature on the **Children's Discovery Trail** in Red Rock Canyon. The half-mile path through Lost Creek Canyon leads to natural rock formations and overhangs that Indians once used as shelters. The trail entrance is near the Willow Spring Picnic Area on the scenic route, but stop at the visitor's center for a guidebook-workbook before starting. The book describes the trail's nine marked sites and asks kids to examine the vegetation, listen to the water music of Lost Creek and smell the bark of a pine tree. It also points out and describes some of the animals that live near the trail.*

Three kinds of rattlesnakes, as well as scorpions and Gila monsters, live in the Red Rock area. Watch where you step and reach, especially along sandstone crevices.

up the access road. Notice that the area appears tamer than the surrounding wild lands—thanks to the convergence of three climate zones and a year-round supply of water from Lake Harriet in the foothills above the ranch.

The permanent outdoor stage on the south side of the access road was built by donations to the volunteer State Parks Cultural Board. During the summer months, community theater and musical concerts are featured. Audiences can sit on their blankets and lawn chairs, spread out picnic-basket dinners and enjoy productions ranging from *The Sound of Music* to *Calamity Jane.*

At the end of the access road you'll find a lush park with extensive lawns, oak trees, a couple of dozen picnic tables, drinking fountains and indoor restrooms for those who prefer the comforts of home. Across the rolling green pasture with its white rail fences, stands an impeccably maintained New England–style ranch house. Built by radio star Chet Lauck (Lum of the "Lum and Abner" show), the ranch was later owned by Vera Krupp, of the German munitions family, and by billionaire Howard Hughes before it became a state park. You can enjoy a free tour of the ranch house, which has all its furniture in place, just as it was in the 1950s.

Nearby is a sandstone-block farmhouse built in the mid-1800s and a reconstructed blacksmith shop, complete with old bellows, tools and cabinets.

Guided tours to Lake Harriet above the ranch are also available. The reservoir, fed by Sandstone Spring, is surrounded by tall marsh grass and trees and is home to dozens of bird species, snakes, lizards, bighorn sheep and other wildlife.

Mount Charleston Area

While the desert floor bakes below, the alpine wilderness of Mount Charleston changes with the colors and climates of four full seasons. Only 30 minutes north of Las Vegas, Mount Charleston and the surrounding Toiyabe National Forest are popular destinations for hiking, backpacking, picnicking and overnight camping, plus skiing during the winter months. Thick bristlecone pines clinging to limestone cliffs 10,000 feet above the desert floor create a stunning backdrop.

A vast array of plant and animal life makes this unique environment home. After you turn off Route 95 and onto Kyle Canyon Road (Route 157), notice the change in vegetation as the elevation increases. Approaching the mountains, you'll see Joshua trees, yuccas and creosote bushes, which have adapted well to the 120-degree summer temperatures and scant rainfall. In the spring, the sides of the road are blanketed with a delicate layer of wildflowers.

As you reach the 5000-foot elevation, piñon pines and junipers take over the landscape, along with scatterings of sagebrush, rabbitbrush and scarlet trumpeter. You probably won't see them from the road, but deer and elk move into this region as the winter snows deepen at higher elevations.

At about 6000 feet, mountain mahogany, oakbrush and ponderosa pine replace the piñon pine and juniper. The stands of pine grow larger as you progress up the mountain. Deer spend their summers in the area, which abounds with bluebell, snowberry and penstemon. At about this point, you'll see a turnoff to the right. This is Deer Creek Highway (Route 158), and leads into Lee Canyon.

The paved roads end at roughly the 7500-foot level, but you can see the forests of bristlecone pine spreading across elevations of 9000 feet and higher. Many of these gnarled veterans are over 5000 years old, predating the majestic redwoods and giant sequoias.

In addition to this varied plant life, the forest is home to the Palmer chipmunk (found nowhere else in the world), bighorn sheep and elk. The area's coyotes, bobcats, foxes and cougars are seldom seen, but their tracks will alert you to their presence.

LOMBARD REMEMBERED

The Spring Mountains just west of the Spring Mountain Ranch State Park were the site of a 1942 plane crash that killed actress Carole Lombard. On a flight to Los Angeles from Indiana, where she had been campaigning for war bonds, Lombard's plane had stopped for refueling in Las Vegas. A few minutes after takeoff, the DC-3 slammed into the snowy slopes near Mount Potosi, killing everyone on board. Lombard's husband, Clark Gable, immediately flew to Las Vegas. After hours of waiting for word from search parties, he set out for the crash site. But, after traveling part of the way up the mountain, he turned around, preferring to remember his wife as he had last seen her. Later that year, a black-spotted orange butterfly indigenous to the cliffs of the Spring Mountains was discovered and named the Carole's fritillary in honor of the actress.

Bring a jacket—the Mount Charleston area enjoys temperatures 20- to 30-degrees cooler than those in Las Vegas.

Humans, too, have found a niche here. On your drive up the mountain you probably noticed cabins and rustic homes perched on sites carved out of the walls of Kyle Canyon. The area has become a colony for nearly two hundred Las Vegans who don't mind the 30-minute commute into the city.

A good first stop is the **Ranger Station** (702-872-5483), where you can pick up maps and information on the area's ecology, sights and history. The large relief map is helpful in planning your outing, whether it be camping, hiking, picnicking or skiing. Drinking water and restrooms are nearby.

Exploring one of the hiking trails, which vary from easy, half-hour walks to two-day treks, is the best way to experience the mountain wilderness. Most of the trailheads are accessible by car and have water and restroom facilities.

Check with the ranger station before starting. Most of the trails are open year-round, but some are closed during winter and early spring. Remember to stay on the marked trails, especially in the higher elevations, where vertical cliffs are dangerous and have claimed lives.

Just a 15-minute walk off Deer Creek Highway, **Desert View Scenic Outlook** provides a breathtaking panorama of the valley and dry lake beds below. Due east is the Sheep Mountain Range, and to the north is Paiute Mesa on the Nevada Test Site. During the 1950s, mushroom clouds from nuclear blasts were photographed from here.

Deer Creek, one of the few streams in the Las Vegas District, flows through the Deer Creek Picnic Area in Lee Canyon, across the highway from the Mahogany Grove picnic area.

Bristlecone Trail begins just above the parking lot at the end of Lee Canyon Highway. The quarter-mile walk circles the ridge with views of the ski area and the spectacular white dolomite limestone cliffs of Mummy Mountain.

Towering majestically at the end of Kyle Canyon Road, **Cathedral Rock** is accessible via a moderate, three-hour hike. You'll pass through stands of pine, fir and aspen on your way to the summit, which offers breathtaking views of Kyle Canyon. Watch your footing, because the trail ends with an abrupt drop of several hundred feet.

Echo Cliff Trail also begins at the Cathedral Rock trailhead and climbs upward through the ponderosa pine and white fir forest above the picnic area. At the base of Echo Cliff, you return along an old road crisscrossing an avalanche path, where the aspens and brush are very colorful in the fall. The trail returns to the upper parking lot in the picnic area.

One of the most scenic areas to visit is **Mary Jane and Big Falls**, in upper Kyle Canyon. The trail starts at the end of Kyle Canyon Road and should take less than four hours to complete. At the lower elevation, lofty pines and white firs are surrounded by vertical cliffs. Soon two trails lead to vantage points near a pair of waterfalls. The best time to view them is in early spring. During the summer there may be only a trickle of water from the cliffs.

Mount Charleston Peak rises to nearly 12,000 feet at the head of Kyle Canyon. If you're not content simply to gaze at its magnificence, and you're an experienced backpacker, there are two trails leading to the summit. One begins in Lee Canyon (11 miles), the other at Cathedral Rock (9 miles). On either hike, plan at least one overnight camp to fully take in the trail's pleasures. (The nine-mile hike can be completed in one day, but you will have little time for exploring and will probably be descending the switchbacks in the dark.) Stop at the ranger station for trail maps and information, and fire permits where necessary.

When the weather turns cold enough to snow, the Mount Charleston Lodge sponsors horse-drawn sleigh rides into the surrounding forest (for a small fee). The frosty jaunt aboard sleighs pulled by two gentle draft horses takes about 20 minutes.

The **Lee Canyon Ski Area** (State Highway 156; 702-872-5462) may open as early as November or as late as January. The season's end may come with the warm March winds or last until May. Good downhill skiing on bunny, intermediate and expert slopes is accessed by three chair lifts, and snow-making equipment ensures that the runs are in powder, not ice. There are also a ski school, rentals, a lounge, a snack bar and a gift shop. For cross-country skiers, there are some magnificent Nordic areas—Scout Canyon, Mack's Canyon, Bristlecone Trail—for touring and mountaineering.

During the winter, especially after a snowfall, snow tires or chains may be required in the Mount Charleston area. Check road conditions by calling the Nevada Department of Transportation (702-486-3116).

SNOW PLAY

The best spot to cavort in the snow is **Foxtail Snow Play Area**, *just off the Lee Canyon Road. The slopes here have been cleared of obstacles and are open to sleds, toboggans and inner tubes. You'll also find restrooms, tables, grills and campfire areas, but you need to bring your own firewood.*

Robber's Roost Cave on Mount Charleston, a limestone overhang, was once used by Mexican bandits as a hideout on their raids in southern Utah and Nevada.

MOUNT CHARLESTON AREA LODGING

The only overnight accommodations in the area are at the **Mount Charleston Hotel** (2 Kyle Canyon Road, Mount Charleston; 702-872-5500, 800-794-3456, fax 702-872-5685). Because it's situated just slightly below the timberline, most of the surrounding scenery is sagebrush and juniper trees, but the hotel's weathered wood exterior, open beam rafters, ponderosa pine pillars and open-pit fireplace with copper hood all contribute to a mountain lodge atmosphere. Guest rooms are of the Best Western variety, with dark earth-tone furnishings and salmon-colored walls, but a few on the top (third) floor offer wood-burning fireplaces and peaked ceilings with exposed beams. The hotel also has a dining room, gift shop, cocktail lounge and (for those who must) slot machine arcade. Moderate.

If you want to rough it, the U.S. Forest Service (702-873-8800) maintains two campgrounds in the area with tent and RV sites: In Lee Canyon, the ten-acre **Dolomite Campgrounds** (Route 156, 18 miles southwest of Route 95) has nature trails and restrooms; the **Kyle Canyon Campgrounds** (Route 157, 17 miles west of Route 95) has chemical toilets and a small grocery store.

MOUNT CHARLESTON AREA RESTAURANTS AND NIGHTLIFE

The Mount Charleston Hotel's **Canyon Dining Room** (2 Kyle Canyon Road; 702-872-5500) features cathedral ceilings with open rafters, walls decorated with mounted trophy heads, tree-trunk pillars and a sweeping 180-degree view of the surrounding hills. Menu specialties include beef, veal, pasta, chicken and scampi. Moderate. Across the partition is the hotel's **Cliffhanger Lounge**, where you can have a drink or dance to a live band on weekends.

The only other place for provisions is the **Mount Charleston Lodge** (end of Kyle Canyon Road; 702-386-6899), a very popular restaurant and bar at the top of Kyle Canyon Road. Despite the name, there are no accommodations here, only sweeping views of the canyon, a circular fireplace, an excellent menu offering game birds, live entertainment on weekends and a charming antique shop next door. Moderate to deluxe.

MOUNT CHARLESTON AREA AND PARKS

Tule Springs, also known as **Floyd Lamb State Park** (9200 Tule Springs Road, at Route 95; 702-486-5413), is a place D. H. Lawrence would love—a still, sylvan lake with ducks and geese on its banks, surrounded by gently sloping hills and towering shade trees. This green oasis is only 15 miles north of downtown Las Vegas on Route 95.

The park, open daily from morning until dusk, attracts anglers, birders, picnickers and hikers. You can feed the ducks on the large and small lakes connected by a stream, stroll around the trimmed lawns on sidewalks or set up your picnic on one of the many tables. Restrooms and drinking fountains are found throughout the park.

A variety of waterfowl pass through on the spring and fall migrations, including ruddy ducks, pintails, white-faced scaup, cinnamon and green-winged teal, Mandarin ducks and Canadian, snow and Ross geese. Imported peacocks wander the grounds, punctuating the air with their squawks (you can hardly say songs; it's more like the angry grate of a rusty gate).

Photographers will find inspiration in the pastoral setting and the old buildings of the **Tule Springs Ranch**. Built in the 1940s as a working ranch, it became a dude/guest ranch where visitors waited out the six-week residency requirement for a quickie divorce. Now, the horse stables, tack rooms, wooden water tower and barn provide a rustic backdrop for artists and photographers.

About six miles north of the Mount Charleston turnoff is **Corn Creek**, located on a well-graded gravel road off Route 95. A former working range and stagecoach stop, Corn Creek is now a field station for the vast Desert National Wildlife Range. This small, rugged oasis is a marvelous site for birdwatching. So diverse is the bird life here that the Audubon Society has included it as part of its adopt-a-refuge program. It is also on the edge of the California flyway and so attracts an astonishing variety of species from hummingbirds to hawks.

ARCHAEOLOGICAL WONDERS

*Named for the large reedlike plants indigenous to the area, **Tule Springs** is one of the few sites in the United States where evidence suggests the presence of humans before 11,000 B.C. Fossils discovered at a site five miles southeast of the park show the presence of several extinct animals—the ground sloth, mammoth, prehistoric horse and American camel, as well as the giant condor. Archaeologists continue working at the fossil site, though it has not been developed for public viewing.*

Corn Creek is a special sanctuary for the once-endangered Nelson desert bighorn sheep.

The natural springs of Corn Creek have formed upper and lower ponds, connected by a gurgling brook. You can walk among the huge cottonwoods, mesquites, willows, fruit trees, cattails and tules clustered around the waterways. There's also a small picnic area with tables, canopies, grills, restrooms and water. An area carved out of the thick, marshy underbrush by caretakers contains houses and horse stables, trimmed lawns and fenced pasture, but these are not open to the public.

The fruited mulberry trees attract evening, blue and rose-breasted grosbeaks, pine crossbills, western and summer tanagers, and orioles. You might see other species such as black-and-white and Wilson's warblers, western bluebirds, flycatchers, thrashers, barn and great horned owls and sharp-shinned and Cooper's hawks.

If you take the footpaths around the ponds, keep an eye out for frogs, toads and lizards. You might even glimpse a coyote or fox on the perimeter of the cultivated area, and a jackrabbit, cottontail or ground squirrel may skitter from the underbrush as you approach.

A walk beyond the ponds takes you to mesquite-filled arroyos, where you might unearth arrowheads left behind by the ancient Indian tribes that once populated Corn Creek. Public restrooms, drinking fountains and a self-service information center are nearby. The area is open from morning until dusk.

Hoover Dam

Long before gambling became king, **Hoover Dam** was the number-one tourist attraction in southern Nevada. Completed in 1935, the dam was touted as the Eighth Wonder of the World—and for good reason. It is one of the world's engineering marvels.

The Hoover Dam project was originally named for President Herbert Hoover in 1930. However, shortly after President Franklin D. Roosevelt took office in 1933, it was renamed Boulder Dam by newly appointed Secretary of the Interior Harold Ickes, who argued that President Hoover had little to do with the project. Then in 1947 a joint resolution of Congress restored the name Hoover Dam, at the same time establishing the precedent of naming dams for presidents in whose administrations they were built.

The horseshoe-shaped plug that holds back two years' flow of the mighty Colorado River is as tall as a 54-story building. The base is 600 feet thick and contains enough concrete to build a two-lane highway from San Francisco to New York. Inside there's as much reinforced steel as in the Empire State Building.

The dam took five years to build, at a cost of $175 million. At the peak of construction, 5000 workers labored night and day. An average of 50 injuries a day and 94 deaths were recorded before the flood gates were closed and Lake Mead began to fill.

Today, Hoover Dam remains southern Nevada's top tourist attraction. Only 20 minutes south of Las Vegas via Route 95/93, the dam is open for tours every day of the year. Begin your visit at the **Exhibit Center** (Route 93, on the Nevada side of the dam; 702-293-8367). Notice the 30-foot-tall Art Nouveau figures outside—the Winged Figures of the Republic, cast in bronze by sculptor Oskar Hansen. Inside, you'll find further evidence of the 1930s architecture influenced by the WPA era: ornate railings, fixtures, floors and doors. The history of the Colorado River, the building of the dam and how it is used for electrical power, flood control and irrigation is told in scale models, movies and brochures.

The guided tour (702-293-8321 or 702-293-8367; admission), which takes about 35 minutes, begins with an elevator ride to the base of the dam. You'll feel the temperature drop as you descend—the interior of the dam averages between 55 and 60 degrees year-round. At the base you'll enter a monumental room housing the seven-story-high turbines that took three years to build and assemble and that generate four billion kilowatt-hours of electricity.

The base of the dam is honeycombed with tunnels. One leads to a 30-foot diversion pipe; another to an outdoor observation deck where you can enjoy a fish-eye perspective of the dam and the rugged canyon it spans. Returning to the top you'll find a snack bar and souvenir shop. If you drive the two-lane road over the dam, you'll find yourself in Arizona.

CASH OR SCRIP?

In order to discourage dam workers from squandering their money in the saloons, brothels and gambling halls of Las Vegas, the U.S. Interior Department recommended that construction companies establish commissaries at the work site and pay their workers in redeemable scrip. But the move caused such outrage by Las Vegas merchants and Nevada lawmakers that the construction firms backed off and gave workers their choice of cash or scrip. Most chose cash and, incidentally, the option of spending it in Las Vegas.

Lake Mead attracts more than 10 million visitors annually.

Lake Mead

Created when the Colorado River was first backed up by Hoover Dam from 1935 to 1938, **Lake Mead** is southern Nevada's second most popular attraction. The sheer size of the lake—822 miles of shoreline and nine trillion gallons of water—and the surrounding jagged canyons and desert sand dunes are reason enough to visit the second-largest lake in the United States. But most people come for the recreational activities: swimming, boating, waterskiing, windsurfing, lying on the beach and exploring the hidden coves and inlets by houseboat. The lake is especially popular with anglers, who take a run at largemouth bass, rainbow, brown and cutthroat trout, catfish and black crappie. Striped bass, which can reach 30 pounds, are the most popular game fish in recent years.

There are a number of ways to reach Lake Mead, but the simplest is through Boulder City, about 20 minutes southeast of Las Vegas. Other, more remote jumping-off points are along the lake's northern finger at Callville Bay, Echo Bay and Overton Beach.

A good way to learn about the lake is to stop at the **Alan Bible Visitor Center** (Highway 93 and Lakeshore Road; 702-293-8906), midway between Boulder City and Hoover Dam. Exhibits and a movie describe the area's history and attractions.

One of the best views of the lake is from the **Hoover Dam cruise boat** (Lake Mead Cruises, 707 Wells Road, Boulder City; 702-293-6180), which leaves from the Lake Mead Marina (322 Lakeshore Road; 702-293-3484) several times a day.

Deep beneath Callville Bay's sheltered waters lie the ruins of **Callville**, an 1864 river-port settlement and the head of steamboat navigation along the Colorado River for a few years. The town, deserted of course, was submerged by the lake when the river was dammed.

About halfway between Echo Bay and Overton Beach is **Rogers Spring**, an oasis created by a warm-water spring. Prehistoric Indians once camped beside the spring, where today's visitors can picnic in a shaded area.

LAKE MEAD LODGING AND RESTAURANTS

At the Lake Mead National Recreation Area (702-293-8907), camping is allowed at **Boulder Beach**, **Callville Bay**, **Echo Bay** and **Temple Bar**. Don't expect much—it's primitive camping with no drinking water (though there are flush toilets).

About a mile north of Boulder Beach, **Lake Mead Marina** (322 Lakeshore Road, Boulder City; 702-293-3484) has hundreds of boat slips and a popular floating restaurant, coffee shop and cocktail lounge.

Developed campsites are available at privately owned grounds nearby. North of Lake Mead Marina, the **Las Vegas Bay Marina** (702-565-9111) has more boat slips, a picnic area and a campground. You can also camp or park your RV at **Callville Bay Resort Marina** (Star Route 10, off Northshore Road, Boulder City; 702-565-8958), which features a coffee shop and cocktail lounge.

The only motel on the Nevada shore of the lake is at **Echo Bay Resort and Marina** (Route 167; 702-394-4000, 800-752-9669, fax 714-833-3541). Along with a restaurant, coffee shop and lounge, the motel offers modern, budget-priced rooms, an RV village and an airstrip for light aircraft.

On the Arizona shore you can rent a room at **Temple Bar Marina** (602-767-3211, 800-752-9669, fax 714-833-3541), which has a modern motel, older cabins with kitchenettes, a café, a cocktail lounge, a campground, a boat-launching ramp, a fuel dock and a store. This is the last outpost for supplies if you plan to boat north of Temple Bar.

LAKE MEAD BEACHES AND PARKS

The best place to spread a beach towel is at **Boulder Beach**, just a few minutes north of the visitor center. The two miles of sandy beach and the sparkling water of Lake Mead attract year-round sunbathers. Picnic areas, campsites, a snack bar and a convenience store are nearby. The clear water and warm temperatures attract divers, who can explore the ill-fated yacht *Tortuga*, near the Boulder Islands, the *Cold Duck*, submerged in 35 feet of water, the remains of Hoover Dam's asphalt factory and the old Mormon settlement of St. Thomas.

CRUISE THE LAKE

*One of the best ways to explore Lake Mead is by cruise boat. **Lake Mead Cruises** (707 Wells Road, Boulder City; 702-293-6180) offers several cruises, the best one being aboard a three-deck paddleboat, the Desert Princess. The 100-foot-long sternwheeler is the largest vessel to ply the waters of the lake and features a snack bar, two glass-enclosed decks, an open promenade deck, an 80-seat dining room, a cocktail lounge and a dancefloor. The late-afternoon cruise features a sunset dinner and stunning views of illuminated Hoover Dam.*

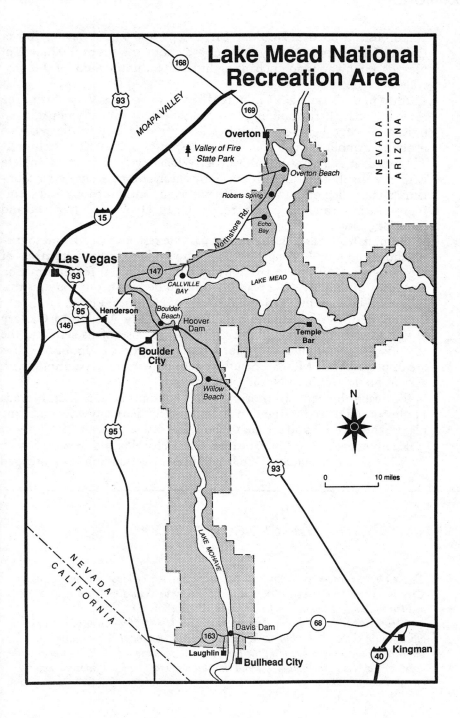

Lake Mead National Recreation Area

Boulder City

Visitors usually discover **Boulder City** as a pit stop on the way to Hoover Dam or Lake Mead. But beyond the gas stations, gift shops and motels of Nevada Highway is an enchanting little town, untouched by the mistakes of civilization.

Although it's only a 30-minute drive from the Las Vegas Strip, the town has no high-rise buildings, bowling alleys, or amusement parks and only one traffic light. And because it is the only city in Nevada that prohibits gambling, there are no casinos, sports books or slot machines.

Instead, it is a slow-paced Mayberry RFD–type of town, complete with a central hotel plaza surrounded by eucalyptus trees and water fountains, an historic hotel, an ice-cream parlor and antique shops—all seemingly lost in a time warp between its Great Depression heritage and the 21st century.

Coming from Las Vegas, you first pass the restaurants, gift and souvenir shops and motels along Nevada Highway. Stop at the **Chamber of Commerce** (1497 Nevada Highway; 702-293-2034) for information and maps of the city. The walking-tour guide points out the sites that have been listed in the National Register of Historical Places.

Next door to the chamber is the **Boulder City Art Guild Gallery** (1495 Nevada Highway; 702-293-2138). Because of its serenity, the town is fast becoming a haven for artists. The works of about 65 artists are displayed here. Most are Southwestern drawings and paintings, with a focus on the southern Nevada wilderness.

To reach the central historic district, continue south along Nevada Highway and then turn right on Arizona Street. Park anywhere near the plaza, where you'll find dozens of shops and restaurants.

Heading the plaza is the **Boulder Dam Hotel** (1305 Arizona Street; 702-293-3510), a stately, Dutch colonial–style building with stepped

---

THE FIRST MASTER-PLANNED COMMUNITY

*Created by the federal government to house the builders of Hoover Dam, **Boulder City** is a geometrically perfect city. It was designed by Saco D. DeBoer, an admirer of Pierre-Charles L'Enfant, who designed Washington, D.C.*

L'Enfant's influence is apparent in the fanlike layout of the city. Government offices sit on the crest of a hill at the base of the fan; commercial, residential and industrial zones spread out from the base. Streets are designed so that through traffic does not traverse residential areas, and the entire town is buffered from the desert by greenbelts and parks.

Near the Echo Bay Resort is a commemorative plaque honoring John Wesley Powell who, in 1869, ended the first river run through the Grand Canyon near here.

gables and white pillars. Inside, the hotel has remained virtually unchanged since it was built in 1933. It was once a hideaway for the rich and famous, and the names of early guests are engraved on brass room-door plaques.

A few doors away stands the stately **Boulder Theater** (1225 Arizona Street; 702-293-3145), the city's first and only movie house. Built in 1932, purportedly to keep dam workers from traveling to Las Vegas' casinos and brothels, the stucco and brick theater features dark wood panels, gold-leaf fixtures, a well-worn, checkerboard tile floor and first-run movies.

Before leaving Boulder City, drive up Nevada Highway to **Denver Street** and turn left for a glimpse of what residential life looked like during the 1930s. The row of homes on the right was built in 1932 for Hoover Dam project managers and supervisors. The old Hollywood Spanish–style houses have changed very little since the Depression era—most have large fireplaces, hardwood floors, sunrooms with casement windows and basements. There's nothing in Las Vegas to match these quaint homes, and they've become popular with many Las Vegans who are willing to do the 30-minute commute into the city.

BOULDER CITY LODGING

At the center of town is the 62-room **Boulder Dam Hotel** (1305 Arizona Street; 702-293-3510), a historical landmark that doubles as the town's only hotel. It is closed for renovations. Call ahead.

Most of the motels on the main highway have clean, budget-priced rooms. A few have kitchenettes, refrigerators or two-bedroom suites. Worth mentioning are the **Sands Motel** (809 Nevada Highway, Boulder City; 702-293-2589), **El Rancho Boulder Motel** (725 Nevada Highway, Boulder City; 702-293-1085) and the **Super 8 Motel** (704 Nevada Highway, Boulder City; 702-294-8888, 800-800-8000, fax 702-293-4344).

BOULDER CITY RESTAURANTS

If you've worked up an appetite exploring this area, try **The Cozy Café** (561 Hotel Plaza; 702-294-0343), which serves simple but tasty dishes—eggs, hamburgers, french fries—and, with its long wood-topped counter, is a popular gathering spot for locals. Budget.

The best Mexican food in town is at **Carlos'** (1300 Arizona Street; 702-293-5828). Though the service is a bit slow, you shouldn't be disappointed with the budget-priced fajitas or chile rellenos.

The Boulder Dam Hotel has hosted such luminaries as Glenn Ford, Bette Davis, Shirley Temple, the Maharajah of India and Crown Prince Olav of Norway.

Bobs All-Family Restaurant (761 Nevada Highway; 702-293-1668), once famous for a six-foot neon rooster on the roof (it's gone), still serves tasty broasted chicken with all the fixin's at budget prices.

There's one restaurant that really captures the flavor of this little town. **Happy Days Diner** (512 Nevada Highway; 702-294-2653) is a genuine 1950s eatery, complete with soda fountain and waitresses in starched-white uniforms. Everything in the place, from the checkerboard floor tile and Wurlitzer jukebox to the Coke glasses and cherry phosphates, is vintage 50s. The food—burgers, rings, fries, chocolate Cokes, grilled cheese sandwiches—and even the prices—$2.99 for the lunch special, $3.99 dinner specials—seem to be caught in a time warp. Expect budget prices at this blast from the past.

Along the main highway are two good spots to eat, both with budget-priced menus. **Two Gals Restaurant** (1632 Nevada Highway; 702-293-1793) serves only breakfast and lunch, and there's usually a line. Selections include avocado and sprouts omelettes, quiches and a number of burgers and sandwiches. **Casa Flores** (930 Nevada Highway; 702-294-1937) is a festive cantina that serves huge portions of chile colorado, papas con huevos and beef fajitas, along with combinations of tacos, enchiladas, beans and rice.

BOULDER CITY SHOPPING

In Boulder City, the plaza and surrounding streets are home to several interesting shops. The **Foxhaus Boutique** (509 Hotel Plaza; 702-293-1411) sells fine gifts, crystal, crafts, candles and kitchenware. A few doors away, **Lacey's Intimate Apparel** (503 Hotel Plaza; 702-293-0882) has a very tasteful collection of, well, intimate apparel. In the corner of the plaza you can enjoy a fresh rhubarb tart or cream cheese muffin and a cup of coffee at **Bobbi Jane's Sweet Treats** (525 Hotel Plaza; 702-293-7310).

Around the corner, on Nevada Highway, are several antique stores. **Ack's Attic** (530 Nevada Highway; 702-293-4035) has a large collection of old kitchen utensils, dolls, metal toys and postcards. Across the street, **J&S Antiques** (527 Avenue B; 702-294-2909) stocks beautiful crystal and porcelain figures, as well as country kitchen utensils and collectibles.

Laughlin Area

The border town of **Laughlin** is a fascinating phenomenon. Located on the west bank of the Colorado River 100 miles south of Las Vegas, Laughlin was once a decrepit bait shop and eight-room motel. It has blossomed into a shimmering riverfront resort and the third-largest gambling center in the state.

Gambling, however, is not Laughlin's only attraction. The river and nearby Lake Mohave are major draws, offering year-round water sports such as swimming, boating, fishing and waterskiing. Also within short driving distance are ghost towns, historic mines and intriguing lost canyons to be explored.

The town is actually a two-mile strip of ten hotel-casinos, a scaled-down version of the Las Vegas Strip. But you won't see any stretch limos or Rolls Royces here; it's mainly RVs and pickup trucks. Known as the Mecca of the Low Roller, Laughlin caters to budget-minded tourists and coin-toting gamblers, most of whom drive in from Arizona and California. Table stakes are of the $1-a-hand variety, and hotel rooms are priced 30 to 50 percent less than their Vegas counterparts.

Most of Laughlin's working population lives across the river in Bullhead City, Arizona's fastest growing city. (The 1990 census pegged the population at 25,000.) There's a small residential section, public library and shopping center west of the casinos in Laughlin, but most hotel workers commute from Bullhead City across the two bridges or by ferryboat.

The best time to visit Laughlin is during the winter and spring months, when daytime temperatures range from 65 to 80 degrees. Temperatures

---

LAUGHLIN'S LAST LAUGH

*The genesis of Laughlin lies in the energy and vision of its namesake, **Don Laughlin**, a former Las Vegas bartender and dealer who, in 1969, bought a bankrupt motel, bar and bait shop for $235,000 and parlayed it into the 660-room Riverside Resort hotel and casino. The resort was so successful that Laughlin spent $10 million of his own money expanding the airport and building a bridge across the Colorado River. Corporate giants soon followed Laughlin's lead, and by the mid-1980s Harrah's, Ramada, Hilton and Circus Circus had begun their own building boom. There are currently nine major hotels in Laughlin serving four million tourists a year.*

in July and August can reach an astounding 120 degrees or more, making this city the hottest spot in the nation.

If you're driving, stop on the way at the old mining town of **Searchlight** for a ten-cent cup of coffee at the Nugget Casino or a sandwich at the '49er Club. The rusting mining equipment and head frames on the hillsides are reminders of the days when this one-street town was the largest city in southern Nevada.

Just a few miles from Laughlin you'll reach a summit overlooking the Colorado River. From here the view of the town is quite stunning, especially at night when the hotel lights glow like burning embers against the dark river.

Continue on the main highway to Casino Drive, and turn right. Stop at the **Laughlin Visitor Center** (1555 Casino Drive; 702-298-3321) for maps, brochures and visitor guides. If you are staying at one of the Laughlin hotels, continue on Casino Drive. All except the Ramada Express are on the river side of the street.

You can park across from the visitor center or at one of the hotels, from which you can walk to the casinos and restaurants. Because traffic on Casino Drive is usually bumper to bumper, especially on weekends, driving from hotel to hotel is not recommended.

If you are used to prowling through the Las Vegas casinos, you'll be pleasantly surprised by the bright and open Laughlin casinos. Huge picture windows are the norm here, so there's plenty of natural light and river views.

The hotels resemble small Las Vegas resorts. There are even a couple of theme hotels. The best is the **Colorado Belle** (2100 South Casino Drive; 702-298-4000), a 600-foot replica of a Mississippi steamboat, complete with three decks and four black smokestacks that are 21 stories tall. In the evening, the paddle wheel turns by strobe light. Inside, the decor is turn-of-the-century New Orleans, with lots of plush red carpeting, glass globe lamps, brass railings and wrought-iron fixtures. The cluster of shops on the mezzanine level has several restaurants, an old-fashioned candy store and wandering clowns to keep your spirits up.

For "Dodge City by the river," try the **Pioneer Hotel** (2200 South Casino Drive; 702-298-2442) next door. The two-story hotel looks like a U-shaped fort, finished with weathered wood panels. The facade of the casino entrance suggests a Wild West boardinghouse. Swinging doors and a wooden porch lead into a hectic casino, decorated with dark wood floors and distressed paneling. On the river side of the hotel is a waving neon cowboy—River Rick—Laughlin's version of Vegas Vic. The hotel grounds facing the river include a lush flower garden, green grass and shade trees. There are also benches for relaxing and watching the ferryboats and jet skiers on the river.

Also worth visiting is the **Best Western Riverside Resort** (1650 South Casino Drive; 702-298-2535). Be sure to check out the antique shop just off the casino. Its small but interesting collection consists of slot machines, jukeboxes, vintage radios and a variety of old neon signs. On display, but not for sale, are antique slots from Don Laughlin's personal collection, including a 1938 vest pocket slot machine and a 1931 slot that paid off in golf balls.

About two miles north of casino row is the **Davis Dam and Power Plant** (602-754-3628), built in 1953 to produce hydroelectric power and regulate water delivery to Mexico. The power plant, on the Arizona side of the river downstream from the dam embankment, is open daily for self-guided tours, which include recorded lectures, illustrated maps and close-up views of the plant's turbines.

Behind the dam lies **Lake Mohave**, which extends 67 miles upstream to Hoover Dam. The long, narrow lake (four miles across at its widest point) provides a multitude of recreational opportunities.

LAUGHLIN AREA LODGING

Although there are nearly 12,000 hotel rooms in Laughlin, busy weekends often attract up to 50,000 visitors. You don't need a calculator to figure the result: reservations are a must. Like their Vegas cousins, the hotels in Laughlin offer the basic amenities—casinos, bars, restaurants, inexpensive buffets and lounge entertainment—and the guest rooms are comparable. Following are a few that provide unusual amenities. All rooms are moderately priced on weekends and budget-priced during the week.

THE SCENIC ROUTE TO LAUGHLIN

If desert driving bores you, try the scenic route over **Christmas Tree Pass**. *The marked 17-mile dirt road leaves Route 95 just south of Searchlight and climbs east through the Newberry Mountains, connecting with Route 163 about six miles west of Laughlin. As you climb toward Christmas Tree Pass, you'll see massive granite outcroppings and stacks of mammoth boulders. With the change in altitude, notice that the sagebrush and cactus give way to the piñon pines for which the area was named. Don't be surprised to see some of the trees decorated with brightly colored cans, paper cups, glass balls or even items of clothing, presumably by local prospectors who have never lost their Christmas spirit.*

For gorgeous river views try the **Edgewater Hotel** (2020 South Casino Drive; 702-298-2453, 800-257-0300, fax 702-298-8165), whose frosty white, 26-story tower has the most rooms fronting the Colorado. All 1470 guest rooms are tastefully decorated with rattan club chairs and white wood furniture, plush green carpets and sand-colored walls accented by Southwestern-print spreads, drapes and ceiling runners. At the dock you can take a free shuttleboat ride to the Arizona bank, or pay for a river cruise on the *Little Belle*.

The covered terrace and pool area at **Gold River Resort and Casino** (2700 South Casino Drive; 702-298-2242, 800-835-7903, fax 702-298-2196), with its palm trees, green lawns and river view, is a great spot for lounging. Inside, the 1000 rooms are bright and airy with a touch of the Southwest—plush carpeting, smoked-glass tables, velour-upholstered chairs and Southwestern-print upholstery. Be sure to check out the casino with its high ceilings and neon mining signs hanging from the rafters.

Just around a bend in the river is **Harrah's Casino Hotel** (2900 South Casino Drive; 702-298-4600, 800-447-8700, fax 702-298-6896), which sits isolated in a minicanyon at the south end of casino row. The cove fronting the hotel offers the only sandy beach on casino row. With a south-of-the-border theme, fiesta colors are splashed throughout the casino, four restaurants, three bars and 1660 guest rooms.

The newest and largest hotel located on the Colorado River is the **Flamingo Hilton** (1900 South Casino Drive; 702-298-5111, 800-352-6464, fax 702-298-5177), where ribbons of pink neon wind through the casino and restaurants. The 2000 guest rooms in the shiny pink twin towers are typically Hilton—spacious, modern and decorated in cool shades of blue and green. The hotel amenities here include six restaurants, a production show and a beautifully landscaped garden overlooking the river.

RIVER OF THE DAMMED

Davis Dam is one of three dams operating to control flooding and produce hydroelectric power along the Colorado River in Nevada, California and Arizona. Along with Hoover Dam to the north and Parker Dam about 80 miles downstream, it forms the Lower Colorado River Dams project. The dams also divert river water to form three lakes: Lake Mead, Lake Mohave and Lake Havasu. Another six large dams in Colorado, Utah and New Mexico also control the waters of the mighty Colorado.

It may not be the Reading, but you can ride the rails on a miniature passenger train at the **Ramada Express** (2121 South Casino Drive; 702-298-4200, 800-272-6232, fax 702-298-6403). The narrow-gauge railroad shuttles you on a ten-minute ride from the parking lot to the casino, which is decorated like a Victorian railroad station. Guest rooms in the 400-room tower behind the casino feature deep earth-tone colors, dark wood furniture and brass lamps and fixtures, while the 1000 rooms in the newer tower feature light-wood furnishings, pastel shades and floor-to-ceiling windows with views of the river and nearby mountains.

If you can't get a room in Laughlin, there is a score of motels in Bullhead City. Most are clean and modern but unexceptional, and room rates tend to run higher than in the Laughlin hotels. Besides the national chains, try the **Park Oasis Motel** (125 Lee Avenue; 602-754-4151, 800-624-2737) and the **Bullhead Riverlodge Motel** (455 Moser Street; 602-754-2250). Both are all-suite motels, ideal for families, and the River-lodge has a boat and fishing dock available for guests' use at no charge. Both moderate.

LAUGHLIN AREA RESTAURANTS

All the Laughlin hotels feature 24-hour coffee shops, inexpensive buffets, snack bars and a variety of restaurants—mostly steak houses. Some of the better dining rooms include **Sutter's Lodge** (2700 South Casino Drive; 702-298-2242) at Gold River Resort and Casino, fashioned after a 19th-century hunting lodge with a veranda and lots of open beams and wood paneling. The specialty on the moderately priced menu is baby back pork ribs. Also featured are steaks, chicken and seafood, and 100 brands of imported beer.

Country cooking is never out of reach at the **Boarding House Restaurant** (2200 South Casino Drive; 702-298-2442) at the Pioneer Hotel, where you can feast on a combination dinner of fried chicken and barbecued ribs. Go easy on the corn bread to save room for homemade strawberry shortcake.

Also worth mentioning are **William Fisk's Steakhouse** (2900 South Casino Drive; 702-298-6832) at Harrah's Casino Hotel for steaks, seafood and Continental cuisine in a Southwestern setting overlooking the river; **Prime Rib Room** (1650 South Casino Drive; 702-298-2535) at the Best Western Riverside Resort, where you can supervise the carving at your table; and the **Alta Villa** (1900 South Casino Drive; 702-298-5111) at the Flamingo Hilton for angel hair pasta and other Italian specialties. All moderate.

LAUGHLIN AREA NIGHTLIFE

Free lounge acts are presented in most of the Laughlin casinos, usually rock or country-and-western groups. The **River Boat Lounge** (2100 South Casino Drive; 702-298-4000) located at the Colorado Belle also features a Dixieland band, singers and dancers in a Bourbon Street Revue each night, and a 12-piece orchestra playing Big Band music on Sunday afternoons.

Most of the celebrity headliners appear at **Don's Celebrity Theatre** (1650 South Casino Drive; 702-298-2535) at the Best Western Riverside Resort, the only theater-sized showroom in Laughlin. Acts range from Roger Miller and Louie Anderson to the Mills Brothers and competition kickboxing. Cover. Also at the Riverside, the **Western Dance Hall** features dancing to country music (live or videotaped), and the **Starview Showroom** hosts a Sunday afternoon big band dance and radio show.

The town's only production show, *American Superstars*, is staged at **Club Flamingo** (1900 South Casino Drive; 702-298-5111) in the Flamingo Hilton. Acts include live tributes to Roy Orbison, Janet Jackson, Charlie Daniels, Whitney Houston, the Blues Brothers and other performers. Cover. **Concert under the Stars** at the Flamingo's outdoor amphitheater usually features nostalgic rock bands. Cover.

For a dose of laughter go to **Sandy Hackett's Comedy Club** (2700 South Casino Drive; 702-298-2242) at Gold River Gambling Hall and Resort. The names of the performers won't make you forget "The Tonight Show," but their jokes will make you forget the slots, at least for a while. Cover.

LAUGHLIN AREA BEACHES AND PARKS

The Colorado River and Lake Mohave provide a multitude of recreational activities, including boating, fishing, waterskiing, scuba diving and windsurfing. Landlubbing hikers will love the desert and canyons surrounding Laughlin, which offer fascinating outings.

The only public beach on the river is at the **Davis Camp County Park** (602-754-4606), about a mile north of Laughlin on the Arizona side of the river. Here you'll find a stretch of sandy beach where you can swim, fish or launch a jet ski. At the south end of the park is a marsh that's home to a variety of birds and other small wildlife.

There's another public beach at **Katherine Landing** (602-754-3272) on Lake Mohave, about three miles north of the dam. The Landing also has a full-service marina, boat launching docks, a campground, a motel, a restaurant and a grocery store. You can rent boats, fishing tackle and water skis here.

Valley of Fire

The jagged sandstone mounds of vermilion, scarlet and mauve at **Valley of Fire State Park** create an eerie pallet, suggestive of a Martian landscape. Unlike Red Rock Canyon, which was created along shifting fault lines, the red sandstone formations at Valley of Fire were formed from great sand dunes during the Jurassic period. Complex uplifting and faulting of the region, followed by 100 million years of erosion, have carved this crimson-hued valley, six miles long and four miles wide, from the desert.

A popular destination for rock hunters, the Valley of Fire is also famous for its petroglyphs—ancient rock art left behind by the prehistoric Basket Maker people and the Anasazi Pueblo farmers who are believed to be North America's earliest peoples. In addition to exploring the majestic sandstone formations—spires, domes and serrated ridges—visitors can hike, camp and picnic.

The state park is a 45-minute drive from Las Vegas via Route 15, or an hour's drive by Northshore Road along Lake Mead. The best time to visit is from late September through early June; summer temperatures are ferocious.

A good first stop is the **Visitor Center** (702-397-2088), where you can pick up maps, trail guides, displays, books and films on the geology, ecology and history of the region. The exhibits explain the natural forces that created this unusual spot. There's also a desert tortoise habitat, where you can see the endangered animals at close range. The driving tour through the valley takes only 15 minutes, but plan to stop at some fascinating sights along the way.

The Cabins were built with native sandstone by the Civilian Conservation Corps in the 1930s as shelter for passing travelers. Picnic facilities and restrooms are nearby.

One of two sites where you can see prehistoric Indian rock art up close is **Petroglyph Canyon**. Follow the self-guided tour along the sandy canyon bottom, and watch for markings on the canyon walls. You should be able to see kachina figures tucked up and away from casual view, as well as dancers holding hands, footprints, clan signs and various animals. Curved and straight lines tie some of the compositions together.

The self-guided trail also leads to **Mouse's Tank**, named for a local Native American who hid from the law here at the turn of the century. The large rock catchment, or tank, at the trail's end collects and preserves rainwater, providing a watering spot for birds, reptiles, mammals and insects.

Atlatl Rock is the park's other major petroglyph site. Named for the ancient spear-throwing sticks depicted in many petroglyphs, Atlatl

Rock has a stairway and scaffold for closer inspection of the extensive rock art. Excavations at the site have uncovered artifacts left by the Virgin Anasazi, Paiute and other Native Americans who once lived along the Colorado River.

Petrified Wood is a collection of 225-million-year-old logs and stumps washed into the area from the ancient forests that once covered this now arid region. Two trails lead to the petrified logs, the most common local fossil.

Other interesting rock formations are the **Seven Sisters**, a close grouping of seven upright figures; the **Beehives**, an unusual sandstone formation eroded by the forces of wind and water; and the **White Domes**, a brilliant contrast of sandstone colors.

Moapa Valley

On your drive to the Valley of Fire you'll pass through **Moapa Valley**, a veritable oasis irrigated by the centuries-old Muddy River. After exiting the interstate you'll discover alfalfa fields, horse ranches and dairies, as well as two one-street towns.

The first one is **Logandale**, a bedroom community on the site of St. Joseph, one of the first Mormon settlements in southern Nevada.

Farther along Route 169 is **Overton**, whose main street spans several blocks of cafés, bars, markets, video stores and a movie theater. If you'd like a hawk's-eye view of the valley, take the paved road leading east out of Overton up the mountain to **Mormon Mesa**, which is a nice place to spread a picnic blanket and enjoy the panorama.

At the south end of town is the **Lost City Museum** (721 South Highway 169, Overton; 702-397-2193), which features a fascinating collection of Anasazi artifacts. The Anasazi, or Ancient Ones, settled the Moapa Valley centuries before any white person set foot in America. The remains of their settlement, which archaeologists call the Lost City, was covered by the waters of Lake Mead, but representative buildings have been reconstructed at the museum. Exhibits consist of pottery, stone tools and weapons, baskets and household items from the Anasazi and other ancient Indian cultures, and a slab of sandstone decorated with petroglyphs—ancient rock drawings—similar to those in the nearby Valley of Fire. The museum also features exhibits relating to the Mormon farmers who settled the valley in 1865. The gift shop has an interesting collection of Hopi Indian cards, drawn by blind artist Jerry Mitchler.

MOAPA VALLEY LODGING AND RESTAURANTS

A good place to camp, dock your sailboat or park your motor home is **Overton Beach Resort** (702-394-4040, fax 702-394-4142), which also features a motel with modest, budget-priced rooms and a coffee shop. In Overton, you can feast on a hearty breakfast or country-style dinner at **Sugar's Home Plate** (300 South Main Street; 702-397-8084), grab a pizza or submarine sandwich at **Tom's Pizza** (198 South Main Street; 702-397-8600), or cool off with an ice-cream cone, malt or other frozen dessert at the **Inside Scoop** (387 South Main Street; 702-397-2055); all at budget prices.

St. George Area, Utah

Imagine a quaint New England town complete with emerald green trees, wood-frame colonial homes and churches with clock towers and spires, then add a backdrop that suggests a miniature, red-hued Grand Canyon. That's the city of St. George, Utah, a delightful change of pace just across the Nevada state line, about 120 miles northeast of Las Vegas.

This little community is a key gateway to Zion National Park, Cedar Breaks National Monument and Snow Canyon State Park. It is also one of the best places in the country to retire because of its weather, scenery and peaceful lifestyle. These attributes make it a great travel destination as well. Throw in plenty of places to explore, shop, dine, stay and play, and you have a fascinating getaway that's a comfortable two-hour drive from Las Vegas.

For those with a yen for nostalgia, St. George is a treasure. There's a wealth of history on nearly every street in the city's central downtown area—the original town settled by Mormon pioneers in the 1860s. Outdoor enthusiasts can hunt, fish, swim or boat at nearby parks and recreational areas, and golfers can tee off on one of eight city golf courses. If

---

THE WEST'S FIRST MORMON TEMPLE

*Only members of the Mormon Church may enter the **St. George Mormon Temple** (450 South 300 East Street; 801-673-5181), a dazzling white edifice that dominates the town. But an on-site visitor center does provide a pictorial history of the temple's construction and other background on the Church of Latter Day Saints. Built in 1871, it predates the Great Salt Lake City temple and is the oldest Mormon temple in use today. Free guided tours of the grounds are also available.*

In 1862, the Mormons planted mulberry trees to grow silkworms—but the experiment failed.

you simply want to experience nature at its best, you will discover one of the planet's most varied landscapes—from lava-crusted craters and billowing sand dunes to granite monuments and mountain meadows.

The city began when Brigham Young sent some 300 families from northern Utah to the southern Utah desert. Young envisioned a huge cotton mission that could supplement the West's supply during the Civil War, which had cut off shipments of cotton from the South. Though initially successful, the cotton mission (and one to grow silkworms) ultimately failed because of its inability to compete in the marketplace after the Civil War. However, a warm climate and a bevy of recreational activities eventually made St. George the fastest-growing city in the state and one of the most popular retirement destinations in the country.

St. George is made for walking. Begin at the **Chamber of Commerce** (97 East St. George Boulevard; 801-628-1658), which was originally built in the 1870s as the Washington County Courthouse. Pick up brochures, a walking-tour guide and maps of the area. In the basement of the square, two-story, red-brick colonial building are dungeonlike cells where cattle rustlers were once jailed. The large room on the second floor was used as a school and courthouse. Other interesting features include 18-inch-thick interior walls, panes of original glass, old chandeliers, original paintings of Zion National Park and the Grand Canyon, an old vault and the exterior cornice work and cupola.

Directly behind the chamber offices is the **Daughters of the Utah Pioneers Museum** (145 North 100 East Street; 801-628-7274), which is filled with relics of the past, including children's toys, lace bonnets, worn tools, yellowed letters and photographs of pioneers. There is also a pioneer dress made from locally produced silk.

The **Mormon Tabernacle** (2 South Main Street; 801-628-4072) was built in 1871 of red sandstone, and has a four-faced clock on a square tower crowned by a slender white steeple. Tour guides explain how limestone for the three-foot-thick basement walls was hand-quarried and red sandstone blocks were hand-cut stone by stone from a nearby site. Take special note of the intricate, plaster-of-Paris ceiling and cornice work, all shipped to California by boat and then hauled by wagon team to St. George.

For a look back to the 1890s, try **Judd's Store** (62 West Tabernacle Street; 801-628-2596), a western-style shop that hasn't changed much since it was built. Notice the gleaming polished wood floors, handmade display cases, pressed tin ceiling and rippled glass windows. Don't leave without sampling some of the baked goods, candies or a float, freeze or banana split from the marble soda fountain.

You can take a guided tour of **Brigham Young's Winter Home** (155 West 200 North Street; 801-673-2517), showcasing beautiful furnishings and memorabilia owned by the second president of the Mormon Church. Huge fruit and mulberry trees still cover the grounds.

Several historic buildings can be found in **Ancestor Square** (42 West St. George Boulevard), along with dozens of shops and restaurants. The **Hardy House**, which is now a Mexican restaurant, was used by the sheriff of St. George during the 1870s. There's even a bullet hole in one of the doors. The **Gardener's Club Hall** served as a meeting place for club members and is still in use today. The one-room **Jailhouse**, believed to have been built by Sheriff Hardy in the 1880s, was constructed from black lava hauled down from the nearby Pine Mountains. The bars on the windows are original.

St. George Art Center (86 South Main Street; 801-634-5850) was built in the 1880s as the Dixie Academy, which grew to become today's Dixie College. The four-story brick building is now used by the city to house art and leisure-related offices.

Also located within St. George is the **Washington County Travel and Convention Bureau** (425 South 700 East, Dixie Center; 801-634-5747), which can provide information on the entire region.

Go north of St. George 25 miles on Route 18 to the town of Central, and you'll find the turnoff to **Pine Valley**, a mountain hamlet with rustic cabins, brick cottages and Victorian homes. At the valley's center is a picturesque, satin white chapel that's believed to be the oldest Mormon chapel still in continuous use.

Just north of the Pine Valley turnoff is a stone marker for the **Mountain Meadows Massacre Site and Memorial**. Here, in 1857, a group of emigrants—120 men, women and children—en route to California was slaughtered by Mormons and Indians. The event is considered a

---

IN SEARCH OF DINOSAUR TRACKS

For evidence that prehistoric creatures once roamed the area, drive to the center of Washington City, about two miles east of St. George, and turn north on Main until you pass under Route 15. Follow the dirt road north, and turn right at the road that goes up the hill to the pink water tank. Park here, then walk up the road to a chained cable gate. Turn right, and walk northeast to a deep wash. Go down into the wash, and follow it downstream until you find a flat, greenish slab of rock. Here you'll find the foot-long tracks that are remnants of another age.

dark period in Mormon history and one the church has tried to live down ever since.

After visiting Pine Valley, backtrack to Route 18 and travel 12 miles south to the **Snow Canyon State Park** (801-628-2255) turnoff. Along the way are numerous extinct volcanic cones and lava fields, many beckoning to be explored. A small park, the canyon itself is a white-and-red mix of Navajo sandstone covered with black lava beds. Elevations range from 2600 to 3500 feet atop the cinder cones. Snow Canyon has served as a location for several films, including *Butch Cassidy and the Sundance Kid*. Grasses, willows, cacti and other shrubbery peer through cracks. Evidence of early human impressions of Snow Canyon can be seen at several pictograph sites within the park.

Leaving the canyon, you'll pass through Ivins and then connect with the rural community of **Santa Clara** three miles west of St. George. Settled by Swiss immigrants, Santa Clara lays claim to the house built by noted missionary, Indian agent and colonizer Jacob Hamblin. Built in 1862, the rough-hewn, red sandstone **Jacob Hamblin Home** (Route 91; 801-673-2161) clearly demonstrates the sturdiness of frontier construction designed to withstand Indian attack, and it showcases a number of 19th-century furnishings and tools.

ST. GEORGE AREA LODGING

There are dozens of chain hotels and motels in St. George, making it simple to find one that meets your requirements and pocketbook. But for a real treat, consider one of the city's bed-and-breakfast inns.

Surrounded by a flower-laden courtyard and manicured lawns, the **Greene Gate Village** (76 West Tabernacle; 801-628-6999, 800-350-6999, fax 801-628-6989) bed-and-breakfast inn is a collection of restored pioneer homes originally built in the 1860s. Three houses sit side by side, flanked by a fountain, swimming pool, hot tub and wrought-iron fence with a green wooden gate. Inside, the village boasts elegant decor—wallpapered rooms, duvets, antique furnishings, plump pillows—and a conscientious staff. Most of the rooms have private baths, and all are furnished in mint-condition antiques. A delicious breakfast is served in a parlor decorated in red velvet, on an oak table embellished with china and silver. Moderate.

For more traditional lodging, there's **The Bluffs Motel** (1140 South Bluff; 801-628-6699, 800-832-5833), which seems to offer two of everything: double queen suites, two televisions, two telephones, even two king suites with private jacuzzis. The 33 rooms are exceptionally well decorated in soft tones and enjoy large bathrooms and living room areas. There's also an outdoor heated pool and jacuzzi. Moderate.

There's a lot of bang for the buck at **Ranch Inn** (1040 South Main; 801-628-8000). More than half the 53 units are classified kitchenette suites, meaning they house a microwave oven, refrigerator, conversation-and-dining area, plus fully tiled bath with mirrored vanity. An indoor jacuzzi, sauna, guest laundry and heated pool round out the inn's amenities. Moderate.

Situated off the main drag, **Ramada Inn** (1440 East St. George Boulevard; 801-628-2828, 800-228-2828, fax 801-628-0505) offers quiet refuge. An expansive lobby provides portal to 90 rooms, each with desk and upholstered chairs. The hotel also has one of the prettiest swimming pool settings, with palm trees surrounding the site. A free continental breakfast is included. Moderate.

The streamlined architecture of **Best Western Coral Hills Motel** (125 East St. George Boulevard; 801-673-4844, 800-542-7733) is reminiscent of "The Jetsons," but the 98 rooms are more down-to-earth with turquoise carpeting, upholstered chairs and dark woods. Indoor and outdoor swimming pools, spas, a putting green and an exercise room are bonuses. Moderate.

Holiday Inn Resort Hotel (850 South Bluff; 801-628-4235, fax 801-628-8157) likes to think of itself as a complete recreational facility. Besides the well-appointed rooms, restaurant and atrium-style lobby (with miniwaterfall), guests are treated to a large indoor/outdoor heated swim-

---

THE SEVEN WIVES INN

*The nicest bed-and-breakfast inn in St. George is the **Seven Wives Inn** (217 North 100 West Street; 801-628-3737, 800-600-3737), consisting of two pioneer homes built in the 1870s. The main house is a wood-frame Victorian with a stone walkway, wrap-around veranda and splendid towering trees. Next door, the smaller, president's house is a colonial with a small swimming pool. All 13 guest rooms have private baths and are decorated in antiques. Most have an outside door leading to a porch or balcony, and some have fireplaces or wood-burning stoves. Each house has a parlor with fireplace, books and games. The best rooms are in the main house and are named after the many wives of the innkeeper's great-grandfather. "Melissa" has a fireplace and a tin bathtub rimmed in oak. "Clarinda" offers an antique pine bed and cane-backed rocker; "Sarah" includes a pair of church pews in front of the fireplace; "Mary Ann" has two iron beds and an oak dresser; "Susan" has a Franklin stove and an outside entrance; and "Jane," located in the attic, was said to be the hiding place of renegade polygamists. Rates include a huge gourmet breakfast in the elegant dining room as welll as use of the swimming pool. Prices are budget to moderate.*

ming pool (you can actually swim in and out of the hotel), whirlpool, tennis court, putting green, minigym, gameroom, video arcade, gift shop and special children's play area. Moderate to deluxe.

ST. GEORGE AREA RESTAURANTS

St. George doesn't lack for choices when it's time to eat. Besides the requisite chains (and none is missing), there are plenty of places that offer a hearty meal at a reasonable cost. At least this side of Utah has heard of the salad bar.

The most popular spot with locals is **Rene's Restaurant** (430 East St. George Boulevard; 801-628-9300), reliable for its home-style cooking in a 1950s-style diner featuring huge windows, white overhead fans and a sign adorned with a neon palm tree. Selections on the moderate-priced menu selections range from pasta and roast turkey to chicken-fried steak and Norwegian salmon. There are also a variety of homemade desserts, mostly fruit pies and thick chocolate cakes, as well as homemade breads and muffins.

Fireplaces, greenery galore and waitresses dressed in early English garb lend a cozy, historic air to **Andelin's Gable House** (290 East St. George Boulevard; 801-673-6796), unequivocally St. George's finest dining establishment. Patrons choose from an elegant five-course dinner or a more moderate menu. Regardless, all are served on pewter and taste delicious. Noteworthy are the roast brisket of beef, orange roughy and chicken pot pie. Save room for dessert. Moderate to deluxe.

In historic Ancestor Square, **Basila's Greek Café** (2 West St. George Boulevard; 801-673-7671) serves classic Mediterranean cuisine in a Greek bistro. Dine on the shaded patio or in an exposed-beam dining room. The best of the specialties include stuffed grape leaves, hummus tahini, loin lamb chops, spinach pie and Mediterranean Greek salad. Budget.

Perched on the third floor of the Tower Building in Ancestor Square, **J. J. Hunan Chinese Restaurant** (2 West St. George Boulevard; 801-628-7219) appears to be the area's choice for Asian cuisine. Seafood, chicken, beef, duck, pork—it's all here, presented in a gracious manner. Budget to moderate.

One of the city's oldest houses is now **Los Hermanos** (46 West St. George Boulevard; 801-628-5989), a cozy Mexican restaurant with exposed wood beams, railroad benches, dark recessed booths and a river-rock floor-to-ceiling fireplace. Choose from the usual selection of tacos, burritos and enchiladas, or try a superb seafood flauta or spicy chile relleno special. A nice touch is the carafe of salsa served with your chips. Prices are budget.

To minimize jealousy, colonizer and polygamist Jacob Hamblin (who eventually counted four wives and 24 children) built identical master bedrooms for his wives.

Service is erratic, but **The Palms Restaurant** (850 South Bluff, inside the Holiday Inn; 801-628-4235) can be a good choice for family dining in a pleasant setting. Besides an extensive salad bar with homemade soups and breads, dinner choices range from roast turkey to mountain trout to chicken teriyaki. The lunch menu comprises sandwiches, hamburgers and salads, while breakfast includes omelettes and griddle items. Budget to moderate.

ST. GEORGE AREA SHOPPING

Shopping in St. George is designed with locals in mind. You'll find a few shopping malls and strip centers but little else. One place of note, however, is the **Artists' Gallery** (5 Ancestor Square, St. George Boulevard and Main Street; 801-628-9293), which carries works by more than a dozen regional artists.

There are also a few antique and collectibles shops worth mentioning. **Holland House** (70 North 500 East; 801-628-0176) has an interesting collection of crystal, china, demitasse sets and Victorian hats and handbags. You'll also find tin toys, lunch boxes and H-O train sets. Try the **Dixie Trading Post** (111 West St. George Boulevard; 801-628-7333) for vintage guns, farm tools, tonsorial accessories, old radios and furniture. **General Store Antiques** (640 East St. George Boulevard; 801-628-8858) offers housewares, perfume bottles, cosmetics cases, Zippo cigarette lighters and pocketknives.

ST. GEORGE AREA NIGHTLIFE

World-class entertainers are showcased through the **Celebrity Concert Series** at Dixie Center (425 South 700 East; 801-628-7003).

The **Southwest Symphony**, a community orchestra, performs throughout the year in the M. C. Cox Auditorium at Dixie Center (425 South 700 East; 801-628-7003), as does the **Southwest Symphonic Chorale**.

Dixie College (225 South 700 East; 801-628-3121) offers a year-round season of plays and musicals utilizing the talents of the Pioneer Players.

You'll think you've stepped back in time at the **Dixie Theater** (35 North Main Street; 801-673-2131), a small, storefront movie house built in the 1950s. The lobby features tables, chairs and a huge fountain-style

If the sand, sage and brilliant wildflowers of Snow Canyon State Park look vaguely familiar, it might just be that you're unconsciously recalling one of the countless Westerns filmed here.

concession stand, and there's a real balcony upstairs. Best of all, you can see a first-run movie for two bucks.

The **Blarney Stone** (800 East St. George Boulevard; 801-673-9191) is a beer bar serving an animated crowd. There's live music on weekends running the gamut from country to pop.

If you prefer a more intimate setting, enjoy a quiet drink in the lounge at the **Hilton Inn** (1450 South Hilton Drive; 801-628-0463).

ST. GEORGE AREA PARKS

Several volcanic cones welcome visitors to **Snow Canyon State Park** (801-628-2255) on Route 18, five miles west of St. George. The black lava rock crusted over red Navajo sandstone makes a striking visual effect in this colorful canyon, considered a treat for photographers. The 65,000-acre park also features picnic areas, restrooms, tent sites, hot showers, electric hookups, a sewage disposal station and a covered, group-use pavilion.

Surrounded by 10,000-foot peaks and ponderosa pines, the **Pine Valley Campground and Reservoir** offers numerous picnicking areas. During the winter, the mountain meadows are dusted with snow, and the reservoir freezes, attracting ice skaters and inner-tubers.

A scenic setting of rocky ridges frames **Gunlock State Park**, a 240-acre reservoir noted for its superb year-round boating, bass fishing, water-skiing and picnicking. Nestled in the rugged ravine of the Santa Clara River, the reservoir's waters abut red rock hills dotted with green shrubbery. Take old Route 91, 16 miles northwest of St. George.

Anglers will love **Quail Creek State Park**, about eight miles east of St. George off the Hurricane exit of Route 15. Stark rock escarpments surround the 590-acre reservoir with a state park set on its west shore. Anglers need only bait their hooks and prepare to reel in bass, trout and catfish. Besides being an ideal site for camping and picnicking, Quail Creek is noted for its waterskiing, boating and windsurfing.

Desert trees and plants crowd the campsites at **Red Cliffs Recreation Site**, a red rock paradise at the foot of Pine Valley Mountain. Maintained by the Bureau of Land Management, the camping area is equipped with picnic tables and restrooms. To get there from St. George, go north on Route 15 about 17 miles to the Leeds exit. From there, it's four-and-one-half miles south.

The Sporting Life

BOATING AND WATERSKIING

You can skip across Lake Mead in a power or ski boat, or simply relax under sail or on the deck of a houseboat. For rentals try the **Callville Bay Resort Marina** (Star Route 10, off Northshore Road, Las Vegas; 702-565-8958), **Lake Mead Marina** (322 Lakeshore Road, Boulder City; 702-293-3484), **Overton Beach Resort and Marina** (Route 167, 13 miles south of Overton; 702-394-4040) and **Echo Bay Resort and Marina** (Route 167, 20 miles south of Overton; 702-394-4000).

In the Laughlin area, waterskiing is permitted along the Colorado River from Laughlin south to Needles. The sparsely populated area just south of Bullhead City is the best choice. You can also waterski on Lake Mohave north of Davis Dam. For boat rentals and equipment try **Lake Mohave Resort** (Katherine Landing, AZ; 602-754-3245).

FISHING

It's open season on all fish year-round at **Lake Mead**, where you'll find an abundance of catfish, bluegill, trout, crappie and striped bass, often tipping the scales at 30 pounds. One of the best spots for bass is near the Las Vegas Boat Harbor because of the wastewater nutrients dumped from the Las Vegas Wash into this section of the lake. Anglers consider the Overton arm of Lake Mead one of the best areas for striped bass; schools of threadfin shad often churn the water in their feeding frenzies. Also worth trying are Calico Basin, the Meadows, Stewart's Point and Meat Hole. For tips on other spots, ask a park ranger or try any of these marinas, which also sell licenses, bait and tackle: **Lake Mead Marina** (322 Lakeshore Road; 702-293-3484); **Las Vegas Boat Harbor** (Henderson; 702-565-9111); **Callville Bay Resort Marina** (Star Route 10, off Northshore Road; 702-565-8958); **Echo Bay Resort and Marina** (Overton; 702-394-4000); and **Temple Bar Marina** (Temple Bay; 602-767-3211).

Fishing is excellent along the Colorado River near Laughlin and Bullhead City. Anglers can fill their creels with striped bass, rainbow trout, catfish, bluegill and crappie. A good spot is the cold water below Davis Dam. There's also good fishing above the dam on Lake Mohave, noted for its rainbow trout and bass.

Trout, bass, bluegill and crappie are plentiful in the St. George area. Try the **Gunlock**, **Enterprise**, **Quail Creek**, **Baker** and **Pine Valley** reservoirs. For more specific locations of prime fishing spots and information on fishing licenses, try **Hurst Ben Franklin** (160 North 500 West, St. George; 801-673-6141) or **McKnight's Sporting Goods** (968 East St. George Boulevard, St. George; 801-673-4949).

WINTER SPORTS

The **Lee Canyon Ski Area** at Mount Charleston offers good downhill skiing on bunny, intermediate and expert slopes, as well as magnificent cross-country skiing at Scout Canyon, Mack's Canyon and Bristlecone Trail. You can rent ski equipment in Las Vegas at **Ski Lee Rentals** (2395 North Rancho Drive; 702-646-0008), **McGhies Ski Chalet** (4503 West Sahara Avenue; 702-252-8077) or **Nevada Bob's** (3631 West Sahara Avenue; 702-362-9904). The **U.S. Forest Service** (2881 South Valley View Boulevard; 702-873-8800) has both maps and information for cross-country skiers. For the latest **ski report**, call 702-593-9500.

Tons of dry powder and a variety of slopes await skiers at **Brian Head Ski Resort** (329 South Route 143, Brian Head, UT; 801-677-2035), about 65 miles northeast of St. George. Catering to both alpine and nordic skiers, Brian Head's seven chairlifts serve mostly intermediate terrain. Cross-country skiers like to glide to colorful **Cedar Breaks National Monument** and beyond. Facilities include chalet accommodations, restaurants and motels nearby. **Pine Valley** becomes a Currier and Ives print when the snow flies, with its frozen reservoir attracting ice skaters and inner-tubers.

RIVER RUNNING

The 11-mile stretch of Colorado River from Hoover Dam to Willow Beach is open year-round to rafts, canoes and kayaks, but the best times are spring and fall. River running requires a permit from the **U.S. Bureau of Reclamation, Lower Colorado Region** (P.O. Box 299, Boulder City, NV 89005; 702-293-8356). For canoe and kayak rentals try **Wilderness Outfitting** (205 Rainier Court, Boulder City; 702-293-7526). It's not exactly white-knuckle rafting, but you can float down the Colorado River from Hoover Dam to Black Canyon and see waterfalls, hot springs and geological formations. Call **Black Canyon, Inc.** (1417 Pueblo Drive, Boulder City; 702-293-3776).

HORSEBACK RIDING

Equestrians can challenge the rugged foothills of Mount Charleston and enjoy views of the desert floor at the **Mt. Charleston Riding Stables** (U.S. Highway 157; 702-872-7009). **Bonnie Springs Ranch Riding Stables** (1 Gunfighter Lane; 702-875-4191) offers access to scenic Red Rock Canyon.

The colorful canyons and valleys around St. George are made for leisurely horseback trips. For trail rides, contact **Diamond Valley Guest**

Ranch (650 North Diamond Valley Road, St. George; 801-574-2281) or **Snow Canyon Riding Stables** (at Snow Canyon State Park, Route 18; 801-875-6677).

GOLF

Serving the Lake Mead, Hoover Dam and Boulder City areas is the **Boulder City Municipal Golf Course** (1 Clubhouse Drive, Boulder City; 702-293-9236).

In the Laughlin area, tee off at the **Emerald River Golf Course** (1155 South Casino Drive, Laughlin; 702-298-0061), **Riverview Golf Course** (2000 East Ramar Road, Bullhead City, Arizona; 602-763-1818), and **Desert Lakes Golf Course** (5835 Desert Lakes Drive, Fort. Mohave, AZ; 602-768-1000), about ten miles south of the Laughlin/Bullhead City bridge off Route 95.

St. George has eight golf courses more per capita than any other city in the Southwest. Four are championship quality: **St. George Golf Club** (2190 South 1400 East Street; 801-634-5854); **Southgate Country Club** (1975 South Tonaquint Drive; 801-628-0000); **Sunbrook** (2240 Sunbrook Drive; 801-634-5866), designed by noted golf course architect Ted Robinson; and **Green Spring** (588 North Green Spring Drive; 801-673-7888), a challenging course set among hills, ravines and gorges.

TENNIS

In the Laughlin area you can hold court at the **Pioneer Hotel** (2200 South Casino Drive, Laughlin; 702-298-2442), the **Flamingo Hilton Hotel** (1900 South Casino Drive, Laughlin; 702-298-5111) and the **Riverview RV Resort** (2000 East Ramar Road, Bullhead City; 602-763-5800).

COWBOY GEORGE AND HIS WAGON TRAIN

*If you're serious about riding, really serious, there's an annual week-long, 150-mile horseback trip from Las Vegas to the old mining town of Pioche. The ride costs about $1000 a person (less if you supply the horse) and usually takes place in April or May. Contact **Cowboy George's High Country Wagon Train** (1466 Bledsoe Lane, Las Vegas, NV 89110; 702-385-7355) for dates and more details.*

In St. George, serve and volley with the locals at **Vernon Worthen Park** (400 East 200 South, 801-634-5869) and **Dixie High School** (350 East 700 South; 801-628-0441).

BICYCLING

In Red Rock Canyon, all mountain bikes and bicycles are prohibited from hiking trails and must stay on the designated roads. The 13-mile **Scenic Loop**, however, is very popular with cyclists and provides a superb, and not very strenuous, ride through the canyon's red sandstone cliffs. Start from the visitor's center, and remember to follow the one-way flow of traffic along the loop. On the first half of your ride you will gain about 1000 feet of elevation, but most of the last half is downhill or flat. At the completion of the loop it's less than a two-mile ride along Route 159 to the visitor's center.

The interesting topography and varied terrain near St. George make for invigorating mountain biking. An intermediate loop ride is **Pine Valley Loop**, a 35-mile trek on dirt road and pavement. Best ridden between April and October, the route is mostly gentle, although hills sneak in on occasion. Give yourself three to five hours. Take Route 18 north 25 miles to the town of Central. Turn right (east) toward Pine Valley Recreation Area. The loop begins on Forest Road 011, six miles from the Route 18 junction. **Snow Canyon Loop** takes riders about 24 miles, passing through the towns of Santa Clara and Ivins before climbing through Snow Canyon State Park. Start the loop at the northwest end of St. George along Bluff. Go west at the Bluff and Sunset Boulevard intersection. Route 91 takes you to Santa Clara, veer north to Ivins, then climb six miles to the park. Route 18 is downhill all the way home.

When the snow melts, mountain bikers find picturesque trails around **Brian Head**. Experts enjoy the single-track rides, while those less inclined to tight spaces go for the dirt roads and double-track trails. A relatively easy ten-mile loop, the **Scout Camp Loop Trail**, begins at the Brian Head Hotel, continues south on Route 143 and then to Bear Flat Road and Steam Engine Meadow. There's a cabin and, you guessed it, an engine on the trail. The trail continues toward Henderson Lake and the namesake scout camp. Another popular ride is **Pioneer Cabin**, about a six-mile journey on a wide dirt road that begins from Bear Flat Road. The 1800s-era cabin has aspen trees growing through its roof. For maps, bike tours, rentals and knowledgeable advice in the Red Rock Canyon area, try **Blue Diamond Bicycles** (14 Cottonwood Drive, Blue Diamond; 702-875-4500) or **McGhies Ski Chalet** (4503 West Sahara Avenue; 702-252-8077). In St. George head for **St. George Cyclery** (420 West 145 North; 801-673-8876). In the Brian Head area, it's **Brian Head Cross Country Ski Center and Bike Shop** (223 West Hunter Ridge Drive, Brian Head; 801-677-2012).

HIKING

Red Rock Canyon offers some of the finest hiking in southern Nevada. One of the best spots is **Pine Creek Canyon** (2 miles), a trek past the creek and sweet-smelling piñon pines to a meadow with the ruins of an historic homestead. You can get a close view of the region's geologic history on the **Keystone Thrust** trail (3 miles), a moderate walk to the older gray dolomite on top of the younger red-and-buff sandstone. An easy trail to the bottom of the canyon at the second **Calico Vista** leads down to the Aztec sandstone and, after seasonal rains, to small pools of water. There is also good hiking at **Sandstone Quarry**, where many small canyons offer a delightful escape from casino life. For maps and trail guides, visit the **Red Rock Visitor's Center** (1000 Scenic Drive; 702-363-1921). For equipment, try **Gary's Backpacking and Mountaineering** (4251 West Sahara Avenue, Las Vegas; 702-368-2225).

In the Laughlin area, bring your hiking shoes and enthusiasm to **Grapevine Canyon**, about six miles west of Davis Dam, just off the Christmas Tree Pass road. Fed by a spring, the canyon is a desert oasis with an abundance of canyon grape, Fremont cottonwood, cattails and rushes, where wildlife come to feed or drink at the shallow stream. Hundreds of petroglyphs—symbolic rock drawings—are evidence that early Native Americans were also drawn to this area. To reach Grapevine Canyon, drive northwest on Route 163 to mile marker 13, about six miles from the dam. Turn right onto Christmas Tree Pass and follow the road for two miles until you reach a sign indicating parking to the left. A trail from the parking lot leads to the canyon entrance, where boulders on either side are carved with an array of petroglyphs.

For a quick though rewarding hike, you don't have to leave St. George. Drive north on Main Street until it dead-ends, turn right and wind to the top of Red Hill. Park at the base of **Sugar Loaf**, the red sandstone slab with the white DIXIE letters, and start walking for a few yards. The view of St. George is nothing short of spectacular.

Nearby Snow Canyon offers several excellent hikes. One of the best is the short walk to **Johnson's Arch** (.3 mile). Along the way look for the names and dates of early settlers carved into the sandstone. At the end of the trail is the arch cut out of the sandstone wall. The trailhead is at the extreme south edge of the park.

Another popular hike is to the **Lava Caves** (0.3 mile) near the north end of Snow Canyon. If you plan on exploring the rugged caves, believed to have once sheltered Indians, take along a flashlight and good judgment. Watch for the sign along the road north of the campgrounds.

About 20 miles east of Cedar City, **Cedar Breaks National Monument** offers two accessible hiking trails. **Alpine Pond Trail** (2 miles) is a loop that passes through a picturesque forest glade and alpine pond fed by melting snow and small springs. The trailhead begins at the Chessmen Meadow parking area. **Wasatch Ramparts Trail** (1 mile) starts just outside the visitor center and ends at a 9952-foot overlook of the Cedar Breaks amphitheater. Along the way, pause at Spectra Point, a 10,258-foot viewpoint.

Transportation

BY CAR

The Red Rock Canyon Recreational Area is a 20-minute drive west from Las Vegas on Charleston Boulevard.

Drive west from downtown Las Vegas on **Route 95** for Tule Springs (Floyd Lamb State Park), about 20 miles; continue to **Route 157** (Kyle Canyon Road) for Mount Charleston, 25 miles; or remain on Route 95 for Corn Creek, 40 miles.

Hoover Dam, Lake Mead and Boulder City are all within a half-hour's drive via Route 95 south of Las Vegas.

Laughlin is an easy 90-mile drive from Las Vegas. Take Route 95 south almost to the California border, and then turn east on **Route 163**.

For the Valley of Fire State Park and Lost City Museum drive east on **Route 15** to **Route 169** and take the south exit, about 50 miles.

To reach St. George drive east on Route 15 across mostly parched desert until you reach the border town of Mesquite, Nevada, about 80 miles from Las Vegas. Continuing east on Route 15 you'll reach the bottom of the Virgin Gorge, a giant gash in the earth where the Virgin River makes its way out of Utah. The 30-mile stretch of highway follows the river through craggy canyons and rock-faced corridors until it reaches St. George, which is set against a background of red-rock plateaus and majestic granite outcroppings.

BY AIR

Scenic Airlines (702-739-1900, 800-634-6801) has two flights daily from Las Vegas to the **Laughlin/Bullhead City Airport** (on the Arizona side of the river).

Sky West/Delta Connection serves **St. George Municipal Airport** and **Cedar City Municipal Airport**.

TAXIS

Taxi service in St. George, Utah is provided by **Pete's Taxi** (801-673-5467).

BY BUS

For trips to Laughlin, **Greyhound Bus Lines** (702-385-1147) offers bus service from its terminal at the Union Plaza Hotel in Las Vegas.

Greyhound Bus Lines can take you from Las Vegas (200 South Main Street; 702-385-1147) to the Southwestern Utah area with stops at St. George (68 West 100 North Street; 801-673-2933) and Cedar City (1355 South Main; 801-586-9465).

CAR RENTALS

Rental agencies at St. George Municipal Airport are **Avis Rent A Car** (801-673-3451) and **National Car Rental** (801-673-5098).

SEVEN

National Parks

The wilderness area immediately surrounding Las Vegas is one of the **187** most magnificent in the country, but it is only a sampling of what awaits visitors willing to venture beyond the Rand McNally lines that separate Nevada from its neighbors. The landscape and geologic features of adjoining states are unlike anything else found on earth. And they're all within quick and easy access of Las Vegas.

Because Las Vegas is the geographic hub of four states—California, Nevada, Arizona and Utah—it is a convenient starting point for visits to some of the most varied, fascinating and beautiful national parks in the country. In this land of astonishing diversity you'll find something new in every direction, from sheer sandstone cliffs and slickrock mesas to secluded beaches on bright blue lakes and vast deserts alive with giant cacti and unusual animals. Within a few hours' drive of Las Vegas you can explore high mountain peaks with lush rolling meadows and deep-slotted canyons harboring lost cities and hidden treasures. In this chapter we've selected four parks that are ideal getaways because of their proximity to Las Vegas as well as their many historic and scenic sights.

About a two-hour drive west of Las Vegas is the austere but quietly beautiful Death Valley National Monument. Equal in size to the combined area of Connecticut and Rhode Island, Death Valley is one of the hottest regions on earth, second only to the Sahara Desert. During the summer months, the average daily high temperature is an astounding 116 degrees.

Nevertheless, visitors are continually drawn to Death Valley, a region rich in history and varied landscape. A museum without air conditioning, Death Valley National Monument is a giant geology lab containing

---

Over 900 plant species subsist in Death Valley, 22 of them unique to the area.

---

salt beds, sand dunes and multitiered hills whose layers are windows on the history of the earth.

In the opposite direction are the geologic marvels of southwestern Utah, a region of mythic diversity. From creosote to ponderosa, from slickrock to mountain valleys, the variety of scenery and natural wonders is unparalleled.

No state has more national parks than Utah, and two of them are within an easy two-and-a-half hour drive of Las Vegas. At Zion National Park and Bryce Canyon National Park you'll find terrain typical of the Colorado Plateau—multicolored mesas, buttes, soaring cliffs, sandstone crags, alpine forests and mountain meadows.

Southeast of Las Vegas is the most spectacular geological marvel of them all, the Grand Canyon. Awesome. Magnificent. Breathtaking. It's easy to slip into hyperbole when trying to describe the Grand Canyon, but it's understandable. Nothing can compare to the immensity of this mighty chasm carved by the Colorado River as it winds through northwestern Arizona.

With more than four million visitors a year, the Grand Canyon is one of the most popular national parks in the United States. Many come to experience the silent grandeur of the canyon and gaze in reverence across its massive cliffs. Others come for the most challenging hiking trails in the country or to explore the narrow canyons and gorges by pack mule. Whatever reason you choose to visit the Grand Canyon, it will be worth the morning's drive from Las Vegas.

Death Valley

Simply stated, Death Valley is the most famous desert in the United States. Set between the lofty Black and Panamint ranges, it is renowned for exquisite but merciless terrain. A region of vast distances and amazingly plentiful plant life, Death Valley holds a magician's bag of surprises.

Hauntingly beautiful, Death Valley received its name in 1849 when a pioneer party—intent on following a shortcut to the gold fields—crossed the wasteland, and barely escaped with their lives. Later, prospectors stayed to work the territory, discovering rich borax deposits during the 1880s and providing the region with a home industry.

Due to the extreme summer temperatures, travel to the valley is not recommended in summer months. Whenever you go, it's always a good idea to carry extra water with you. The best time to see the park is from November through April. In late February and March (with average

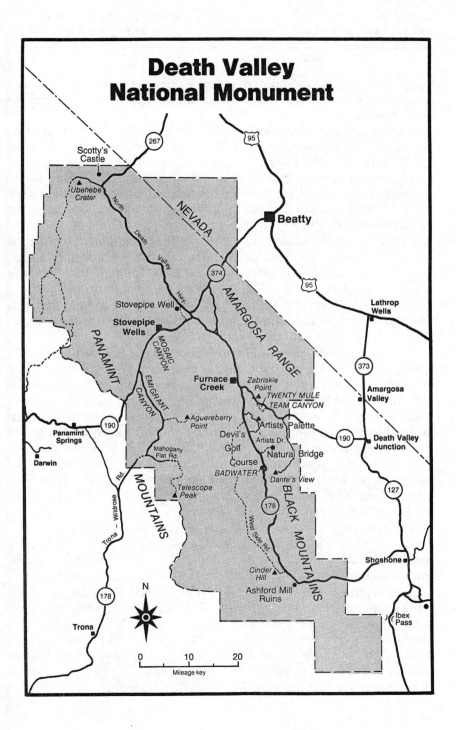

Death Valley
National Monument

267

95

Scotty's
Castle

Ubehebe
Crater

NEVADA

Beatty

North

Death Valley Hwy.

374

AMARGOSA RANGE

95

Stovepipe Well

Lathrop
Wells

Stovepipe
Wells

PANAMINT

MOSAIC CANYON

EMIGRANT CANYON

Furnace
Creek

Zabriskie
Point

TWENTY MULE
TEAM CANYON

373

Amargosa
Valley

190

Aguereberry
Point

Artists Palette

Panamint
Springs

Devil's
Golf
Course

Artists Dr.

190

Death Valley
Junction

Darwin

Mahogany
Flat Rd.

Natural Bridge

BADWATER

Dante's View

127

Trona – Wildrose Rd.

Telescope
Peak

MOUNTAINS

178

West Side Rd.

BLACK MOUNTAINS

178

Cinder
Hill

Shoshone

N

Ashford Mill
Ruins

Ibex
Pass

Trona

0   10   20

Mileage key

Death Valley National Monument's parched yet fascinating terrain ranges from a low of 282 feet below sea level at Badwater to mountains rising 11,000 feet.

---

highs of 73 degrees, dropping to a cool 46 degrees at night), the desert comes alive with spring blossoms such as Death Valley sage, rock *mimulus* and Panamint daisies.

A fitting prelude to dusty, desiccated Death Valley lies along the southern gateway to this fabled destination. Here, stretching north along Route 127 from the town of Baker, is a chain of dry lakes. Once part of Lake Mojave, an ancient body of water that drained over 3500 square miles, these lake beds are now flat expanses baked white in the sun. **Silver Dry Lake**, which appears to the west four miles outside Baker, was an Indian habitat more than 10,000 years ago.

To the east rise the Silurian Hills, backdropped by the Kingston Range. If you see a snow-domed mountain in the far distance, it's probably 11,918-foot Charleston Peak, 60 miles away in Nevada. Those pretty white hills with the soft curves are the Dumont Dunes, 30 miles north of Baker.

Beyond Ibex Pass, as the road descends into another ancient lake bed, you'll pass **Tecopa Lake Badlands**, where erosion has carved fascinating formations from soft sedimentary rock.

A side road leads several miles to **Tecopa Hot Springs** (619-852-4264), a series of rich mineral baths once used by Paiute Indians. Today this natural resource has been transformed into a bizarre tourist attraction. If there is a last outpost before the world ends, this is the place. A white mineral patina covers the ground everywhere, as if salt had been shaken across the entire desert. Water sits in stagnant pools. Wherever you look—against a backdrop of rugged, stark, glorious mountains—there are trailers, hundreds of trailers, metal refuges against the Mojave sun, painted white like the earth and equipped with satellite dishes. In a kind of desert monopoly game, if you collect enough mobile homes you can hang a sign out front and call it a motel.

The inhabitants of these tin domiciles are on permanent vacation. This is, after all, a health resort; people walk about in bathrobes. They wander from the private baths at the trailer parks and motels to the public baths, which, in the single saving grace to this surreal enclave, are free.

A good place to start your **Death Valley National Monument** tour is the southern entrance to the park off Route 178. Crossing two low-lying mountain passes as it travels west, Route 178 (Badwater Road) turns north upon reaching the floor of Death Valley. Within a couple of miles lie the ruins of **Ashford Mill**, built during World War I when gold mining enjoyed a comeback. The skeletons of several buildings are all that remain of that early dream.

A nearby vista point overlooks **Shoreline Butte**, a curving hill marked by a succession of horizontal lines. Clearly visible to the naked eye, these lines represent the ancient shorelines of Lake Manly, which covered the valley to a depth of 600 feet and stretched for 90 miles. Formed perhaps 75,000 years ago when Pleistocene glaciers atop the Sierra Nevada began melting, the lake dried up about 10,000 years ago.

For a close-up look at a cinder cone, follow nearby West Side Road, a graded thoroughfare, downhill for two miles. That reddish-black mound on your left is **Cinder Hill**, residue of an ancient volcano.

The main highway continues through the heart of the region to **Mormon Point**. From here northward, Death Valley is one huge salt flat. As you traverse this expanse, notice how the Black Mountains to the east turn from dark colors to reddish hues as gray Precambrian rocks give way to younger volcanic and sedimentary deposits.

Continue on to that place you've been reading about since third-grade geography: **Badwater**, at 282 feet below sea level, is the lowest point in the Western Hemisphere. Take a stroll out onto the salt flats and you'll find that the crystals are joined into a white carpet that extends for miles. Despite the brackish environment, the pool itself supports water snails and other invertebrates. Salt grass, pickleweed and desert holly also endure here. Out on the flats you can gaze west across the valley at **Telescope Peak**, 11,049 feet high. Then be sure to glance back at the cliff to the east of the road. There, high in the rocks above you, a lone sign marks Sea Level.

The water that carved **Natural Bridge** (off Route 178, about two miles along a gravel road and up a half-mile trail) was quite unlike those stagnant pools on the valley floor. Indeed, it cascaded from the mountains in torrents, punched a hole in the underlying rock and etched this 50-foot-high arch. Behind the bridge, you can still see the lip of this ancient waterfall. Also notice the formations along the canyon walls that were left by evaporating water and bear a startling resemblance to dripping wax.

Artists Drive, a nine-mile route through the Black Mountains, is one of Southern California's most magnificent roads. The hills are splashed with color—soft pastels, striking reds, creamy browns—and rise to sharp cliffs. Along the way at **Artists Palette**, the hills are so vividly colored they seem to pulsate. It's a spot admired by photographers from around the world, a place where the rainbow meets the badlands.

If you'd like a scientific explanation for all this beauty, the artistic medium is oxidation: Chloride deposits create the green hues, manganese oxides form the blacks, and the reds, yellows and oranges are shades of iron oxide. These contrasting tints are most spectacular in the slanted light of the late afternoon sun.

Mushroom Rock, the sculptor's answer to Artists Palette, rises on the right several hundred yards after you regain Route 178. A boulder of basalt lava, it was carved by windblown sand.

Legend has it that Badwater got its name from a surveyor whose mule refused to drink here, inspiring him to scratch "bad water" on the map he was charting.

Up in **Golden Canyon**, erosion has chiseled chasms into the bright yellow walls of a narrow gorge. Climb the three-quarter-mile trail, and you arrive in a natural amphitheater, named for the iridescent quality of the canyon walls, which are the embodiment of sunlight.

In this entire wasteland of wonders the only major center of civilization is **Furnace Creek**, where a gas station, a campground, restaurants and two hotels create a welcome oasis. The **Death Valley National Monument Visitor Center** (619-786-2331) is a good resource for maps and information. It houses a museum re-creating the history of Native Americans and early prospectors. There are also mineral displays and an oversize relief map of the valley.

The nearby **Borax Museum** features the oldest house in Death Valley, a sturdy 1883 structure built by a borax miner. There's also a wonderful collection of stagecoaches as well as a huge Rube Goldberg contraption once used to extract gold deposits from rock.

While the yellow metal symbolizes the romance of desert prospecting, the lowly borax mineral proved of much greater value to Death Valley miners. Important as a cleaning agent, the white crystal was first discovered in 1881. Eventually, it inspired its own romantic images, with 20-mule teams hauling 36-ton wagonloads across 180 miles of desert to the railhead in Mojave.

A two-and-one-half-mile trail climbs from Golden Canyon to **Zabriskie Point** (most folks follow Route 190, which leads southeast from Furnace Creek). Everyone inevitably arrives at this place, as though it were a point of pilgrimage for paying homage to nature.

What else can a mortal do, confronted with beauty of this magnitude? In the east, amber-hued hills roll like waves toward the horizon. To the west extends a badlands, burnished by blown sand to fierce reds and soft pastels. All around, the landscape resembles a sea gone mad, waves of sand breaking in every direction, with a stone tsunami, Manly Beacon, raised high above the combers, forever poised to crash into Death Valley.

Poetic as it sounds, these mustard-colored hills are dry mud, lake-bed sediments that were deposited 2 to 12 million years ago, then uplifted to their present height. But in the early morning and late afternoon, when the place is suffused with color, Zabriskie Point demonstrates that humble origins are of little consequence.

For a close-up view of those mud hills, follow the nearby dirt road through **Twenty Mule Team Canyon**. It winds almost three miles through a former borax-mining region.

Backtracking to Furnace Creek, Route 190 proceeds north toward the upper end of Death Valley. The history of the region's most valuable mineral is further revealed at the **Harmony Borax Works**. Surrounded by the ruins of Death Valley's most successful borax plant is an original 20-mule-team rig.

At the very end of Death Valley, when you've gone as far north as you can without bumping fenders with the Nevada border, you'll find the strangest feature in the entire park—a castle in the desert. It's a place called **Scotty's Castle** (admission), though Scotty never owned it. In fact Scotty swindled the fellow who did own it, and then became his lifelong friend. Sound preposterous? Perhaps.

It seems that Walter "Death Valley Scotty" Scott, a former trick rider in Buffalo Bill's Wild West Show, once convinced a Chicago millionaire, one Albert Johnson, to invest in a nonexistent gold mine. Johnson traveled west to see the mine, discovered that the dry desert clime helped his fragile health, forgave Scotty and decided during the 1920s to build a mansion in the sand.

The result was a $2 million Moorish castle, a wonderfully ridiculous building with wrought-iron detailing, inlaid tile, carved-beam ceilings, expensive antiques—and nothing else for miles around. Scotty, the greatest storyteller in Death Valley history, told everyone it was his castle. Hence the name. Somehow it reminds me of Hearst Castle in San Simeon, a place too gaudy to appreciate but too outrageous to ignore.

Ubehebe Crater, eight miles from Scotty's lair, is one of the park's natural wonders. A half-mile in diameter and reaching a depth of 450 feet, this magnificent landmark was created by a single explosion. The force of the volcanic steam scattered debris over a six-square-mile area and blew the crater walls so clean that one side retains its original sedimentary colors. Whether the crater dates back 10,000 years or is only a few hundred years old is currently being debated by geologists. They do agree, however, that other nearby craters have been formed in the last few centuries.

SALTING AWAY THE DUNES

*About a mile from the Natural Bridge you'll find **Devil's Golf Course**. Rather than a sand hazard, this flat expanse is one huge salt trap, complete with salt towers, pinnacles, and brine pools. The sodium chloride here is 95 percent pure, comparable to table salt, and the salt deposits are three to five feet thick. They were formed by a small lake that evaporated some 2000 years ago; below them, earlier deposits from larger lakes extend down 1000 feet beneath the surface.*

From the crater, a winding gravel road leads 27 miles to **The Race-track**, another of nature's magic acts. This two-mile mud playa, set at the bottom of a dry lake, is oval-shaped like a race course. In fact, an outcropping at the north end is dubbed "The Grandstand." The racers, oddly enough, are rocks, ranging in size from pebbles to boulders. Pushed by heavy winds across the mud-slick surface, they leave long, faint tracks that reveal the distances they have raced.

Stovepipe Wells, Death Valley's other village, is even smaller than Furnace Creek. A motel, restaurant, store, gas station and campground comprise the entire town. Six miles east of the village, a graded road departs Route 190 and travels four miles past **sand dunes** before joining North Death Valley Highway, the road to Scotty's Castle. Alive with greenery, these undulating dunes support numerous plant species, including creosote, mesquite and pickleweed. Coyotes hunt prey in the sandhills, and there are kit foxes, lizards and kangaroo rats.

Farther along rests the old **Stovepipe Well** from which the village derived its name. Used by prospectors crossing Death Valley, the well was fitted with a tall stovepipe so travelers could see it even when sand blanketed the area.

One person found neither well nor stovepipe. **Val Nolan's grave**, a simple resting place within crawling distance of the well, consists of a pile of stones and a wooden marker. Carved into the grave is an epitaph that graphically reveals Val Nolan's last days: "A Victim of the Elements."

DEATH VALLEY LODGING

Furnace Creek Ranch (619-786-2345, fax 619-786-2514) is a 224-unit resort sprawling across several acres and featuring three restaurants, a saloon, a general store and a swimming pool. Guest accommodations include duplex cabins (moderate), which are fully furnished but lack

---

A VIEW FROM THE TOP

*To get above it all, venture to **Dante's View**, a 5475-foot perch with a panoramic 360-degree vista. From this vantage point the salt flats and trapped pools of Death Valley are like a bleak watercolor. Although the Panamint Mountains wall off the western horizon, a steep half-mile trail (up the knoll north of the parking lot) leads to a point where you can gaze beyond the Panamints to the snow-thatched Sierra Nevada. Here, in a single glance, you can see Badwater and Mount Whitney, the lowest and highest points in the contiguous United States.*

At Burned Wagons Point (historic marker) in Stovepipe Wells, a desperate party of '49ers killed their oxen and dried the meat by burning their wagons.

---

extra amenities, and standard rooms (deluxe), which are plusher, more spacious and feature televisions and refrigerators.

The poshest place in the area is **Furnace Creek Inn** (619-786-2345, fax 619-786-2514), a 70-room hotel set on a hillside overlooking Death Valley. This Spanish-Moorish-style building, built of stone and adobe, is surrounded by flowering gardens. Palm trees shade the grounds, and a stream feeds three koi ponds. There are two restaurants, tennis courts and a spring-fed swimming pool. Guest rooms are quite comfortably furnished and most have fireplaces. Ultra-deluxe, including breakfast and dinner.

DEATH VALLEY RESTAURANTS

There are five restaurants in Furnace Creek (all can be reached at 619-786-2345). The least expensive food in all Death Valley, except for dishes you cook around your campfire, is in the **Wrangler Buffet** at Furnace Creek Ranch.

The **'49er Coffee Shop** next door has omelettes, hot sandwiches and burgers, and dinners such as pork chops and fried trout. With its wood-plank walls and ranch atmosphere, this is a good place for a moderately priced meal.

The **Wrangler Steakhouse** serves filet mignon, barbecued chicken, broiled halibut, ribs and pork chops every evening. Cozy and informal, the "house" consists of an unassuming room decorated with Mexican rugs, plus a small dining patio. Moderate to deluxe.

The fine dining places are up at Furnace Creek Inn. At **L'Ottimos** you feast on shrimp scampi, veal scallopini and pasta primavera, all prepared tableside. Dinner only. Deluxe.

Upstairs at the **Inn Dining Room**, candlelight and a beamed ceiling create a more formal atmosphere. Gentlemen are requested to wear jackets during dinner, and the menu is fixed-price. You can choose from among nearly 40 entrées, including sole Oscar and medallions of beef. Breakfast is served daily (no lunch), with a champagne brunch on Sundays. Ultra-deluxe.

In Stovepipe Wells, you'll find a spacious **Dining Room** (619-786-2387) embellished with Indian rugs and paintings of the Old West. The cuisine matches the ambience, an all-American menu featuring fried chicken, rainbow trout, steak, veal piccata and cod. Moderate.

Standing guard over the entrance to Zion National Park is the Watchman, a 2,600-foot monolith of sandstone and shale.

DEATH VALLEY NIGHTLIFE

The Furnace Creek Inn includes the **Oasis Lounge** (619-786-2345) among its elegant facilities. Featuring live entertainment nightly, it's a lovely spot to enjoy a quiet evening.

The **Badwater Saloon** (619-786-2387) in Stovepipe Wells hosts jukebox dancing. With western-style decor and a dancefloor, it's a night owl's oasis.

The finest entertainment for many miles is at the **Amargosa Opera House** (Death Valley Junction; 619-852-4316). This amazing one-woman show is the creation of Marta Becket, who performs dance pantomimes in a theater she personally decorated with colorful murals. Her performances run every Friday, Saturday and Monday from November to April, and every Saturday in October and May. Locally renowned, she's extremely popular, so call for reservations.

Zion National Park

From towering sandstone cliffs to deep slotlike canyons, **Zion National Park** (Route 9, Springdale, UT; 801-772-3256; admission) has it all. Sheer rock walls surround the verdant floor of Zion Canyon, where lush hanging gardens and waterfalls stand in marked contrast to the surrounding desertlike terrain of stark rock formations and etched red rock. Couple all this with some nearby historic buildings and movie-set towns that have been featured in hundreds of films, and you have a rewarding getaway only 155 miles northeast of Las Vegas.

It's easy to see why the popularity of Zion, grandfather of Utah's national parks, has skyrocketed the past few years. Easily accessible year-round, with an endless variety of hiking trails geared to all abilities, this "heavenly city of God" is a park for all people.

Covering 147,000 acres, the park was carved almost single-handedly by the Virgin River, which flows along the canyon floor. Cottonwoods, willows and velvet ash line the river, providing an ever-changing kaleidoscope of colors as one season follows another. To avoid the crowds and traffic, time your visit for November through April. Otherwise, expect lots of cars, nonexistent parking and plenty of company.

Be sure to stop at the **Visitor Center**, where rangers are happy to provide maps, brochures and backcountry permits. Naturalist-guided walks, evening programs and patio talks are scheduled from late March to November. Specific dates and times are posted at the center.

Depending on your time and specific interest, you can drive, bicycle or take a guided tram tour through Zion. But don't miss out on the fabulous sights that await just off the roads. Zion is best appreciated close up, and you'll miss the true majesty of the park if you don't wander around.

Zion Canyon Scenic Drive takes visitors about six-and-a-half miles into the heart of Zion Canyon with its 2000-to-3000-foot-high walls, carved inch by inch by the Virgin River cutting through the Markagunt Plateau. Just past the entrance you're likely to spot **West Temple**, the highest peak in Zion's southern section. Notice the delineated strata of the rock as it rises 4100 feet from base to peak.

One of the first places you might want to pause is **Court of the Patriarchs** viewpoint. From here you can see reverently named monuments like the Sentinel, the Patriarchs (a series of three peaks called Abraham, Isaac and Jacob), Mount Moroni, the Streaked Wall, the Spearhead and the sheer-walled sandstone monolith Angels Landing, perched

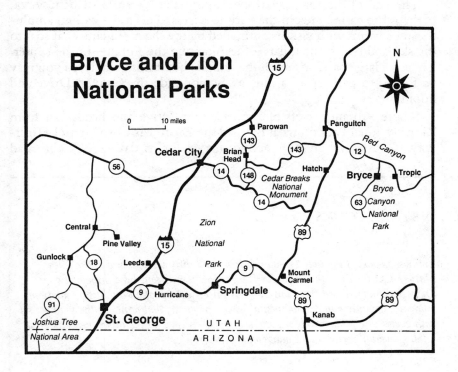

1500 feet above the canyon bed. To the east and above are two other monuments, Mountain of the Sun and the Twin Brothers.

Emerald Pools parking area, two-and-a-half miles up the Scenic Drive, offers access to a trail network serving both the upper and lower pools. A creek from Heaps Canyon sends water cascading down waterfalls into pools below. Yuccas, cacti and scrub oaks line the trail to the upper pool, and the path affords views of shaded, north-facing slopes rich with ponderosa pine, aspen and Douglas fir. If you happen to visit Zion in the fall, this is a prime spot to see the changing colors.

The **Grotto Picnic Area** is the perfect place to take a break from exploring the park. Here in the cool shade of broadleaf trees and Gambel oaks you'll find fire grates, picnic tables, water and restrooms.

Driving down the road you'll spot the **Great White Throne** on the east side. Notice how this 2400-foot megalith ranges in color from a deep red at the base to pink to gray to white at the top. The color variations occur because the Navajo sandstone has less iron oxide at the top than at the bottom.

A bit farther is a short, paved walk that leads to **Weeping Rock**, where continuous rain "weeps" across a grotto. Even on a hot day, the spot remains cool. Here, as in other parts of Zion, you should see lush, hanging cliff gardens thick with columbine, shooting stars and scarlet monkeyflower.

The end of the road, so to speak, comes at **Temple of Sinawava**, perhaps the easiest area in the park to access. This huge natural amphitheater swarms with visitors enthralled by the sheer red cliffs that soar to the sky and two stone pillars—the Altar and the Pulpit—in the center. There's a large parking area at the temple, but it fills quickly, so you may be forced to park up to a mile away alongside the Canyon Drive and hoof it in.

Route 9 branches off of Zion Canyon Drive and heads east from Zion National Park on what is called the **Zion–Mount Carmel Highway**. Considered an engineering marvel for its day (1930), the road

---

KIDS' NATURE TOURS

*Youngsters ages 6 through 12 can get down and dirty with nature at the **Zion Nature Center** through the Junior Ranger Program. From June through Labor Day, park rangers and the Zion Natural History Association conduct a variety of outdoor adventure and environmental science programs that acquaint the younger set with everything from the flight pattern of a golden eagle to the difference between a Utah beavertail cactus and a maidenhair fern.*

Pay close attention and you might spot the Zion snail at Weeping Rock, a creature found in the park and nowhere else.

snakes up high precipices and around sharp, narrow turns before reaching the high, arid plateaus of the east. If you've ever ridden Disneyland's Matterhorn, you'll love the mile-long, narrow, unlit tunnel. Rangers control traffic through the darkened tube, stopping drivers when an oversized truck or recreational vehicle is passing through. Even with some delays, the tunnel is a treat, with huge, windowlike openings allowing sunlight to stream in every so often and affording unparalleled views of the vermilion cliffsides. And was that the Abominable Snowman behind that rock?

On the other side of the tunnel lies the park's "slickrock" territory. It's almost like a time warp connecting one country to another.

Canyon Overlook is an easy, half-mile self-guided walk on the Zion–Mount Carmel Highway just east of the tunnel. Unlike the lush Zion Canyon floor, this area showcases plants and animals that make rock and sand their home. The overlook itself provides views of lower Zion Canyon, including the Streaked Wall with its long, black marks sharply contrasting with the red canyon walls; West and East Temples, giant stone monoliths with templelike edifices perched on top; and the massive, multicolored cliff called Towers of the Virgin.

Don't miss **Checkerboard Mesa**, a prime example of sandstone etched over time with horizontal lines and vertical fractures to resemble a mountainous playing board. You stay on Route 9 out of Zion National Park to connect with Route 89 and head south toward the Arizona border.

Continuing on Route 89, you'll pass what looks like a giant dinosaur jutting out of a mountainside. That's **Moqui Cave** (admission), which claims the largest collection of dinosaur tracks in the Kanab area. Other displays include Indian artifacts, foreign money and fluorescent minerals. Open only from April through October.

Located farther south, Route 89 heads toward the base of the colorful Vermilion Cliffs and **Kanab**, a town known as "Little Hollywood" for the more than 200 movies, most of them grade-B Westerns, filmed in the area. Today, Kanab is a crossroads for travelers headed to Lake Powell, the Grand Canyon or the Bryce area and has numerous motels and restaurants.

Heritage House (100 South Main; 801-644-2542) is an 1886 restored pioneer mansion built of brick and red rock and is one of the 13 homes making up the Kanab walking tour. You can find brochures at Heritage House or at Kanab's city offices (40 East 100 North; 801-644-2534).

ZION AREA LODGING

Massive vermilion cliffs surround **Zion National Park Lodge** (801-586-7686, fax 801-586-3157), located in the heart of the park. A huge, manicured lawn and shade trees welcome guests to the property, which includes motel-style rooms, suites and cabins. While standard furnishings are the norm, location is everything. Cabins afford more privacy and feature fireplaces and private porches. Dining room, snack bar and gift shop are on-site. Moderate to deluxe.

Rooms at **Flanigan's Inn** (428 Zion Park Boulevard, Springdale; 801-772-3244, 800-765-7787, fax 801-772-3396) range from okay to very nice indeed. Those on a budget might opt for the smaller, somewhat plain rooms. If you place a value on spaciousness, splurge on the larger, suitelike rooms done in oak furnishings with tile baths, bentwillow wallhangings and ceiling fans. Regardless of room, hotel guests can partake of the swimming pool and excellent restaurant. Budget to moderate.

American and English antique furniture fills **Under the Eaves Guest House** (980 Zion Park Boulevard, Springdale; 801-772-3457). Constructed of sandstone blocks from nearby canyon walls, the home resembles a cheery English cottage. Three rooms have private baths, another two share. Full breakfast is served each morning, and guests can sip a cup of tea in the outdoor gazebo that fairly bursts with flowers or soak in the soothing outdoor spa. Moderate.

Located in a quiet neighborhood, **Harvest House Bed and Breakfast** (29 Canyon View Drive, Springdale; 801-772-3880) is sure to please even the most demanding. All four rooms are exquisitely decorated in what the owners term "urban eclectic." Expect bright, airy spaces full of

---

HOLLYWOOD, ZION STYLE

*Some movie-set towns are still evident throughout the Zion area. Because most sit on private property, it's safest to check with the **Kane County Travel Council** (41 South 100 East, Kanab; 801-644-5033) for the latest information on which are open to the public. In Kanab, a bit like the Universal Studios tour is **Lopeman's Frontier Movie Town** (297 West Center; 801-644-5337), a replica of a Wild West movie set that caters to groups but lets individuals tag along. Here, marshals in white hats battle black-hatted villains during mock gunfights. You can walk along the boardwalk and peer into the false storefronts. Shops, a snack bar and historic exhibits are also on-site. The town is open only from April through October, and hours are intermittent. It's best to call ahead.*

wicker furniture, private baths, plush carpeting and balconies with an unparalleled view of Zion National Park. Beverages are available anytime from the dining room wet bar, and there's an extensive library of art and cookbooks. Moderate to deluxe.

Tree-shaded lawns and gardens mark the Best Western **Driftwood Lodge** (1515 Zion Park Boulevard, Springdale; 801-772-3262, 800-528-1234, fax 801-772-3702). Forty-eight oversized rooms bring the outdoors inside with oak furniture and gray-blue accents. A dining room, gift shop and outdoor swimming pool are nice pluses. Moderate.

Nothing fancy, but good home cooking and warm hospitality are hallmarks of **Zion House Bed and Breakfast** (801 Zion Park Boulevard, Springdale; 801-772-3281). Two rooms offer private baths, two others share. Guests can swap tales of park adventures in the comfortable living room. Family-style breakfast is served. Budget to moderate.

Just a short drive to Zion National Park, **Best Western Weston's Lamplighter Motel** (280 West State, Hurricane; 801-635-4647, 800-528-1234, fax 801-635-0848) is a good alternative when Springdale accommodations fill. The 32 units are attractively furnished with small sitting areas, and a pool/jacuzzi provides respite after a day of touring. Moderate prices.

If you must overnight in Kanab, plan to stay at the **Shilo Inn** (296 West 100 North; 801-644-2562, 800-222-2244). The 118 minisuites are nicely decorated in soft blues and pinks; most include microwaves and refrigerators. Extra amenities, including free continental breakfast and fresh fruit, raise the complex well above the motel crowd. Plus there are a swimming pool and spa, gift shop, video-game room and guest laundry. Moderate.

ZION AREA RESTAURANTS

Right in the heart of Zion National Park, **Zion Lodge Restaurant** (801-772-3213) satisfies every appetite with bountiful breakfasts, hearty lunches and gourmet dinners. Hamburgers, salads, seafood and steak are pleasantly presented amid the beauty of Zion. Reservations required for dinner. Budget to moderate.

You can't miss with breakfast, lunch or dinner at **Flanigan's Inn Restaurant** (428 Zion Park Boulevard, Springdale; 801-772-3244). The bright, airy establishment serves up healthy portions of everything from Rocky Mountain trout to Dixie ham steak, as well as pasta, chicken and beef dishes. Reservations recommended for dinner. Budget to moderate.

Consistently good is the **Driftwood Restaurant** (1515 Zion Park Boulevard in the Driftwood Lodge, Springdale; 801-772-3224) with its wraparound windows providing a glorious view of Zion. Utah mountain trout, crispy chicken and flame-broiled steaks top the dinner menu. For dessert there's a bountiful selection of homemade pies and cheese-cake. Breakfast fare includes eggs, pancakes, muffins and the like. Budget to moderate.

The rustic appearance of **Bit and Spur Saloon and Mexican Restaurant** (1212 Zion Park Boulevard, Springdale; 801-772-3498) belies what many consider Utah's best Mexican restaurant. Besides standard favorites like chile rellenos and tostada supreme, the menu features deep-dish specials such as sour-cream enchilada, chicken enchilada and pasta diablo. It's dinner only, amigos. Moderate.

ZION AREA NIGHTLIFE

The **Grand Circle Multimedia Sound and Light Show** is a treat for the senses at Dixie College's O. C. Tanner Amphitheater (Springdale; 801-673-4811; admission), May through September. The production takes viewers on an odyssey through Zion National Park and other nearby national gems. The amphitheater also provides other top entertainment.

There are dances every Saturday night and talent shows during the week at the **Old Barn Theater** (50 North 100 East, behind Parry Lodge; 801-644-2601) in Kanab.

ZION AREA PARKS

All that's missing is the surf at **Coral Pink Sand Dunes State Park** (12 miles off Route 89 between Springdale and Kanab; 801-874-2408). This is Mother Nature's sandbox just aching to be frolicked in by young and old alike. Some of the dunes reach several hundred feet in height. A resident park ranger is on hand to answer questions about this unusual area, and there are a few interpretive signs as well. But those who prefer sand to water will revel in the inviting dunes.

Bryce Canyon National Park

A child's jumbo-sized crayon box couldn't contain all the pastels, reds, violets, greens and blues found in the unspoiled land of **Bryce Canyon National Park** (801-834-5322; admission), located about 210 miles north-east of Las Vegas in southwestern Utah. Famous for its stupendous rock formations that seem to change color with the blink of an eye, Bryce offers a maze of trails that wind in and around its many wonders.

Set on the jagged edge of the Paunsaugunt Plateau, Bryce is a national park that really does defy superlatives. There are 12 huge bowls of spires

Bryce's rock formations are 50 to 60 million years old.

and pinnacles, and even the gigantic summertime crowds can't distract from the natural amphitheaters in the Pink Cliffs layer of the earth. Who'd have ever thought there were this many shades of red or shapes of rock? The sands and shales of Bryce, some softer than others, are the result of eons of erosion wearing away the limestone.

Located at nearly 8000 feet above sea level, the park's 35,000-plus acres receive more than their fair share of snow during the winter. Some say that the rocks are at their most beautiful in winter when they're covered with dollops of snow.

Bryce was once covered by an inland lake, and geologists figure rivers and streams carried silt and sediment from throughout the region to the lake, depositing it in layers. These layers became compacted, as more layers were added, until forces within the earth caused the lake bottom to rise. As the different levels of earth emerged and became exposed, they took shape and turned colors. Red and yellow hues were due to iron oxides. The purples came from manganese. White reveals an absence of minerals in that part of the rock.

At sections of the park like Silent City and other natural amphitheaters, the rock figures take shapes that resemble chess pieces, a preacher, a woman playing the organ or faces that might be seen on Easter Island.

Sculptured rock forms come in countless profiles, the most famous of which have been named "hoodoos." These, too, are ever-changing because of rainwater and snow seeping into the cracks of the rock, thawing and wearing away the layers.

Bryce Canyon's nooks and crannies are best explored on foot. If time is a factor, it's wise to drive to the overlooks on the 21-mile park road for a sweeping look at the big picture. Start at the **Fairyland Point** lookout about two miles north of the visitor center to see the imaginary creatures, the looming **Boat Mesa** and the mysterious **Chinese Wall** in Fairyland Canyon. The rather strenuous Fairyland Loop Trail also begins here.

For a concentrated collection of formations, travel to the park's nucleus, and stop at either the **Sunrise** or **Sunset Point** lookout to view the figures reminiscent of chess pieces in **Queen's Garden**.

The Rim Trail, which skirts the canyon edge for 11 miles, takes you to **Inspiration Point** and the eerie army of stone "people" called the **Silent City**. From the Rim Trail at this point it's possible to see the **Wall of Windows** and the majestic **Cathedral**.

Continuing south for another two-and-one-half miles takes you to **Bryce Point**, which offers breathtaking views of the whole Bryce Am-

None of this region's main thoroughfares, like Center, Main and Tabernacle, goes by the name "Street." Why? Ask the locals—you may just make a friend in the process.

phitheater. Three hiking trails (the Rim, Under-the-Rim and Peekaboo Loop) may be accessed from here. Horses share the Peekaboo Loop and take riders past profiles such as the **Alligator** and **Fairy Castle**.

From the main park road continue south for seven miles to **Farview Point** to gaze at the natural wonders stretching hundreds of miles outside of Bryce. The flat-topped mesa to the north is the Aquarius Plateau. South of the park are the distinctive White Cliffs.

Natural Bridge, with a huge opening in a rock, stands out distinctly about two miles south of the Farview lookout. It's another two miles to **Ponderosa View Point**, where you can pick up the Agua Canyon connecting foot trail while seeing the lovely pink cliffs.

Drive the final two miles to **Rainbow Point** and **Yovimba Point**, and end up at the park's highest places, towering more than 9000 feet above sea level. A little more barren and rugged than other sections of Bryce, these two overlooks serve as trailheads for several hiking paths. It's worth the short jaunt on the **Bristlecone Loop Trail** to see the rare, gnarled trees up close and personal.

To explore the multimillion-year-old wonders of Bryce fully, begin the sometimes arduous 22-mile **Under-the-Rim Trail** from here, and travel north on a two- or three-day excursion. Camping in the park's backcountry is especially rewarding, as the stars tend to put on quite a show in this rarefied, high-altitude air.

The closest real town to the park is **Tropic**—hometown to Ebenezer Bryce, who is credited with discovering Bryce Canyon while searching for stray cows. There is a back route to Bryce from Tropic for foot travelers only, off the Peekaboo Loop trail. The easier way to go is by returning to Route 12 and traversing the ten miles or so through lovely **Tropic Canyon**. A recently discovered natural bridge is on the east side of the highway, about three-tenths of a mile north of the Water Canyon Bridge.

Stop for a snack or to rest your legs in Tropic, a special village that remains true to its name. Flowers seem to dance in the gardens, and old trees stretch their limbs languorously. At the south end of town is **Ebenezer Bryce's old log cabin**, which houses Indian artifacts.

If you drove to Bryce Canyon by way of Springdale (Route 9) or Cedar Breaks National Monument (Route 14), consider returning through **Panguitch**, where Route 143 will take you back to the interstate at Parowan. It's only a few additional miles, and the handsome, historic town is worth it.

A short walking tour through the center of town will give you a chance to see buildings left behind by early pioneers who founded the town in 1864. Begin the tour at the **Garfield County Courthouse** (55 South Main), built for just over $11,000 in 1907. Cross to the **Houston home** (72 South Main), which was constructed of extra-large bricks fired in a Panguitch kiln. The home's lumber and shingles came from a local sawmill. Two blocks north you'll find the town's **first jail** (45 South Main), built in 1890 under the supervision of a probate judge. The tiny, one-room structure was constructed of two-by-fours.

The building on the corner of 1st North and Main is a classic bit of architecture called the **Garfield Exchange**. It has housed just about every kind of business you can think of, from general merchandise to furniture, groceries and now a gift shop.

Prominent on Center is the **Panguitch Social Hall Corporation** (35 East Center), which was first built in 1908 but burned shortly thereafter. On the same spot, using some original materials, another social hall was built. Now it houses the Panguitch Playhouse. Next door is a library that was built in 1908, thanks to a generous donation from Andrew Carnegie.

Finally, the city's **Daughters of the Utah Pioneers Museum** (Center and 1st East; 801-538-1050), is a lovely brick monolith on the site of the old bishop's storehouse. Back in the mid-19th century, members of the Mormon Church paid their tithes with cattle and produce, which were kept on this lot. Now, visitors trace the region's history here.

BRYCE AREA LODGING

Cheap, clean and very basic describes the budget-priced **Color Country Motel** (526 North Main, Panguitch; 801-676-2386, 800-255-6518, fax 801-676-8484) with its flowered bedspreads and scenic vistas on the walls.

THE HISTORIC BRYCE CANYON LODGE

*The only one of the original trio of National Park Service properties that hasn't been devastated by fire, the **Bryce Canyon Lodge** (Bryce Canyon Park; 801-586-7686) is listed on the National Register of Historic Places. The three types of rooms— suites, cabins and doubles—fit most budgets and tastes. Splurging on a suite is a treat. These rooms ooze romance, from the white-wicker decor to Cleopatra chairs to the makeup mirror. Quaint log cabins have gas fireplaces, porches and dressing areas. Regular rooms are furnished in Southwestern style. Open only from spring until late fall, the lodge tends to book well in advance. Moderate to deluxe.*

A step up in quality and price is the **Best Western New Western** (180 East Center, Panguitch; 801-676-8876), natty and renovated in paisley patterns and scalloped carpeting with spotless housekeeping and a cool pool for those toasty summer days. Moderate.

There's nothing like a full-service resort when you really feel like getting away from it all. **Best Western Ruby's Inn** (Route 12, Bryce Canyon; 801-834-5341, 800-468-8660, fax 801-834-5265) operates as a world of its own, with a general store, liquor store, campground, helicopter pad, riding stables, even its own post office on site! An international clientele can be found anytime. Rooms are decorated in Southwestern decor, and the staff remains friendly even after a long tourist season. Moderate to deluxe.

A kitchen and fireplace within cozy, knotty-pine rooms are what the **Bryce Lodge** (Route 12, near Bryce Canyon; 801-834-5361, fax 801-834-5464) can offer its guests. The hotel's 50 rooms are open for groups as well as individuals. Moderate.

Another very comfortable residence is the **Bryce Point Bed and Breakfast** (61 North 400 West; 801-679-8629), about eight miles east of Bryce in the perpetually flowering town of Tropic. Guests enjoy a private entrance and private baths. Each of the four rooms features handmade oak cabinets and picture windows facing the garden. Moderate.

BRYCE AREA RESTAURANTS

You expect country cooking at a place named **Foy's Country Corner** (80 North Main, Panguitch; 801-676-8851), and that's just what you get. Good juicy hamburgers, chicken-fried steaks, halibut and a salad bar highlight the menu. Budget.

When it comes time to settle down and have a semifancy meal, there's little doubt that the top choice in this area is the beautiful old log restau-

---

PICTURE PERFECT

*Named for its photogenic value by the National Geographic Society, **Kodachrome Basin State Park** (801-679-8562) is 2240 acres of vividly colored sandstone chimneys, towering rock spires and arches. Stop at the Trail Head station, a little store, for maps and advice. Kodachrome is chock full of petrified geyser holes, 65 at last official count, believed to be freaks of nature and unique to this area. Utah's most recently discovered arch, a 90-footer named **Shakespeare**, can be seen by taking a ten-minute hike on Chimney Rock Trail, one of six in Kodachrome. Located seven miles south of Cannonville, which is a few miles east of Tropic along Route 12.*

rant in the **Bryce Canyon Lodge** (801-834-5361), the National Park Service concession. Service is quick and attentive though hardly fussy, the cuisine continental but not generic. Homemade breads and Levi-busting desserts complement the generously portioned entrées. Prices are moderate.

Equipped to serve and satisfy large groups, the **Best Western Ruby's Inn** (Route 12, Bryce Canyon; 801-834-5341) presents satisfying—though surely not imaginative—fare at budget-to-moderate prices in its spacious dining room. A menu of Continental cuisine features steaks and chops for dinner. The dining room can be a little noisy when large groups converge. During the busy summer months, the adjacent **Red Canyon Room Deli** is a convenient spot for quick and tasty on-the-go budget meals.

The booths are inviting, the coffee steaming and the pies and soups fresh and delicious at **Bryce Lodge** (Route 12, northwest of Bryce Canyon National Park entrance; 801-834-5361), which also offers specials every evening. Budget to moderate.

Had a local not made the recommendation, I'd never have stumbled onto the very modest **Pizza Place** (North Main, Tropic; 801-679-8888). A wisecracking chef kept the starving wolves at bay, appeasing our ravenous hunger with an order of wonderfully gooey and stringy mozzarella cheese sticks before the main event—a hefty, generously topped, sweet-crusted pizza that could be the tastiest pie this side of Chicago. Budget.

BRYCE AREA SHOPPING

An enticing smell of potpourri tickles the nose upon entering **Favorite Pastimes** (415 East Center, Panguitch; 801-676-2608). Quilts and wreaths, bookends and knickknacks are carefully selected, if not hand-made themselves.

It may seem corny, but you gotta love **Old Bryce Town** (Route 12, across from Ruby's Inn; 801-834-5337), filled with shops and services. Among them, the **Canyon Rock Shop** (801-834-5337) has a huge selection of polished stones, fossils and petrified wood, plus a place to pan for gold! The **Western Store** (801-834-5337) has a great selection of pseudo-Stetsons so you can step out on the range and not feel like a total city slicker.

Wind chimes line the front porch and Navajo rugs are omnipresent inside the **Bryce Canyon Trading Post** (Routes 12 and 89; 801-676-2688), a good place to pick up the requisite postcard, T-shirt or turquoise stone.

Hometown folks have gotten together to create gifts for **Gerry's Creative Cottage** (221 West 100 South, Tropic; 801-679-8553). Craft supplies are available if you'd rather make it yourself.

BRYCE AREA NIGHTLIFE

The **Panguitch Playhouse** (Center) hosts summer musicals as well as special events.

Don't be surprised if angry Indians come a'chasing when you're riding in the covered wagon train en route to a hoedown and sing-along. The **Chuck Wagon** (Route 12, Bryce Canyon; 801-834-5202) operates out of the Ruby's Inn complex during the summer season. Expect a huge country supper served in a dutch oven amid the pines before kicking up your heels in the foot-stompin' hoedown. It's a hoot.

Rodeos featuring local talent are held nightly except Sunday throughout the summer at the **Rodeo Grounds** (801-834-5341) across from Ruby's Inn in Bryce Canyon. Barrel racing, bull wrasslin', roping and riding make for a full evening.

During winter weekends **Best Western Ruby's Inn** (801-834-5341) offers live music in its Red Canyon Room.

BRYCE AREA PARKS

One of the top fishing areas in the region, **Panguitch Lake** (Route 143, about 17 miles south of Panguitch; 801-865-3700) has ten miles of shoreline and boats for anglers eager for rainbow, cutthroat and brown trout. Facilities include public boat ramps, boat rentals, tourist cabins, a general store and a snack shop.

You can fish or spread a picnic blanket at **Tropic Reservoir and King's Creek Campground** (801-676-8815) or simply relax near the old sawmill remains. The park is located on an unmarked road off Route 12, about three miles west of Bryce Canyon junction.

Often overlooked because of its proximity to Bryce Canyon, **Red Canyon** (Route 12 about four miles east of Route 89; 801-676-8815) is a lovely collection of sculptured pink, red and scarlet rocks in a scenic but compact park.

Grand Canyon

No matter how many spectacular landscapes you've seen in your lifetime, none can quite compare with the Grand Canyon. For centuries, it posed the most formidable of all natural barriers to travel in the West, and to this day no road has ever penetrated the wilderness below the rim. Despite all photographs you take, paintings you make or postcards you buy, the view from anywhere along the Grand Canyon rim can never be truly captured.

The Grand Canyon is as long as any mountain range in the Ro   as the highest of the Rocky Mountains is tall.

The North Rim and the South Rim of the G essentially separate destinations, more than 200 miles apart by road. This chapter covers the developed national park areas on both rims and, for the adventuresome, hiking possibilities in the canyon as well as two lesser-known areas of the Grand Canyon that are challenging to reach— Toroweap Point in the Arizona Strip and the scenic area below the Indian village of Supai.

The Grand Canyon comes as a surprise. Whether you approach the North Rim or the South Rim, the landscape gives no hint that the canyon is there until suddenly you find yourself on the rim looking into the chasm ten miles wide at the top and a mile down to the Colorado River, winding through the canyon's inner depths like a silver thread. From anywhere along the rim, you can feel the vast, silent emptiness of the canyon and wonder at the sheer mass of the walls, striated into layer upon colorful layer of sandstone, limestone and shale.

The Grand Canyon is 277 miles long, extending from the western boundary of the Navajo Reservation to the vicinity of Lake Mead and Las Vegas. Only the highest section of each rim is accessible by motor vehicle. Most of **Grand Canyon National Park** (admission), both above and below the rim, is a designated wilderness area that can be explored only on foot or by river raft.

More than five million years ago, the Colorado River began carving out this canyon that offers a panoramic look at the geologic history of the Southwest. Sweeping away sandstones and sediments, limestones and fossils, the river made its way through Paleozoic and Precambrian formations. By the time humans arrived, the canyon extended nearly all the way down to schist, a basement formation.

The **North Rim** of the Grand Canyon receives only about one-tenth the number of visitors the South Rim gets. (For visitor information, the North Rim has a visitors' desk staffed by rangers at the Grand Canyon Lodge; 602-638-7864.) Snowbound during the winter because it is 1200 feet higher in elevation, the North Rim is open only from mid-May through October, while the South Rim is open year-round.

The North Rim does not have the long, heavily traveled scenic drives that the South Rim has. The main road into the park dead-ends at the lodge and other tourist facilities at **Bright Angel Point**. The only other paved road is **Cape Royal Scenic Drive**, a 23-mile trip through stately ponderosa pine forest that takes you to several of the national park's most beautiful viewpoints—**Point Imperial**, **Vista Encantadora**, **Walhalla**

---

n the Hopi belief system, the Grand Canyon is said to be the sipapu, *the hole through which the earth's first people climbed from the mountaintop of their previous world into our present one.*

Overlook and **Cape Royal**. Another road, unpaved and passable only in a high-clearance vehicle, runs 17 miles to **Point Sublime**. Other viewpoints on the North Rim are reached by foot trails. (Information on these can be found in the "Hiking" section at the end of the chapter.)

Extremely adventuresome motorists can visit a separate area along the North Rim of the Grand Canyon, **Toroweap Point**, by leaving Route 89A at Fredonia, about 75 miles north of the North Rim entrance. Don't forget to fill up the gas tank in Fredonia, because you won't see another gas station for nearly 200 miles, and bring along some extra water. Next, proceed west for 15 miles on Route 389 to **Pipe Springs National Monument** (602-643-7105). Take time to see the monument. The remote, fortresslike old Mormon ranching outpost, which had the only telegraph station in the Arizona Territory north of the Grand Canyon, was home to the Winsor family and their employees, thus its historical nickname, Winsor Castle. The ranch buildings and equipment are well preserved, and the duck pond provides a cool oasis. Volunteers costumed in period dress re-create the pioneer lifestyle during the summer months.

From Pipe Springs, backtrack six miles to where an unpaved road turns off to the south. It goes 67 miles to the most remote point that can be reached by motor vehicle on the Grand Canyon rim. The road is wide and well maintained, easily passable by passenger car, but very isolated. You will not find a telephone or any other sign of habitation along the way. You may not see another car all day. Several other dirt roads branch off, but if you keep to the road that goes straight ahead and looks well used, following the "Toroweap" and "Grand Canyon National Monument" signs whenever you see them, it's hard to get lost. Have fun experiencing this wide-open countryside, as empty as all of Arizona used to be long ago.

There is a small, primitive campground at **Toroweap Point** but no water. As likely as not, you may find that you have the place all to yourself. The elevation is 2000 feet lower than at the main North Rim visitor area, so instead of pine forest the vegetation around Toroweap Point is desert scrub. Being closer to the river, which is still some 3000 feet below, you can watch the parade of river rafts drifting past and even eavesdrop on passengers' conversations.

The **South Rim** of the Grand Canyon is the busy part of the park. From **Grand Canyon Village**, the large concession complex where

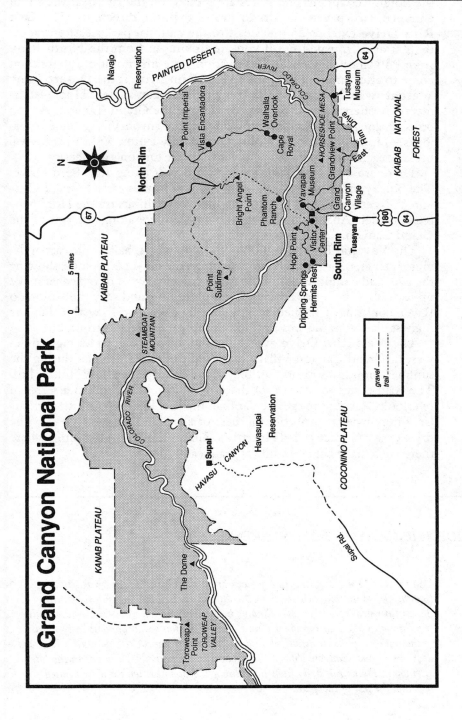

the hotels, restaurants and stores are located on the rim near the south entrance, two paved rim drives run in opposite directions. The **East Rim Drive** extends 25 miles east to the national park's east entrance, the entrance you will use if you are driving in from the North Rim, Lake Powell or the Navajo Reservation. The first point of interest you come to after entering the park on East Rim Drive is the **Desert View Watchtower**, built in the 1930s as a replica of an ancient Hopi watchtower. It offers the first panoramic view of the Grand Canyon. As you proceed along East Rim Drive toward Grand Canyon Village, other overlooks—**Lipan Point, Zuni Point, Grandview Point, Yaki Point**—will beckon, each with a different perspective on the canyon's immensity.

There are two interesting museums to visit along East Rim Drive. The **Tusayan Museum** (602-638-2305), 23 miles east of Grand Canyon Village near the park's east entrance, has exhibits on the Hopi people and their Anasazi ancestors who used to live along the rim of the Grand Canyon.

The **Yavapai Museum** (602-638-7890), about half a mile east of the visitor center, offers detailed information on the canyon's geology, showing the ages and compositions of the many colorful layers of rock that make up its walls. You'll also find explanations of how and why the Colorado River could have formed the canyon by slicing its way through the highest plateau in the area instead of simply meandering around it.

The **West Rim Drive**, which follows the canyon rim for eight miles west of Grand Canyon Village, is closed to private vehicles during the summer months. Visitors can bicycle or board a free park shuttle bus. The road clings to the rim of the canyon as it takes you to a series of overlooks, each more spectacular than the last. **Pima Point**, in particular, offers what is probably the best of all Grand Canyon views. The drive ends at a place called **Hermit's Rest**, a former tourist camp where there are a snack bar and a hikers' trailhead.

RIDE THE CANYON BALL EXPRESS

*You can take a nostalgic trip into yesteryear on the **Grand Canyon Railway** (Route 40, Williams; 602-635-4000, 800-843-8724; admission). A turn-of-the-century steam train leaves Williams in the morning for a two-and-a-half-hour trip through Coconino National Forest, tracing the route that brought early tourists to the national park. It arrives around noon at the historic 1908 Santa Fe Railroad depot in Grand Canyon Village. The return trip departs for Williams in the late afternoon. Trains run daily from June through September, with a more limited schedule the rest of the year.*

The Powell Memorial honors Major John Wesley Powell, the one-armed adventurer who first surveyed the Grand Canyon for the U.S. government in 1869—in a wooden boat.

The **Grand Canyon Visitor Center** (602-638-7888) is located about one mile east of Grand Canyon Village. Leave your car in the village and walk to the visitor center on the paved, magnificently scenic Rim Trail (or, if you're not spending the night at park lodgings, park at the visitor center and walk to the village). Be sure to see the central plaza display of boats that have been used to explore the Grand Canyon. A burned fragment is all that remains of one of the original wooden boats used by Major Powell in 1869. Other wooden boats are of more recent vintage. There is also one of the original inflatable river rafts used by the woman who, in 1955, invented white-water rafting as we know it today.

Just outside the park's south entrance, the town of Tusayan has an **IMAX Theatre** (602-638-2203) that shows films about the Grand Canyon on a seven-story, 82-foot-wide wraparound screen with six-track Dolby sound. The **Over the Edge Theatre** (602-526-4575) also features Grand Canyon films. Why one should wish to watch a movie when the real thing is just a few minutes away is not immediately apparent, but in fact the theaters add an extra dimension to the Grand Canyon experience by presenting river-rafting footage, aerial photography and close-up looks at places in the canyon that are hard to reach.

GRAND CANYON AREA LODGING

On the North Rim of the Grand Canyon, the only lodging within the park is the **Grand Canyon Lodge** (602-638-2611), consisting of a beautiful 1930s-vintage main lodge building overlooking the canyon, and a number of cabins—some rustic, others modern, a few with canyon views. Clean and homelike, both rooms and cabins have an old-fashioned feel. About half the units have television sets, and a few have fireplaces. Rates vary from budget to moderate. North Rim accommodations are in very high demand, so reservations should be made far ahead. They are accepted up to 23 months in advance. Reservations are booked through **TW Recreational Services Inc.** (451 North Main Street, Cedar City, UT 84720; 801-586-7686), which also handles reservations for the lodges at Bryce Canyon and Zion national parks.

Aside from the national park lodge, the closest accommodations to the North Rim are 44 miles away at **Jacob Lake Inn** (602-643-7232). This small, rustic resort complex surrounded by national forest offers both motel rooms and cabins, including some two-bedroom units,

---

Some staff members of El Tovar Hotel still wear the traditional black-and-white uniforms of the famous "Harvey Girls."

---

all priced in the budget range. Again, reservations should be made well in advance.

The South Rim offers many more lodging choices, most in or near Grand Canyon Village. The phone number for all South Rim accommodations is 602-638-2401. Reservations at any of them can be made up to 23 months in advance by writing Grand Canyon National Park Lodges (P.O. Box 699, Grand Canyon, AZ 86023).

Top of the line is the deluxe-priced **El Tovar Hotel**. Designed after European hunting lodges, El Tovar was built by the Fred Harvey Co., a subsidiary of the Santa Fe Railroad, in 1905. The lobby retains its original backwoods elegance, with a big fireplace, massive wood ceiling beams and dark-stained pine decor throughout. The rooms were renovated in the 1980s. All have full baths, color televisions and telephones.

More affordable historic lodging is available nearby at **Bright Angel Lodge**. The main log-and-stone lodge was built in 1935 on the site of Bright Angel Camp, the first tourist facility in the park. Its lobby features Indian motifs and a huge fireplace. Rooms are clean and modest, and most have televisions and phones. Besides rooms in the main building, the lodge also rents several historic cabins on the canyon rim, some with fireplaces. Budget to moderate.

Also in Grand Canyon Village, on the rim between El Tovar and Bright Angel Lodge, are the modern twin stone lodges, **Thunderbird Lodge** and **Kachina Lodge**. Located on the rim trail, these caravansaries are within easy walking distance of the restaurants at the older lodges. Rooms all have televisions and phones. Moderate.

The largest lodging facility in the park, **Yavapai Lodge** is situated in a wooded setting about half a mile from the canyon rim, near the park store, across the road from the Visitor Center and about a mile from Grand Canyon Village. Rates are moderate, and the contemporary rooms are equivalent in quality to what you would expect for the same price at a national chain motor inn.

The newest option is **Maswik Lodge**, set away from the canyon rim at the southwest end of Grand Canyon Village. The lodge presents a variety of motel-style room choices as well as cabins. Some of the rooms have televisions. Budget to moderate.

An elegant modern rustic building, with the look of a ski lodge and a lobby boasting multistory picture windows, **Moqui Lodge** is managed as part of the national park lodge system although it is located in Kaibab National Forest just outside the park entrance. Moderate.

Just outside the South Rim entrance gate, the community of **Tusa-yan** has several motels and motor inns that are not affiliated with the national park. Rates are in the moderate range at all of them. If you cannot get reservations at one of the national park lodges, try one of the typical chain motels such as the **Red Feather Lodge** (602-638-2414), **Best Western Grand Canyon Squire Inn** (602-638-2681) or **Quality Inn Grand Canyon** (602-638-2673).

GRAND CANYON AREA RESTAURANTS

At the North Rim, the **Grand Canyon Lodge Dining Room** (602-638-2611) offers moderately priced breakfast, lunch and dinner selections. The food is good, conventional meat-and-potatoes fare and the atmosphere—a spacious, rustic log-beamed dining room with huge picture windows overlooking the canyon—is simply incomparable. Reservations are required for lunch and dinner. The lodge also operates a cafeteria serving budget-priced meals for breakfast, lunch and dinner in plain, simple surroundings.

The South Rim offers a wider variety of restaurant options. The most elegant is **El Tovar Dining Room** (602-638-2401, ext. 6384). Entrées such as filet mignon and crab legs béarnaise are served on fine china by candlelight. The ambience is classy, but casual dress is perfectly acceptable. Deluxe.

PHANTOM RANCH

No survey of lodgings at the Grand Canyon would be complete without mentioning Phantom Ranch. Located at the bottom of the canyon, this 1922 lodge and cabins is at the lower end of the North Kaibab Trail from the North Rim and the Bright Angel and South Kaibab Trails from the South Rim. It can be reached only by foot, mule or river raft. Cabins are normally reserved for guests on overnight mule trips, but hikers with plenty of advance notice can also arrange lodging. Prices, included in overnight mule trips, are in the moderate range. Bunk beds are available by reservation only in four budget-rate ten-person dormitories for hikers. There is no television at the ranch and only one pay phone. There is outgoing mail service, however, and mail sent from Phantom Ranch bears the postmark, "Mailed by Mule from the Bottom of the Canyon." Meals are served in a central dining hall, which becomes a beer hall after dinner. Do not arrive at Phantom Ranch without reservations! You can reserve space up to a year in advance by calling 602-638-2401 or writing Grand Canyon National Park Lodges (P.O. Box 699, Grand Canyon, AZ 86023).

One of the best dining bets in the area is the Moqui Lodge Cowboy Cookout (602-638-2424), where a chuck wagon–style barbecued beef dinner is followed by a Western music show nightly in the summer season.

More informal surroundings and moderate prices are found at the **Bright Angel Restaurant** in the Bright Angel Lodge. Menu selections include chicken piccata, grilled rainbow trout and fajitas. Cocktails and wine are available. Adjoining the Bright Angel Lodge, the **Arizona Steakhouse** specializes in steaks and seafood and has a good, large salad bar. You can watch the chefs cook in the open kitchen while you eat. Moderate. The phone number for these and all other South Rim Grand Canyon restaurants is 602-638-2361. Reservations are not required.

In the Yavapai Lodge, across the highway from the visitor center, the **Yavapai Grill** serves fast food—burgers and fries, hot dogs, chicken nuggets—while the **Yavapai Cafeteria** offers a changing selection of breakfast, lunch and dinner items. Both are in the budget range. Nearby in the general store, **Babbitt's Delicatessen** features sandwiches, salads and fried chicken box lunches to go or eat on the premises.

There are two other cafeterias in the park—the **Maswik Cafeteria** at Maswik Lodge, at the west end of Grand Canyon Village, and the **Desert View Trading Post Cafeteria**, 23 miles east of the village along the East Rim Drive. Both serve a changing selection of hot meals. Ice cream, hot dogs and soft drinks are available at the **Hermit's Rest Snack Bar** at the end of the West Rim Drive, as well as at the **Bright Angel Fountain** near the trailhead for the Bright Angel Trail. All are budget.

Outside the park entrance, the town of Tusayan has nearly a dozen eating establishments ranging from McDonald's to the beautiful, moderately priced **Moqui Lodge Dining Room** (602-638-2424), which specializes in Mexican food.

GRAND CANYON AREA SHOPPING

Of several national park concession tourist stores on the South Rim of the Grand Canyon, the best are **Hopi House** (602-638-2631), the large Indian pueblo replica across from El Tovar Hotel, and the adjacent **Verkamp's Curios** (602-638-2242). Both have been in continuous operation for almost a century and specialize in authentic Indian handicrafts, with high standards of quality and some genuinely old pieces.

Other Grand Canyon shops, at least as interesting for their historic architecture as for their wares, include the old **Kolb Studio**, originally a 1904 photographic studio and now a bookstore, and the **Lookout Studio**, which has rock specimens and conventional curios. Both are in

Grand Canyon Village. Other souvenir shops are the **Hermit's Rest Gift Shop** (at the end of West Rim Drive) and the **Desert View Watchtower** (East Rim Drive).

GRAND CANYON AREA NIGHTLIFE

On the South Rim, there is dancing nightly at the **Yavapai Lounge**, and **El Tovar Lounge** has a piano bar. In general, though, Grand Canyon National Park does not have much in the way of nightlife. We suggest taking in one of the ranger-produced slide shows presented in the amphitheaters on both the North Rim and the South Rim or simply sitting in the dark along the canyon rim and listening to the vast, deep silence.

GRAND CANYON AREA PARKS

The 1,500,000-acre **Kaibab National Forest** (602-635-2681), an expanse of pine, fir, spruce and aspen forest, includes both sides of the Grand Canyon outside the park boundaries. Most recreational facilities are near the North Rim, where they supplement the park's limited camping facilities. Wildlife in the forest includes mule deer, wild turkeys and even a few bison. The national forest visitor center is at Jacob Lake, located on Route 89A at the Route 67 turnoff.

A nice spot for picnics and camping is **Lee's Ferry, Glen Canyon National Recreation Area** (602-645-2471), halfway along the most direct route between the North and South Rims. Historically, Lee's Ferry was the first crossing point on the Colorado River, established by John D. Lee in 1871. Lee, a Mormon, was a fugitive at the time, wanted by federal authorities for organizing the massacre of a non-Mormon wagon train from Arkansas. He lived here with one of his 17 wives for several years before he was tracked down and killed by federal marshals. Today, Lee's Ferry is the departure point for raft trips into the Grand Canyon. It's located in Marble Canyon about two miles off Route 89A, 85 miles from the North Rim entrance and 104 miles from the east entrance to the South Rim.

Sporting Life

FISHING

The lakes and streams in the Zion and Bryce areas are stocked with trout and other game fish. Try **Fish Lake**, where mackinaw and trout are the catch of the day, and **Panguitch Lake**, which is nearly as popular in winter for ice fishing as it is as a summer resort.

Boats, bait, tackle and licenses can be secured through the **Beaver Dam Lodge** (Shore Road, Panguitch Lake, UT; 801-676-8339) and **Deer Trail Lodge** (Panguitch Lake, UT; 801-676-2211).

HORSEBACK RIDING

In Death Valley, **Furnace Creek Ranch** (619-786-2345) rents horses and offers wagon and carriage rides from October through May.

Riding through southwestern Utah's "Color Country" on leisurely horseback trips is one of the best ways to explore steep canyons. The horses are likely to be as surefooted as mules at the Bryce Canyon and Zion National Park concessions, the only horse rides allowed into parks—the others are relegated to the peripheries. For trail rides, contact **Bryce-Zion Trail Rides** (Zion Lodge, 801-772-3967; or Bryce Lodge, 801-834-5219) or **Best Western Ruby's Inn** (Route 12, Bryce Canyon; 801-834-5341).

At the Grand Canyon, the **Moqui Lodge stable** (602-638-2891) in Tusayan, near the park's south entrance, offers a selection of guided rides to remote points along the South Rim. Most popular is the four-hour East Rim ride, which winds through Long Jim Canyon to a viewpoint overlooking the Grand Canyon. One- and two-hour rides are also available. Horseback rides do not go below the canyon rim, but burro trips do.

There are many ways to see the Grand Canyon but the classic tour is by mule. Trips range from one-day excursions as far as Plateau Point to two- and three-day trips to the bottom of the canyon, which cost several hundred dollars a person including meals and accommodations at Phantom Ranch. Mule trips depart from both the North Rim and the South Rim. Reservations must be made well ahead of time—as much as a year in advance for weekends, holidays and summer months. For South Rim departures, contact **Grand Canyon National Park Lodges** (P.O. Box 699, Grand Canyon, AZ 86023; 602-638-2361). For North Rim departures, contact **Grand Canyon Trail Rides** (P.O. Box 128, Tropic, UT 84776; in summer, 602-638-2292; the rest of the year, 602-679-8665).

JEEP TOURS

For a backcountry adventure, try touring **Kolob Terrace Road**, a two-lane, paved path along the fringes of Zion National Park's west side. The route provides overviews of the Left and Right Forks of North Creek, climbing through dense evergreen forests past Tabernacle Dome and Firepit Knoll. North Creek canyons, Pine Valley Peak and the Guardian Angels are just a few of the other scenic sights. Kolob Terrace Road

---

The beach area on the river below Glen Canyon Dam is situated at the confluence of the Colorado and Paria Rivers, which often have distinctly different colors, giving the water a strange two-toned appearance.

---

starts at the town of Virgin, about 14 miles from Zion's main entrance on Route 9.

WINTER SPORTS

Fish Lake on Route 25 attracts snowmobilers, while sledding and tubing fans head toward **Red Canyon** on Route 12 or **Coral Pink Sand Dunes** near Kanab, Utah.

Cross-country trails are groomed on the rim of **Bryce Canyon**. But within the park skiers can break trail and wander through literally thousand of acres of wilderness, beyond the red-tipped fantasyland of rock spires and figures. Rentals and maps may be secured through **Best Western Ruby's Inn** (Route 12, Bryce Canyon, UT; 801-834-5341).

Brian Head Ski Resort (329 South Route 143; 801-677-2035), 12 miles north of Zion National Park, is renowned for the volume of light, dry snow it receives. Catering to both alpine and nordic skiers, Brian Head's seven chairlifts serve mostly intermediate terrain.

BICYCLING

Death Valley may seem like the last place to ride a bicycle, but it's actually quite pleasant from October to April. The main road in the park is paved, and there's little traffic. The side roads to some of the sights are gravel, however, and require a mountain bike. **Furnace Creek** is a good starting point: It's an easy ride from here to Badwater and Artists Drive, though the latter destination requires uphill pedaling. For an even more challenging ride you can venture up, up, uphill to **Dante's View**; plan on an all-day effort, and bring provisions (especially water!).

Cyclists are starting to discover southwestern Utah for its sights, interesting topography and varied terrain. An easy ride is Route 9 from Springdale through **Zion National Park** (11 miles). In fact, a bicycle is one of the best ways to tour Zion Canyon Scenic Drive from the south visitor center to the Temple of Sinawava, a massive rock canyon.

For a pleasant ride through meadows and pine forests, try **Dave's Hollow Trail** (4 miles), near Bryce Canyon National Park. At the boundary line to the park, about one mile south of Ruby's Inn, is a dirt road that heads west. Follow the road about one-half mile, then turn right about three-fourths of a mile along the trail. This begins a ride along a mellow, double-track trail that ends at the Forest Service station.

At the South Rim of the Grand Canyon, the **West Rim Drive** is closed to private motor vehicles during the summer months but is open to bicycles. This fairly level route, 16 miles round-trip, makes for a spectacular cycling tour.

Although trails within the Grand Canyon National Park are closed to bicycles, **Kaibab National Forest** surrounding the North and South Rims offers a wealth of mountain biking possibilities. The forest areas adjoining the park are laced with old logging roads, and the relatively flat terrain makes for low-stress cycling. One ride the National Forest Service recommends in the vicinity of the South Rim is the **Coconino Rim Trail**, which starts near Grandview Point and continues for more than ten miles north through ponderosa woods.

For other suggestions, stop at the Tusayan Ranger Station just outside the South Rim entrance or the National Forest Information Booth at Jacob Lake or contact **Kaibab National Forest Headquarters** (800 South 6th Street, Williams, AZ 86046; 602-635-2681).

Toward the west end of the Grand Canyon on its North Rim, visitors to **Toroweap Point** will find endless mountain biking opportunities along the hundreds of miles of remote, unpaved roads in the Arizona Strip.

BIKE RENTALS   For rentals and knowledgeable advice, try **Zion Canyon Cycling Company** (998 Zion Park Boulevard, Springdale, UT; 801-772-3929) or **Best Western Ruby's Inn** (Route 12, Bryce Canyon, UT; 801-834-5341).

HIKING

Zion National Park is considered one of the best hiking spots in the nation, with a variety of well-known trails. A comprehensive list is included in the Zion National Park brochure. Regardless of which trail you choose, expect the unexpected—a swamp, a waterfall, a petrified forest or splashes of wildflowers.

You can also expect lots of company on **Gateway to the Narrows Trail** (1 mile), which traces the Virgin River upstream to Zion Canyon Narrows, one of the tight stretches where 20-foot-wide canyons loom 2000 feet overhead. The concrete path winds among high cliffs and cool pools of water. This easy trail begins at the Temple of Sinawava parking area.

For a more moderate hike, continue past the end of the paved path of Gateway to the Narrows and continue along the **Orderville Canyon Trail** (2.8 miles). Much of the trip involves wading through the Virgin

River, at times four feet deep, but if you don't mind wet feet the narrows is an amazing contrast of Navajo sandstone arches, grottoes and fluted walls looming over tight chasms. Be aware that the level of the river can change, so watch for "danger level" signs, or check with park rangers for river conditions.

Angel's Landing (2.4 miles) is a strenuous hike that begins at the Grotto picnic area and offers incredible views over the sheer drops of Zion Canyon. Because the trail is built into solid rock with a 1500-foot dropoff over the last half mile, it isn't recommended for the faint of heart or anyone with "high" anxiety.

Another heavily visited trail system starts at the **Emerald Pools** parking area. The easy, paved trail (.3 mile) to Lower Emerald Pool is shaded by cottonwood, box elder and Gambel oak. The trail ends at a waterfall with the pool below. The more stout-of-heart can venture to the Upper Pool (1.3 miles), by a rough and rocky trail.

Considered one of the most strenuous hikes within Zion, **West Rim Trail** (13.3 miles) takes two days, culminating at Lava Point. Hikers are blessed with scenic vistas including Horse Pasture Plateau, a "peninsula" extending south from Lava Point, surrounded by thousand-foot cliffs. Lightning strikes are frequent on the plateau, and uncontrolled wildfires have left some areas robbed of vegetation. The trailhead starts at the Grotto picnic area.

Bryce Canyon is hiking central because it's so beautiful and accessible. If you're uneasy around hordes of people, either set out early or late in the day or plan to spend a few days in the backcountry to wander into castles and cathedrals, animal farms, temples, palaces and bridges.

The outstanding **Under-the-Rim Trail** (11 miles) connecting Bryce Point with Rainbow Point could be turned into a multiday trip if side canyons, springs and buttes are explored to their full potential.

Riggs Spring Loop Trail (4 miles) starts at Yovimpa Point and takes best advantage of the Pink Cliffs. More moderate than the Riggs Spring Loop Trail is the **Bristlecone Loop Trail** (.5 mile) that begins atop the plateau and leads to sweeping views of spruce forests, cliffs and bristlecone pines.

One of the most famous trails—and rightly so—within the Bryce boundaries is **Queen's Garden** (.8 mile). Start from Sunrise Point and dive right into this amazing amphitheater. Taking a spur to the **Navajo Loop Trail** (an additional mile) brings you into the Silent City, a hauntingly peaceful yet ominous army of hoodoos. The trail ends at Sunset Point.

In the park's northern section is the **Fairyland Loop Trail** (4 miles). Moderately strenuous, the loop provides views of Boat Mesa and the fantasy features of the fairy area. Near the splitting point for the horse trail is the monolith known as Gulliver's Castle. An easier route is **Rim**

Trail (up to 11 miles) along the edge of the Bryce Amphitheater, which can be taken in small or large doses.

The ultimate hiking experience in **Grand Canyon National Park** is an expedition from either rim to the bottom of the canyon and back. With an elevation change of 4800 feet from the South Rim to the river, or 5800 feet from the North Rim, the hike is as ambitious as scaling a Rocky Mountain Peak. Plan at least two, preferably three, days for the trip. An overnight wilderness permit is available free of charge at the visitor centers.

The main trail into the canyon from the North Rim is the **North Kaibab Trail** (14.2 miles), which starts two miles north of Grand Canyon Lodge and descends abruptly down Roaring Springs Canyon for almost five miles to Bright Angel Creek, where you'll find several swimming holes. The trail follows the creek all the way to Phantom Ranch at the bottom of the canyon. Allow a full day for the hike from the rim to the ranch and two days to hike back to the rim, stopping overnight at Cottonwood Camp, the midway point. Because of heavy snows on the rim, the trail is open only from mid–May through mid–October.

On the South Rim, **Bright Angel Trail** (7.8 miles to the river or 9.3 miles to Phantom Ranch) starts at Grand Canyon Village, near the mule corral. The most popular trail in the canyon (daily mule rides take this route), it has the most developed facilities, including resthouses, a ranger station, emergency phones, water and a campground midway down at

---

HAVASU CANYON TRAIL

*For the adventuresome, an intriguing Grand Canyon experience accessible only by foot is found at the west end of the canyon. The **Havasu Canyon Trail** (16 miles) is entirely within the Havasupai Indian Reservation. Take the Supai turnoff located near Peach Springs. From there, the Supai Road goes for 62 miles before the pavement ends. In another 11 miles, the road dead-ends. A foot trail descends 2000 feet in eight miles to the Indian village of **Supai** where about 500 people live. (All hikers must check in at tribal headquarters.) From there, the main trail continues for about four miles more into Havasu Canyon, which includes a series of three high waterfalls—the 75-foot Navajo Falls, 100-foot Havasu Falls and 200-foot Mooney Falls—with large pools ideal for swimming. The tribe can arrange a horseback trip back to the starting point. Whether you plan to stay in the campground or the modern lodge at Supai, advance reservations are essential. For camping information, write **Havasupai Tourist Enterprise**, Supai, AZ 86435, or call 602-448-2121. For lodging listings, see the "Grand Canyon Area Lodging" section.*

Indian Garden, where the Havasupai Indians used to grow crops. The shortest and steepest trail into the canyon is the **South Kaibab Trail** (6.4 miles to Phantom Ranch), which begins at the trailhead on East Rim Drive, four-and-a-half miles from Grand Canyon Village.

Several less-used trails descend from the South Rim, intersecting the **Tonto Trail** (92 miles), which runs along the edge of the inner gorge about 1300 feet above river level for the length of the Grand Canyon. The **Grandview Trail** (3 miles), an old mine access route that starts at Grandview Point on East Rim Drive, goes down to Horseshoe Mesa, where it joins a loop of the Tonto Trail that circles the mesa, passing ruins of an old copper mine. There is a primitive campground on the mesa. The **Hermit Trail** (8.5 miles) begins at Hermit's Rest at the end of West Rim Drive and descends to join the Tonto Trail. Branching off from the Dripping Springs Trail, which also starts at Hermit's Rest, the **Boucher Trail** (11 miles) also goes down to join the Tonto Trail and is considered one of the most difficult hiking trails in the park. Ask for detailed information at the park rangers' counter in the South Rim Visitor Center.

Without descending below the canyon rim, hikers can choose a variety of trails ranging from short scenic walks to all-day hikes. On the North Rim, the easy, paved, handicapped-accessible **Transept Trail** (2 miles) runs between the campground and the lodge, then continues gradually downward to Bright Angel Point. The **Uncle Jim Trail** (2.5 miles) starts at the same trailhead as the Roaring Springs Canyon fork of the Bright Angel Trail, two miles north of the lodge. The **Ken Patrick Trail** (10 miles) forks off the Uncle Jim Trail, continuing straight as the shorter trail turns south, and eventually reaches a remote point on the rim where it descends to follow Bright Angel Creek until it joins the Bright Angel Trail.

On the South Rim, the paved, handicapped-accessible **Rim Trail** (1.5 miles) goes from the Kolb Studio at the west side of Grand Canyon Village to the Yavapai Museum. A one-third-mile spur links the Rim Trail with the visitor center. At each end of the designated Rim Trail, the pavement ends but unofficial trails continue on for several more miles, ending at Hopi Point near the Powell Memorial on West Rim Drive and at Yaki Point, the trailhead for the South Kaibab Trail, located on East Rim Drive.

Visitors to remote Toroweap Point on the North Rim may wish to try the **Lava Falls Trail** (2 miles), which begins as a jeep road midway between the old ranger station and the point. Although the trail is not long, it is rocky, edgy and very steep, descending 2500 feet to the Colorado River and the "falls"—actually a furious stretch of white water formed when lava spilled into the river. Allow all day for the round-trip hike, and do not attempt it during the hot months.

Transportation

BY CAR

There are several entry points to Death Valley National Monument, 135 miles northwest of Las Vegas. The fastest approach is to take **Route 15** south to **Blue Diamond Highway (Route 160)**, then drive west to Pahrump, about 65 miles. Exit on **Route 372**, and continue to **Route 178**, which leads to the park's south entrance. You can also enter the park along its eastern boundary at Death Valley Junction by driving northwest from Las Vegas on **Route 95** and turning south on **Route 373** at Lathrop Wells.

To reach Zion and Bryce Canyon national parks, drive east from Las Vegas on Route 15 past St. George, Utah, about 140 miles. For Zion, exit on **Route 9** and drive to the park's main entrance, one mile north of Springdale. For Bryce Canyon, remain on Route 9 until you reach **Route 89**, then exit and drive north past the beautiful Cedar Breaks National Monument to **Route 12**. Exit and continue southeast on Route 12 until you reach **Route 63**, which leads to Bryce Canyon's main entrance.

The Grand Canyon's North Rim is about 275 miles from Las Vegas. Drive east on **Route 15** to the **Route 9** exit north of St. George, Utah, about 130 miles. Continue east on Route 9 through the towns of Hurricane and Springdale, then turn south on Route 89 at the Mount Carmel junction. **Route 67**, which forks off of **Route 89** at the resort village of Jacob Lake, ends at the North Rim.

To reach the canyon's South Rim, drive southeast on **Route 93** through Boulder City to Kingman, Arizona, about 90 miles, then east on **Route 40** to Williams. Exit and drive north on **Route 64** and **Route 180** to Grand Canyon Village, about 260 miles from Las Vegas.

BY AIR

Visitors may fly into **St. George Municipal Airport** or **Cedar City Municipal Airport** via Sky West/Delta Connection.

Airlines with flights from Las Vegas to **Grand Canyon Airport**, located in Tusayan near the south entrance to the national park, include America West, Air Nevada, Air Vegas and Western Airlines. A shuttle service runs hourly between the airport and Grand Canyon Village.

BY BUS

For Grand Canyon National Park, **Navajo-Hopi Tours** (399 South Malpais Lane, Flagstaff, AZ; 602-774-5003) provides bus service to the Grand Canyon South Rim, and **Greyhound Bus Lines** (200 South

Main Street, Las Vegas, NV; 800-231-2222) stops at the bus terminal in Flagstaff (399 South Malpais Lane; 602-774-4573).

BY TRAIN

Amtrak's "Southwest Chief" (1 East Santa Fe Avenue, Flagstaff, AZ; 800-872-7245) serves Flagstaff and Kingman daily on its route between Chicago and Los Angeles. The westbound passenger train stops in Flagstaff late in the evening, so arriving passengers will want to make hotel reservations in advance with a deposit to hold the room late. Amtrak offers a complimentary shuttle bus service to the Grand Canyon for its Flagstaff passengers.

CAR RENTALS

Rental cars available at the Grand Canyon Airport are **Budget Car Rental** (602-638-9360) and **Dollar Rent a Car** (602-638-2625).

AERIAL TOURS

Many **"flightseeing"** tours offer spectacular eagle's-eye views of the Grand Canyon. Air tour companies with flights from Las Vegas' McCarran Airport include **Adventure Airlines** (702-736-7511) and **Las Vegas Airlines** (702-647-3056). Tour flights from the Grand Canyon Airport near Tusayan are offered by **Grand Canyon Airlines** (P.O. Box 3038, Grand Canyon, AZ 86023; 602-638-2407), **Air Grand Canyon** (P.O. Box 3399, Grand Canyon, AZ 86023; 602-638-2686) and **Windrock Aviation** (P.O. Box 3125, Grand Canyon, AZ 86023; 602-638-9591).

Even more thrilling are the Grand Canyon **helicopter tours** offered by **Papillon Grand Canyon Helicopters** (P.O. Box 455, Grand Canyon, AZ 86023; 602-638-2419), **Kenai Helicopters** (P.O. Box 1429, Grand Canyon, AZ 86023; 602-638-2412) and **AirStar Helicopters** (Grand Canyon Airport; 602-638-2622).

EIGHT

Reno–Tahoe

The Reno–Tahoe area in Northern Nevada is the state's other main gambling destination, but it offers travelers a totally different destination experience than its cousin Las Vegas to the south. Visitors, about 11 million annually, are attracted not only by the gambling but also by the region's natural wonders, including pine-tree-bordered Lake Tahoe, one of the world's most beautiful volcanic crater lakes, cradled in the Sierra Nevada Mountains' Carson Range.

The largest among North America's alpine lakes, Lake Tahoe is situated at an elevation of 6225 feet and surrounded by forests and peaks that reach as high as 10,000 feet. The lake itself is 22 miles long and 12 miles wide, with an average depth of 989 feet. It is fed by 63 creeks, rivers and streams and has a water capacity four times that of Lake Mead (the largest man-made lake in the world).

Surrounding the lake are hundreds of thousands of acres of preserved wilderness with an abundance of year-round recreation: sightseeing, hiking, camping, nature walks, fishing, boating, bicycling, golf, tennis, windsurfing and skiing.

The Truckee River flows out of Lake Tahoe and travels northeast along Route 80, passing through the Reno–Sparks area, about 35 miles away. The river continues on until it empties into Pyramid Lake, sacred to the Native American tribes whose lands border it.

Reno is nestled in a long, urbanized valley known as Truckee Meadows, which also includes the Reno suburb of Sparks. Famous as "The Biggest Little City in the World," Reno has a population of about 134,000 and a downtown district that is home to most of its attractions.

Sitting in the shadow of the Sierra Nevada mountain range to the west, Reno enjoys a four-season climate in which the temperature seldom exceeds 100 degrees. During the hottest months—July and August—the highs average in the low 90s, and in the winter the average daily high is 45 degrees.

Visitors are drawn to the Reno area for its natural beauty; mild, sunny climate; gaming-resort hotels offering contemporary comfort, pleasures and entertainment; and the area's fascinating history dating to the gold rush of 1849, the laying of the Central Pacific Railway in the 1860s, the Virginia-Truckee (V&T) Railroad in the 1870s and the operation of Mark Twain's *Territorial Enterprise* in nearby Virginia City.

Reno is host to several famous spectator events, including the Reno Championship Air Races held in September, touted as the most thrilling and daring of its kind. Also during September, balloonists converge on the town for the annual Great Reno Balloon Race, which sends more than a hundred colorful hot-air balloons into the sky. In June, cowboys from throughout the West visit the city for the annual Reno Rodeo, one of the most prestigious events of its kind in the country.

The city of Reno began to take shape during the 1870s after the completion of the V&T Railroad, which connected it with Nevada's capital, Carson City. The rapid growth was reflected in downtown brick buildings, spreading residential areas, a theater, a state university that moved to Reno from Elko in 1885, and a new iron bridge across the Truckee River.

Reno's mushrooming population, urged on by silver strikes in Tonopah and gold strikes in Goldfield and Rhyolite during the first five years of the century, instilled in its upright citizens a desire for respectability. This resulted in a short-lived backlash against the rowdy town's permissiveness, including a ban against alcohol two years before national Prohibition.

However, the Roaring Twenties era overturned the temporary moral strictures and restored the town's identity as the center of a new Wild West when Mayor E. E. Roberts refused to enforce laws in gambling, drinking, whoring and sinning in general. Meanwhile, the Victory Highway over the Sierras in 1925 and the first airline service in 1927 made the town more accessible than ever.

Following the Crash of '29, the 1930s in Nevada were just as bleak as for the rest of the nation, complicated by a devastating three-year drought that killed off cattle ranching and the state's economy. Legislators tried pulling out of the slump once again by offering quickie divorces and legalized gambling. In the mid 1930s, visionaries Raymond "Pappy" Smith and William Harrah built casinos here, and helped turn around Las Vegas' image from one of sleaze to that of good, clean fun.

Then in 1947 the Reno City Council redlined gambling to prevent the unbridled casino growth observed in Las Vegas at the time. When

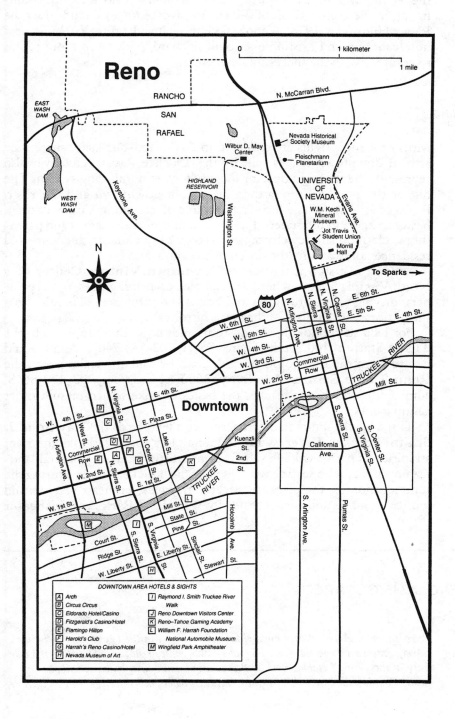

Reno

0   1 kilometer
           1 mile

RANCHO

SAN

RAFAEL

N. McCarran Blvd.

EAST
WASH
DAM

Nevada Historical
Society Museum

Wilbur D. May
Center

Fleischmann
Planetarium

HIGHLAND
RESERVOIR

UNIVERSITY
OF
NEVADA

WEST
WASH
DAM

Keystone Ave.

Washington St.

Evans Ave.

W.M. Kech
Mineral
Museum

Jot Travis
Student Union

Morrill
Hall

N

To Sparks →

80

W. 6th St.

W. 5th St.

W. 4th St.

W. 3rd St.

W. 2nd St.

N. Arlington Ave.

N. Sierra St.

N. Virginia St.

N. Center St.

E. 6th St.

E. 5th St.

E. 4th St.

Commercial
Row

TRUCKEE RIVER

Mill St.

S. Sierra St.

S. Virginia St.

S. Center St.

California
Ave.

S. Arlington Ave.

Plumas St.

Downtown

N. Virginia St.

E. 4th St.

W. 4th St.

West St.

N. Arlington Ave.

Commercial
Row

N. Sierra St.

N. Center St.

Lake St.

E. Plaza St.

Kuenzli
St.

2nd
St.

W. 2nd St.

E. 1st St.

TRUCKEE
RIVER

W. 1st St.

Mill St.

State St.

Pine St.

Court St.

S. Sierra St.

S. Virginia St.

E. Liberty St.

Sinclair St.

Holcomb
Ave.

Ridge St.

W. Liberty St.

Stewart
St.

[B] Circus Circus
[C] Eldorado Hotel/Casino
[D] Fitzgerald's Casino/Hotel
[A] Arch
[J] Reno Downtown Visitors Center
[F] Harold's Club
[E] Flamingo Hilton
[G] Harrah's Reno Casino/Hotel
[K] Reno–Tahoe Gaming Academy
[L] William F. Harrah Foundation
[I] Raymond I. Smith Truckee River
[M] Wingfield Park Amphitheater

DOWNTOWN AREA HOTELS & SIGHTS

[A] Arch	[I] Raymond I. Smith Truckee River
[B] Circus Circus	Walk
[C] Eldorado Hotel/Casino	[J] Reno Downtown Visitors Center
[D] Fitzgerald's Casino/Hotel	[K] Reno–Tahoe Gaming Academy
[E] Flamingo Hilton	[L] William F. Harrah Foundation
[F] Harold's Club	National Automobile Museum
[G] Harrah's Reno Casino/Hotel	[M] Wingfield Park Amphitheater
[H] Nevada Museum of Art	

the red line was lifted in the early 1970s, gambling really took off, culminating in the construction of the Las Vegas-like MGM Grand (now the Reno Hilton) in 1978. Reno's skyline changed immediately as new hotels shot up and existing ones built skyward, packing in more rooms to compete with the successful newcomer.

Reno

Most of Reno's sights are clustered in a two-and-one-half square mile area of downtown that is split by the Truckee River. The river also represents the starting point for the city's street numbering system. The higher the number, the farther away from downtown and the river. Reno's version of "The Strip" covers five blocks along Virginia Street, between 2nd and 6th streets. Here you'll find souvenir stores and pawnshops, clothing and jewelry stores, a score of restaurants, and some old residence hotels among the dozen or so casino-hotels.

A good first stop is the **Reno Downtown Visitors Center** (275 North Virginia Street), where you can pick up maps, guides, travel planners, driving tours, brochures and books about the area. There's also a small room with displays of the area's historical and geological sights.

For help with booking rooms, tours and shows in town, head to the **Ticket Station** (100 South Virginia Street; 702-348-7403). And if you'd like to learn the fine points of card, craps or roulette dealing, visit the **Reno-Tahoe Gaming Academy** (300 East 1st Street; 702-329-5665; admission), which also teaches the basics of poker, baccarat and other casino games.

Three blocks south on Sierra Street you'll come to the **Raymond I. Smith Truckee River Walk**, a public plaza that overlooks the river and features native wildlife reliefs, eight artistic fountains, natural landscaping and gazebo seating with vistas of the Truckee River. During the summer months, the plaza has street performers, pushcart vendors and musical concerts and dances at nearby **Wingfield Park Amphitheater**

RENO'S FAMOUS ARCH

*Reno's famous **Arch**, always highlighted in movies set in the town, spans Virginia Street, between Fitzgerald's and Harold's Club, with its slogan "The Biggest Little City in the World" emblazoned by thousands of white light bulbs and ribbons of neon. First installed in 1927, the arch has been redesigned three times in its lifetime.*

Reno, the "tough little town on the Truckee," endured frontier justice until police were introduced in 1889.

(2 North Arlington Avenue; 702-334-2077), which features grass seating around an open-air stage.

The oldest casino in town is **Harold's Club** (250 North Virginia Street; 702-329-0881), marked by a wall mural depicting gold rush pioneers camped at a river bank. Founded in 1935 by the Smith family, Harold's originated the modern view of gambling as family entertainment, and instituted safeguards against cheating on both sides of the table, notably the original eye-in-the-sky, one-way glass and catwalk system. Harold's was also the first to offer casino staples like free drinks, comps, charters and junkets, and they hired the first female dealers, further enhancing casino respectability.

If you need a change in luck, visit the **Lucky Forest** (255 North Virginia Street; 702-786-3663) on the second floor of Fitzgerald's Hotel & Casino. The mini-museum displays talismans of good fortune from horseshoes and rabbit's feet to Aladdin's lamp and *Ho Tei*, the Chinese god of good luck.

If you can't get enough of retro nostalgia—and who can?—visit **Eddie's Fabulous Fifties Casino** (45 West 2nd Street; 702-329-1950) where you can bebop to tunes by Elvis, Jerry Lee, Ben E. and the Everlies on the PA system. You can even sit in the bar in back-seat halves of '50s convertibles.

Like its three-ringed cousin in Las Vegas, **Circus Circus** (500 North Sierra Street; 702-329-0711) offers free circus acts and midway games daily. Under the big top you can watch jugglers, Chinese acrobats, clowns, high- and low-wire aerialists and trapeze artists in spangled tights zoom overhead while you try to decide whether to double down your blackjack hand.

Art lovers should head for the **Nevada Museum of Art** (160 West Liberty Street; 702-329-3333; admission) housed in a contemporary building. Exhibits rotate every six to eight weeks and focus on 19th and 20th century Great Basin, Native American and fine art, photography weaving and basketry.

Other galleries with an emphasis on art produced in the surrounding Great Basin and Sierra Nevada regions include **Artists Co-Operative of Reno** (627 Mill Street; 702-322-8896) and **River Gallery** (15 North Virginia Street; 702-329-3698).

Travel from downtown north on Virginia Street up a hill to 11th Street and you'll encounter the **University of Nevada, Reno** (East 9th and North Virginia streets; 702-784-1110), a 200-acre campus with luxuriant grassy areas shaded by 100-year-old oak trees. Brick-paved walkways and old brick buildings are counterpoints to contemporary architecture and Manzanita Lake reflecting a graceful willow tree. The university's **Jot Travis Student Union** (702-784-6505) borders one edge of the lake and houses a dining commons and bookstore, which offers a depth of titles on the West and the complete University Press list. If you're a college logo fanatic, the store also sells UNR T-shirts, sweatshirts, mugs, pennants, cards, souvenirs and sundries.

Just east of the campus' Getchell Library, the **W. M. Kech Mineral Museum** (702-784-6988), in room 108 of the Mackay School of Mines, recalls mining's important role in the growth of Nevada. Quantities of mineral specimens crowd the display cases in this airy, well-lighted room, ranging from gold, silver, copper and lead to borax, sulfides, oxides, quartzites and geodes. Upstairs, the mezzanine exhibits display a geological breakdown of minerals and some fossils from around the world, plus miners' tools, machines, scales and diagrams.

Across the football field-sized Quadrangle stands **Morrill Hall**, built in 1887, and named after the congressman who established the college land-grant system. The four-story building once housed the entire school and now is home to the alumni office and the University Press. From its tower, carillon bells toll for special occasions. The other buildings around the central Quad were built between 1906 and 1945, and feature the Jeffersonian Revival style: Victorian architecture with Gothic and Italianate detail.

Set aside a few hours to take in the **Nevada Historical Society Museum** (702-688-1190; admission) at the north end of the campus. The museum is packed with fascinating artifacts, photographs and car-

---

THE HISTORY OF THE HORSELESS CARRIAGE

*If you prefer eight-cylinder nostalgia, head over to the **William F. Harrah Foundation National Automobile Museum** (10 South Lake Street; 702-333-9300; admission), a futuristic building that houses a century's worth of automobile history. Included are more than 200 antique, vintage, classic and special-interest automobiles, many from Harrah's original collection. Many of the cars are displayed on sets designed to represent the era from which they came: for instance, a '50s-style diner and gas station for a 1955 Ford T-bird, and a blacksmith's shop for an original "horseless carriage." There's also a multi-media theater that runs a fast-paced, high-tech history of the automobile and features real cars on stage, plus rotating exhibits that display specialty cars, such as British sports cars from Morgans to MG's to Aston Martins.*

In the late 1920s, Reno was not only the divorce, but also the marriage capital, outdoing California's three-day waiting period for marriage with its no-waiting period.

tographs delineated in a timeline from 13,000 year-old primitive man and the Desert Archaic culture of 8000-1000 B.C., through the Paiute, Shoshone and Washoe eras, up to initial contact with Europeans in the 1820s. The exhibits reveal how in only 25 years the earliest white explorers, followed by wagon trains from the east, settlers and the Comstock strike and Pyramid Lake battles, managed to completely overwhelm the Native cultures. The exhibit continues with the history of the mining boom, military arrival, Pony Express, telegraph and railroad, which carry the visitor on into the 20th century. Look for books in the gift shop and changing exhibits in the adjacent gallery.

Next door, the university's **Fleischmann Planetarium** (702-784-4811) may be small, but it exhibits globes of the Earth and moon, a large relief map of the Sierra area and a cloud display. Try out the gravity well in the Hall of the Solar System, the instruments in the gift shop and view the stars through the large telescope on certain clear nights. The Star Theater (admission) offers fascinating astronomy shows.

The sprawling Rancho San Rafael Park just a short stroll across Virginia Street is home to the **Wilbur D. May Center** (1502 Washington Street; 702-785-5961), named after the industrialist and heir to the May Department Store fortune who was one of Reno's major supporters during the 1920s and '30s. He was also a world traveler who circled the globe more than 40 times, with many of his souvenir artifacts from exotic ports displayed in the **Wilbur D. May Museum** (702-785-5961; admission). Designed after May's own Western-style ranch house just outside of Reno, the museum displays include a shrunken head, weavings, glass, silver, masks, ivory and ceramic pieces from all over the world. His hunter's trophy room is filled with horned, antlered and fanged creatures from other continents, and the conference room exhibits black-and-white photos of the installation of Nevada's portion of the transcontinental telephone line: 400 miles through the Sierras.

In back of the museum you can wander through the **Wilbur D. May Arboretum and Botanical Garden** (702-785-4153), which displays both native and ornamental plants along an assortment of paths. Plants are labeled and correspond to information in the brochure you can pick up at the garden's entrance. An added attraction is the Song Bird Garden, which gives song bird suitors ideas on how to attract the musical birds.

Next door, kids will love the **Wilbur D. May Great Basin Adventure** (702-785-4064; admission), a mini theme park that traces the Great Basin's history from prehistoric times to the present. Included are a di-

The Reno Hilton Theater boasts the largest stage in the state.

nosaur pit, mining building, discovery room, petting zoo, pony rides and a log flume ride.

Just a few miles from downtown, the **Liberty Belle Saloon & Restaurant** (4250 South Virginia Street; 702-825-1776) provides a glimpse of a genuine Western-style saloon with its dark wood furnishings, brass fixtures and tiffany lamps. The place is owned by Frank and Marshall Fey, grandsons to Charles Fey, who is credited with inventing the three-reel slot machine. On display are several of the inventor's original machines, including the Liberty Bell, the first automatic-paying, three-reel slot, now valued at more than $60,000. There are more modern slots on display (and for play), and you can buy books about the history of the one-armed bandit.

For a taste of a cowboy's life, visit **Bull Creek Ranch** (1850 West Old Highway 40; 702-345-7600; admission), a working cattle ranch nestled in the Sierra Nevada foothills nine miles west of downtown Reno. Bring your chaps and spurs because the activities are not for dudes: cattle drives, roping, cutting and branding.

RENO LODGING

Unlike the megaresorts in Las Vegas, the hotels in Reno are smaller— with a handful of exceptions—with less emphasis on fantasy themes and showroom entertainment to lure guests. Instead, the focus is on gambling, with most of the hotel's amenities and promotions centered around the casinos.

The summer months are busiest, especially from May through October, when most of the area's seasonal events are held. During this time it's best to book ahead for one of the city's 25,000 guest rooms. During the winter months, hotels frequently offer room packages and bargain rates to attract visitors.

The largest hotel in the city is the **Reno Hilton** (2500 East Second Street; 702-789-2000, 800-648-5080, fax 702-789-2130), with 2000 modern guest rooms in its 25-story tower. Most feature print drapes and spreads, with plaid upholstered furniture and redwood entertainment centers. Some rooms have picture windows offering sweeping views of the mountains. The 100,000-square-foot casino is the city's largest. Other hotel facilities include a health club, outdoor pool, eight tennis courts, two movie theaters, 50-lane bowling alley, six restaurants and an outdoor "aquagolf" driving range. Deluxe.

A smaller version of its Las Vegas namesake, **Circus Circus Hotel Casino** (500 North Sierra Street; 702-329-0711, 800-648-5010, fax 702-329-0599) has its signature neon clown out front and 1625 budget-priced rooms in its two pink towers. Most of the guest rooms have brightly colored carpeting, upholstery and wall coverings, as well as views of the river and mountains. Hotel amenities include a casino, three restaurants, free circus acts and midway on the mezzanine level, lounge and a children's play area.

Everybody's Irish at **Fitzgerald's Casino/Hotel** (255 North Virginia Street; 702-786-3663, 800-648-5022), at least on St. Patrick's Day, when the beer runs green and the Blarney stones are eroded by kisses. The Irish theme is year-round, however, so you can always count on leprechauns, four-leaf clovers and emerald green wall art in the public areas. The hotel's 351 moderate-to-deluxe-priced rooms are tastefully decorated in subdued earth-tones of light brown and green, with drapes and bedspreads done in cool pastels. The hotel features a casino, restaurant and Lucky Forest charm display.

You'll find some of the nicest rooms in town at the newly remodeled **Eldorado Hotel/Casino** (345 North Virginia Street; 702-786-5700, 800-648-5966, fax 702-348-9269), a glitzy resort whose casino and restaurants are always packed with visitors and locals alike. The hotel's 800 guest rooms are spacious affairs with light wood furniture, Southwestern patterned upholstery and bedspreads and pastel carpeting. In addition to the bustling casino, which boasts the world's largest roulette table, the hotel features a pool and jacuzzi, a popular buffet and seven restaurants. Moderate to deluxe.

Nearly a clone of its alter-ego in Las Vegas, the **Flamingo Hilton Reno** (255 North Sierra Street; 702-322-1111, 800-648-4882, fax 702-785-7086) ignites the downtown area with its pink-neon flamingos and feathers along its block-long marquee. The 604 rooms, however, are decorated in subdued Hilton greens and blues, with dark wood furniture

---

REINVENTING RENO

It was Reno's divorce trade more than gambling that turned the economic tide and set the stage for Raymond "Pappy" Smith, who in the mid '30s set up Harold's Club, chased out the cheaters, hookers and drunks and advertised Nevada casinos as good clean fun. William Harrah built his hotel on cue from Smith's success and by the end of World War II Reno's population had swelled to almost 30,000 based on the marriage and divorce industries and the swarm of tourists who descended to partake of the newly respectable casino games.

and headboards. In addition to a rambling casino and penthouse restaurant, the hotel features showroom entertainment with the celebrity tribute, "American Superstars." Moderate to deluxe.

The most Las Vegas-like of all Reno resorts is the **Peppermill Hotel Casino** (2707 South Virginia Street; 702-826-2121, 800-282-2494, fax 702-826-5205), which features neon art and signs, plastic plants, silk flowers and movie-set trees throughout the casino and restaurants. For the budget-conscious, 105 guest rooms are available in the older Motor Lodge and G-building. The rooms are small, and adorned with the traditional bed and desk. Newer and larger accommodations can be found in the Annex and Tower. Moderate to deluxe in price, the 527 rooms are decorated with pastel color schemes, Southwest paintings, wooden desks and furniture. Hotel amenities include a casino, four-star dining at Le Moulin, health club and a heated pool and whirlpool.

Built by Bill Harrah in 1937, **Harrah's Reno Casino/Hotel** (219 North Center Street; 702-786-3232, 800-648-3773, fax 702-788-2815) is one of the city's oldest gambling resorts. It also represents the founder's devotion to detail and dedication to his guests. The 565 guest rooms are the largest in town, and tastefully decorated with light wood furniture, floral print quilts and blue-and-turquoise color schemes. Some of the rooms feature the best views of the snow-capped Sierras. Hotel guests are entertained by celebrity headliners, first-class dining, a pool and health club and a video arcade. Moderate to deluxe.

If you want to get away from the gambling atmosphere and still enjoy hotel amenities, try the **Holiday Inn/Convention Center** (5851 South Virginia Street; 702-825-2940, 800-736-6001, fax 702-826-3835). The 153 budget-to-moderate-priced rooms are standard fare with dark wood furniture and floral prints, but the pool is inviting and you can bring your pet if you like.

Just a short drive from downtown, **John Ascuaga's Nugget** (1100 Nugget Avenue; 702-356-3300, 800-843-2427, fax 702-356-4198) in Sparks is a modern, 29-story monolith with the Sierra Nevadas as a backdrop. Most of the 1000 guest rooms are located in the tower, and feature rose-colored floral prints, white-washed wood furniture and sweeping views of snow-capped peaks. The older garden rooms in the five-story Courtyard tower are motel-like with earth-tone carpeting and polished wood furnishings. Facilities at the hotel include an 80,000-square-foot casino, celebrity showroom, health club, a deli and six restaurants, including the popular John's Oyster Bar, and a magnificent indoor/outdoor Olympic-sized swimming pool decorated with slate walkways, towering plants and partially enclosed by glass walls. Prices fall in the moderate range.

Other hotel-casinos worth trying are the **Riverboat Hotel & Casino** (34 West Second Street; 702-323-8877, 800-888-5525, fax 702-

348-0926), which features 297 moderately priced rooms and an 1890s Mississippi riverboat-style casino; the **Sands Regency Hotel/Casino** (345 North Arlington Avenue; 702-348-2200, 800-648-3553, fax 702-348-2226) for its 1000 moderately priced rooms, casino, pool, jacuzzi and health club; and the 586-room **Clarion Hotel Casino** (3800 South Virginia Street; 702-825-4700, 800-723-6500, fax 702-826-7860) which offers moderate-to-deluxe rates, gambling, a pool, health club, a video arcade and RV parking.

You'll find only two guest rooms at the **South Reno Bed and Breakfast** (136 Andrew Lane; 702-849-0772), but they are tastefully decorated with antique furniture, poster beds and scenic wall tapestries. Also in the house is a book-paneled parlor with card games, and a pool in back. Deluxe.

There are also a score of motels in town, including national chains such as **Motel 6** (1901 South Virginia Street; 702-827-0255), **Easy 8** (255 West Fifth Street; 702-322-4588), **Days Inn** (701 East Seventh Street; 702-786-4070) and **Rodeway Inn** (2050 Market Street; 702-786-2500). Or you might want to try a locally run motel, such as **Bob Cashell's Horseshoe Lodge** (222 North Sierra Street; 702-322-2178), the **Gatekeeper Inn** (221 West 5th Street; 702-786-3500) or the **Truckee River Lodge** (501 West 1st Street; 702-786-8888), advertised as Reno's only nonsmoking lodging. All are moderately priced and are certified by the Northern Nevada Motel Association.

RENO RESTAURANTS

While the hotels have their share of bargain-priced, all-you-can-eat buffets, Reno restaurateurs pride themselves on presenting fine dining at

---

DELECTABLE DINING

*A local favorite for years, **Le Moulin** (2707 South Virginia Street; 702-826-2121) in the Peppermill has a modernized country French atmosphere with indirect neon lighting and recessed chandeliers casting a warm, red-white glow off etched glass dividers. Each table and booth has its own candle, and the walls are adorned with paintings of waterfowl and other wildlife. Wild game, incidentally, is offered every night as an opener or entrée. Other tasteful appetizers include smoked salmon, oysters on the half shell and crab ravioli in saffron broth. Main courses include fresh fish, prime rib, châteaubriand, rack of lamb, and abalone doré. Save room for the crème brulée and white chocolate cheesecake. Moderate to deluxe.*

reasonable prices. Listed here are some of the city's best hotel dining rooms, along with a few unique neighborhood eateries.

La Strada (345 North Virginia Street; 702-786-5700) in the Eldorado has a country house atmosphere with dark wood pillars and beams, faux leather booths and wood tables and chairs. Diners can watch through glass walls as the chef prepares moderately priced fish, fowl and veal specialties, plus homemade pasta and pizza in the wood-burning oven. Also in the Eldorado, **The Vintage** (702-786-5700) offers fine dining on châteaubriand, coq au vin, scampi, duckling, and steak Diane, all prepared tableside and deluxe priced. If you prefer meat and plenty of it, try the moderately priced **Grill** (702-786-5700), which specializes in mesquite grilled barbecue beef ribs and baby back pork ribs. You can also feast on duckling, chicken and lamb, roasted on the oak and mahogany-fueled rotisserie.

Another favorite with steak lovers is the **Prime Rib Company** (221 South Virginia Street; 702-324-7777) in the Pioneer Inn, where you can gorge on a slab of USDA choice prime rib, or camp out at the soup and salad bar (be sure to try the clam chowder when available) for less than five bucks. Also at budget prices is a one-pound T-bone steak dinner with all the trimmings, plus seafood and pasta dishes.

If you can't get enough beef, head for the **Hickory Pit Steak House** (500 North Sierra Street; 702-329-0711) in Circus Circus, where the emphasis is on moderately priced prime rib, New York and porterhouse steaks. In the rambling dining room you can also sample doggie-bag portions of crab, lobster and traditional pasta dishes.

Located in the Clarion Hotel, **Café Alfresco** (3800 South Virginia Street; 702-825-4700) is patterned after a sidewalk Parisian bistro. The restaurant features hanging plants, marble-top tables and white-cane chairs. The menu's focus is Italian: pastas and pizzas fixed in a wood-burning stove. Also noteworthy are the meal-sized salads. Budget to moderate.

Although it may seem out of place, **John's Oyster Bar** (1100 Nugget Avenue; 702-356-3300) in John Ascuaga's Nugget brings a taste of San Francisco to the semi-arid Sierra Nevada foothills. Patterned after a sailing ship, the restaurant is decked out with dark woods, alcoves, a mast and plenty of rigging. The specialty is oysters on the half shell, and the tables have the right accessories: eye-blistering horseradish, bottles of tabasco and saltines. Other popular specialties include pan roasts, oyster stews, cioppinos and seafood Louies. Moderate.

Some of the best Mexican food in town is served at **Miguel's** (1415 South Virginia Street; 702-322-2722), a budget-priced cantina with tile floors, booth seating and colorful artifacts on the walls. The Mexican specialties include sizzling beef or chicken fajitas prepared tableside, and combination dinners topped by a zesty chili relleno served with rice, beans and flour tortillas.

Reno's population doubled between 1960 and 1980 to 100,000. Today its population is more than 133,000.

For a taste of the Far East, try the **Siamese Hut** (1775 Mill Street at Kietzke Lane; 702-786-7747), which serves up incendiary Thai cuisine at budget prices. Don't let the modest dinette tables and faux plants fool you—the storefront café is popular with locals and usually packed. Among the specialty dishes are pad Thai, noodles with shrimp, scallions and carrots in a sweet sauce; and the hot and spicy prik king, meat (choice of beef, chicken, pork or shrimp) and vegetables bathed in a pungent curry sauce.

A popular hangout of the downtown lunch crowd is **Café Soleil** (100 West Liberty Street, Suite 150; 702-324-1500), a tiny bistro on the first floor of the Porsche Building. The house specialty is a roasted bell pepper sauce that is ladled over pasta (try the mushroom ravioli), meat and pork loin dishes. Be sure to try the squash with maple syrup and cinnamon sauce. Moderate.

Vegetarians will find the **Blue Heron** (1091 South Virginia Street; 702-786-4110), the city's only vegetarian restaurant, to their liking. For lunch, try the vegetarian tempeh burgers and falafel, and for dinner there's an assortment of veggie plates, salads and designer baked potatoes. This wood-paneled eatery also features a small bakery that sells fresh-baked muffins, breads and cookies. Budget.

A great spot for breakfast or lunch is the **Bagel Deli** (2600 South Virginia Street; 702-825-8866), where you can choose from a variety of bagels, topped with special cream cheese spreads, including green onion, strawberry, avocado, and date and honey, to name a few. Budget.

The three-mile stretch of Wells Avenue between Mill Street and South Virginia Street is home to a variety of fine restaurants, but the best is **Rapscallion Seafood House** (1555 South Wells Avenue; 702-323-1211), a cozy affair with dark wood panels, brocade-patterned booths and soft, indirect lighting. The specialty here is fresh seafood with entrées such as swordfish, yellowfin tuna and the house favorite, Rapscallion stew, a spicy blend of fish filet, clams, oysters, tomatoes, leeks, garlic and white wine. Moderate to deluxe.

If you like thick-crust pizza, try **J.J.'s Pie Company** (555 West Fifth Street; 702-786-5555), a storefront eatery with funky wooden tables and weird pictures on the wall. But the moderately priced pizzas, which come in a variety of sizes, have a perfect crust—thick, but not doughy, with just the right amount of crispness on the edges. Choose from the usual selection of toppings, including a tasty vegetarian number that will make you forget pepperoni. Before you finish, dip the crusty remnants into a bit of honey for a faux Italian version of Mexican sopapillas.

The Gambler's Bookstore (99 North Virginia Street) offers 1000 titles about gambling, sports, antique slots and a myriad of how-to guides on casino games.

If you crave a good burger, head to **Bailywick's** (101 East Pueblo Street; 702-786-7154), a hyperactive little joint with formica counter-tops, generic wall art and not a golden arch in sight. The specialty is budget-priced, half-pound burgers, which are topped with anything the kitchen has on hand. For wimps, there's a more subdued one-third pounder. To ensure a cholesterol meltdown, be sure to order a side of fries, which appear more broasted than fried, and are served with ranch dressing.

RENO SHOPPING

The downtown district has a number of souvenir shops, jewelry stores, pawnbrokers and clothing stores in which to roam. You can find vintage collectibles at **Washoe Antiques** (1215 South Virginia Street; 702-322-3009) in the Antique Mall. The collection of Reno memorabilia sometimes includes old cast-iron slot machines, craps felt layouts, old punch cards and other gambling artifacts.

If your wardrobe needs a jump start, head to **Parker's Western Clothing** (151 North Sierra Street; 702-323-4481), a warehouse-sized emporium that's been in business since 1919 and specializes in Western-style men's and women's apparel, plus boots and leather goods.

You can pore over locally produced arts and crafts at **Crafter's Mall** (100 North Sierra Street; 702-333-2818), where local artisans display their cloth, lapidary, florals, wood, ceramic and leather craftwork.

The shopping arcade at the **Reno Hilton** (2500 East Second Street; 702-789-2000, 702-789-2046 for arcade manager) has 40 stores and boutiques in which to wander. Most are on the high-end of men's and women's apparel, jewelry, upscale children's ware and toys and designer shoes.

If you mall addicts need a fix, try the **Park Lane Mall** (310 Plumb Lane; 702-825-7878), which is anchored by Sears and Weinstock's department stores. Here you'll find the standard mix of clothing shops, shoe stores, record and tape stores, gift and card shops, and a Nevada store that sells books about the region and locally produced ceramics, wall art and other gifts.

RENO NIGHTLIFE

Most of Reno's nightside entertainment is found in the larger hotel-casinos, but there are a few gems hidden in and around downtown.

A road version of the popular Las Vegas production show *Splash* plays indefinitely at the **Hilton Theater** at the Reno Hilton (2500 East Second Street; 702-789-2285). The aquacade of music and dance takes place in and around a water tank with mermaids, high divers, synchronized swimmers and laser light effects. The hotel's **Goldwyn Ballroom** hosts popular headliners such as Brett Butler and Mark Russell, the **Just for Laughs** comedy club features stand-up comics often fresh from late-night TV appearances, while the **Confetti Cabaret** hosts lounge-type acts. No cover. During the summer months, you can enjoy a concert under the stars at the **Outdoor Amphitheater** with headliners such as James Taylor and The Gipsy Kings. Cover charge for all shows.

You'll also find headliner entertainment at **Sammy's Showroom** (219 North Center Street; 702-786-3232) in Harrah's. Featured performers have included Phyllis Diller, Floyd Cramer, the Coasters and the Drifters. In between headliner engagements, the showroom is home to two fast-paced music and dance revues, *Hit City* and *High Voltage*. Cover.

Headliners such as Juice Newton frequently play the **Celebrity Showroom** (1100 Nugget Avenue; 702-356-3300) at John Ascuaga's Nugget, which also offers combination show-dinner packages at its Rotisserie, Steakhouse Grill and Trader Dick's, a very good Chinese restaurant. Cover.

The **Flamingo Showroom** at the Flamingo Hilton (255 North Sierra Street; 702-322-1111) is host to *American Superstars*, an impersonator's tribute to such celebrities as Madonna, Sammy Davis, Jr., the Blues Brothers, Charlie Daniels and Billy Ray Cyrus. Unlike some impersonator shows, this one is performed live (no lip sync); cover. The hotel's

---

RETRO ROCKIN'

As much a shrine to rock and roll as a nightclub, **Dick Clark's American Bandstand Club** *(236 North Virginia Street; 702-786-2222) on the second floor of Harold's Club features a huge dancefloor flanked by two bars and overhead track lighting, all surrounded by walls covered with music memorabilia from Clark's personal collection. When you tire of bebopping to hits from the '50s to the '90s, you can watch classic "American Bandstand" footage from the original television show on TV monitors, or examine platinum and gold records, bandstand costumes, vintage concert posters and rare photographs. Also on the walls you'll find Gloria Estefan's chaps, Rod Stewart's soccer ball, Paula Abdul's tap shoes, Chubby Checker's boots and Mick Jagger's jacket. Just how—and why—Clark acquired these mementos remains a mystery. Cover.*

penthouse-level **Top of the Hilton** features breathtaking bird's-eye views of Reno and a comfortable lounge/piano bar. No cover. The **Showspot Lounge** features entertaining singers and small musical groups.

Other popular spots for celebrity entertainment are the **Center Stage Cabaret** (3800 South Virginia Street; 702-825-4700) located in the center of the casino at the Clarion Hotel (no cover); the **Cabaret** (345 North Virginia Street; 702-786-5700) in the Eldorado; and the **Convention Showroom** (2707 South Virginia Street; 702-826-2121) in the Peppermill; both with cover.

The **Firelite Lounge** (55 East Nugget Avenue; 702-358-6900) in the McCarran House hosts entertainment for all tastes, including Monday night football, karaoke night on Wednesday and live entertainment Friday and Saturday. No cover.

A nightspot with a local clientele is **Easy Street** (505 Keystone Avenue; 702-323-8369), a converted movie theater where you can dance to deejay hosted Top-40 hits. Cover.

Rounding out the dance halls is the **Rodeo Rock Café** (1537 South Virginia Street; 702-323-1600), a barn-like ballroom where you can two-step to deejay-driven country hits. If you're *really* feeling frisky you can take a turn on the mechanical bull. But before you do, keep this in mind: there's a reason they make you sign a disclaimer. Cover.

For quieter liaisons try the **Blarney Stone Pub** (255 North Virginia Street; 702-786-3663) in Fitzgerald's, an Irish-themed lounge decorated in handcrafted mahogany and Emerald Isle artwork and memorabilia. There's also a map that displays the coats of arms from all 32 counties in Ireland. Choose from a wide selection of Irish potables, including Harp and Guinness ales in bottles, Watney's on tap, plus Irish coffee and Carolan's Irish Cream Liqueur.

Lake Tahoe Area

Lake Tahoe and its surrounding alpine wilderness is one of the most popular year-round resorts in the world. Most famous for its winter sports, resorts such as Kirkwood, Soda Springs, Tahoe Donner and Squaw Valley exalt Tahoe's reputation as a skier's paradise.

In addition to 15 world-class alpine (downhill) resorts, the area is home to eight nordic (cross-country) skiing centers, and thousands of acres of scenic terrain, varying from gentle meadows to spacious bowls and challenging chutes, ideal for sledding, sleigh rides or just playing in the snow.

When the snow melts in late spring and the aspens take on new foliage, Lake Tahoe is transformed into an evergreen wilderness spotlit by chiseled granite mountains, all serving as a backdrop for the blue waters of the lake itself.

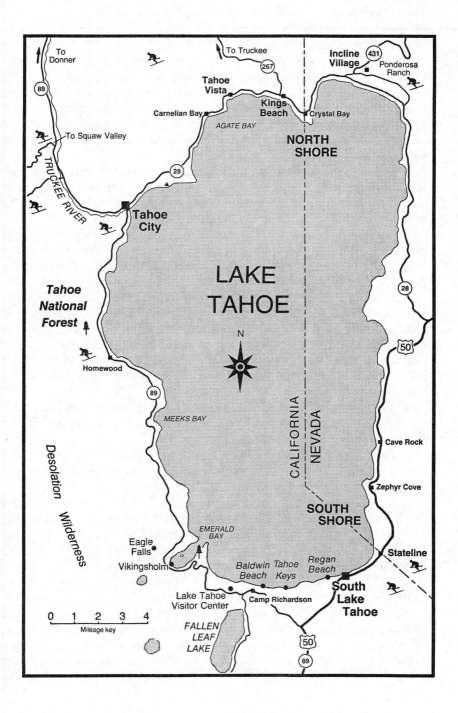

The best way to see Lake Tahoe is to drive the 72 miles around it.

The largest of North America's alpine lakes, Lake Tahoe straddles the California-Nevada border just 35 miles south of Reno. About 42 miles of its shoreline lie in California, and about 29 miles are in Nevada. The largest of the lake's settlements and the highest concentration of year-round residents are located at South Lake Tahoe. The north shore of the lake is home to a number of popular vacation-home communities, many very upscale.

All around the lake are breathtaking natural wonders: two-story-high boulders perched on sunken cliffs; secluded coves and inlets and transparent crystal bays; and clusters of rocks barely emerging from the water to naturally enclose white sandy beaches.

Of course there are also the man-made wonders: championship golf courses, boat docks and marinas, picnic and recreation areas; a stunning example of Norse castle architecture; the fabled Ponderosa Ranch, once the set for the "Bonanza" TV series; and, believe it or not, casinos.

To reach Lake Tahoe from Reno take **Route 395** south ten miles to **Route 431** (the Mount Rose Highway), then head west. The highway climbs slowly until you reach the base of the Sierras, then quickly increases its ascent. The highway crests at about 8200 feet and on your descent into the Lake Tahoe basin you'll begin to glimpse patches of the lake's crystal blue waters. Watch for vista points where you can pull off the highway for panoramic views of the lake.

If you miss the sign, the Incline Green Championship Golf Course is the first indication that you have reached **Incline Village**, one of the North Shore's most affluent resort communities.

Continue to Lake Shore Drive, turn left, then marvel at the palatial estates on the lake side of the road, estates that some owners probably unabashedly call "summer cabins."

Drive west on Route 28 for about six and a half miles until it veers south into the lakeside community of **Crystal Bay**, which straddles the Nevada-California border. In addition to resort homes, a golf course and two beaches, Crystal Bay is home to four small lodge-style casinos, the largest of which, the **Cal–Neva Lodge Resort** (2 Stateline Road, Crystal Bay, NV 89402; 702-832-4000), has a line painted across a rock wall in its lobby, denoting the state line.

Return to the highway and drive west past the intersection of Route 267 to **Kings Beach**, a summer hot spot that is a mecca for vacationers, who crowd the sandy beach, motels and fast-food outlets, creating a scene reminiscent of Santa Monica's Venice Beach. In addition to the souvenir shops, sporting good stores and bikini boutiques, you'll find some interesting art galleries and a few good restaurants. Kings Beach is also the site of the Pro Arts Festival held during July and August, when local artists and craftspeople set up in canvas-covered stalls and sell hand-crafted jewelry, leather, wood carvings, Native American rugs, oil paintings, stained glass, sculpture and other objects of art.

You'll find less crowded beaches and two marinas a couple of miles west at **Tahoe Vista**, one of the North Shore's newer communities. There are also a few older motels, some first-class restaurants and the old Kellogg Mansion, built from native stone after the turn of the century for the legendary cereal king. Today it is home to the La Playa restaurant.

Route 28 angles south along the lake's west shore and passes through **Carnelian Bay** on its way to **Tahoe City**, the largest and oldest of the North Shore communities.

With most of the businesses and attractions clustered near the inter-section of Route 28 (West Lake Boulevard) and Tonopah Road, Tahoe City is ideal for walking. Worth visiting is **Fanny Bridge** which spans the mouth of the Truckee River, the lake's only outlet, and connects with a dam built in 1910 to regulate the lake's output. Just a few feet from the dam's outlet gates is the **North Lake Tahoe Historical Society Museum** (open May through September), where you'll find old photographs depicting the area's history, Native American artifacts, tools, clothing and early logging and railroad equipment. You can also buy books about the area, plus greeting cards decorated by local artists. In the summer of 1995, a second building will open showcasing Native American basket work. A few hundred feet north is **Watson's Log Cabin**, built in 1880 on the lake's shore as the honeymoon retreat for Tahoe pioneers Robert and Stella Watson. Today the cabin is operated by the

---

THE OLD WEST REVISITED

The **Ponderosa Ranch** (100 Ponderosa Ranch Road, Incline Village, NV 89451; 702-831-0691; admission; open May through October) will be familiar to many as the setting for many of the episodes of the famed "Bonanza" TV series. First opened to the public in 1967, the Ranch is home to an Old West town complete with general store, Silver Dollar Saloon, ice cream parlor, horse-drawn carriages and displays of historic firearms, ranching equipment and other antiques. The most popular attraction is the **Cartwright House**, a rambling log home with some beautiful period furnishings including a hand-carved dining table and coat rack on which hang the hats of the Cartwrights. "Bonanza" buffs will recognize the living room's massive stone fireplace, and perhaps recall scenes of Ben Cartwright lecturing Little Joe or arguing with Hoss in front of it.

Historical Society as a museum. If you feel the urge to shop, walk 100 yards inland from the lake to **The Cobblestone Mall**, a replica of a Swiss Alpine village with stucco walls, dark wood beams and eaves and a clock tower on one of its turrets.

Tahoe City is a jumping-off point to several excellent ski resorts, including the famous **Squaw Valley**, about nine miles west of the lake, and the site of the 1960 Winter Olympics. From Tahoe City, take Route 89 west to Squaw Valley Road and turn left. At the turnoff you'll see the Olympic five-ring insignia and Olympic torch flickering above it. Whether or not you're a follower of the games, it's difficult to suppress the feeling of reverence the sight creates.

The valley is surrounded by a number of mountain peaks, which in the winter provide some of the country's best skiing. The highest is Granite Chief at 9050 feet. Nestled at the center of the valley is the ski lodge, from which an aerial tram slides up 8200 feet to a hilltop restaurant at High Camp. In addition to the ski lifts and lodges, Squaw Valley is home to an excellent golf course, several upscale condominium complexes and a lavish resort complex with luxury rooms, tennis courts and three swimming pools.

Route 89 wends its way south along Lake Tahoe's western shore, twisting and turning around granite outcroppings and often emerging onto some of the lake's most picturesque vistas: lush evergreens that cascade down the mountainsides to the water's edge. Most of the West Shore's tiny resort communities are only seasonally inhabited, so you'll find fewer commercial facilities, but an abundance of recreational opportunities. There are two alpine ski areas along the route, as well as four fully equipped marinas, miles of hiking trails and bike paths, plus well-appointed lodges and resorts.

VIKINGSHOLM

*A walk down a mile-long trail near Emerald Bay will bring you to one of Lake Tahoe's most unusual sights, **Vikingsholm**, a composite of Norwegian castle architecture. Nestled among towering pines, the castle features a stone-and-mortar facade and sharply peaked shake roofs, and is noted for its hand-carved woodwork on the back and inside. One of the wings is constructed from wood and its roof is covered with sod, which sprouts colorful native wildflowers during the spring months. During the summer you can take a guided tour of the castle, which contains authentic reproductions of early Viking furnishings, including a hand-painted bridal chest and life-size wooden sculpture.*

Carnelian Bay is named for the reddish, semi-precious stones that are abundant in the area.

About 20 miles south of Tahoe City lies the well-photographed **Emerald Bay**, at the center of which is the lake's only island, Fanette Island, a jagged, granite outcropping with peaks that reach 150 feet above the lake's surface. Atop Fanette Island sits a stone tea house. Named for its transparent blue-green waters, the bay is a popular mooring spot for the lake's cruise boats. From the picnic area at the head of the bay you have a perfect view of **Eagle Falls**, which tumbles into the lake over three rocky embankments.

From Emerald Bay, Route 89 travels southeast through the turn-of-the-century village of **Camp Richardson**, where there are a number of excellent wooded campgrounds, and along the lake's southern shore on its way to the junction of Route 50.

Turn left on Route 50 and head northeast to the bustling metropolis of **South Lake Tahoe**, which is home to about 25,000 year-round residents, more than half the valley's total population. Here you'll also find most of the lake's tourist-oriented businesses—high-rise hotel/casinos, motels, souvenir shops, restaurants and even a few Vegas-style wedding chapels. Route 50 becomes Lake Tahoe Boulevard, the city's main drag, and it's here you'll find its visitors center, chamber of commerce and small museum.

Continue east on Route 50 (Lake Tahoe Boulevard) and at the lakeshore you'll come to the oldest section of the city, with the uninspiring name of **Bijou**. Nevertheless, this vibrant commercial district offers the most opportunities for exploring, if you like designer jewelry and clothing stores, antique shops and art galleries, as well as some nice motels and restaurants. At one of the two marinas you can take a cruise on the glass-bottomed *Tahoe Queen* or, in the winter months, drive south to the internationally famous Heavenly Valley ski resort.

Bijou is also a connecting point to the densely populated tourist mecca of **Stateline**, which spans the Nevada-California border. The California side of Stateline resembles any modern tourist town with scores of souvenir and specialty shops, cafés, sporting good stores, shopping centers and dozens of motels that beckon potential guests with their red neon "vacancy" signs. It's a different scene on the Nevada side, however, where a one-quarter-mile strip of Lake Tahoe Boulevard is home to five glitzy resort casinos: Harrah's Tahoe, Harvey's Resort Hotel, Caesars Tahoe, Bill's and the Horizon Casino Hotel.

Route 50 continues north along the lake's eastern shore and passes through **Zephyr Cove**, named for the gale-like afternoon winds. The

The M.S. Dixie II, a Mississippi paddlewheeler, offers sightseeing and dinner cruises out of Zephyr Cove.

cove is home to a sandy beach and marina. There are also riding stables, campgrounds, a cluster of shops, a general store and motel just off the highway.

A few miles north of Zephyr Cove, the highway passes through a tunnel in **Cave Rock,** a volcanic outcropping that is believed to have once been a battle site for the Paiute and Washoe tribes. The rest stop just below the highway provides some picturesque views of the lake. Don't be surprised to see local anglers along the banks casting for cutthroat trout known to inhabit the crystal waters.

Route 50 continues north to the old logging camp of Glenbrook, then veers east at the junction of Route 28 on its way to Carson City, Nevada's state capital. To return to Reno, take Route 28 and continue to Incline Village, then retrace your route out of the Lake Tahoe Basin and back to Reno.

LAKE TAHOE AREA LODGING

Most of the lake's larger resort hotels are located at South Lake Tahoe, with a handful on the North Shore. In between, the lake's smaller communities are home to dozens of rustic motels and motor inns that offer clean, comfortable rooms at mostly moderate prices.

If your taste leans toward luxury in grand style, head for **Harrah's Lake Tahoe Casino Hotel** (Highway 50, Stateline, NV 89449; 702-588-6611, 800-648-3773, fax 702-788-3274), with its 18-story tower and 540 ultra-deluxe rooms, most of which have stunning lake and mountain views and two marble-tiled bathrooms, each equipped with a phone and color TV. Hotel amenities include an indoor swimming pool, 70,000-square-foot casino, health club, hot tubs and four superb restaurants.

It's hard to believe the towering **Harvey's Resort Hotel & Casino** (Highway 50, Stateline, NV 89449; 702-588-2411, 800-427-8397, fax 702-588-6643) across the street was once the hokey Wagon Wheel Saloon, but it's true. In 1944 Harvey and Llewellyn Gross opened a one-room log cabin with a six-stool counter, three slot machines, two blackjack tables and the only 24-hour gas pump between Carson City and Placerville. Today that operation has expanded into a 22-story, 740-room resort with well-appointed guest rooms decorated with Colonial and French Provincial furnishings, pastel color schemes and boasting marble-tiled bathrooms. All rooms also contain stocked bars and refrigerators. Deluxe to ultra-deluxe.

Set on the shore with its own sandy beach, **Caesars Tahoe** (55 Highway 50, Stateline, NV 89449; 702-588-3515, 800-648-3353, fax 702-586-2068) is one of the state's most glitzy resort-casinos. Continuing the Roman theme started by its sister resort in Las Vegas, Caesars Tahoe features an entrance decorated with sandstone, brick and fieldstone, and its 15-story tower rises above towering pine trees. The 440 guest rooms are bright and spacious with light wood furniture and brass-and-black lamps and fixtures, soft pink color schemes, oyster-shell headboards and marble countertops and circular tubs in the bathrooms. Many have balconies and most offer magnificent views of the lake and surrounding forests. In addition to the lively casino, hotel amenities include six restaurants, a celebrity showroom, lagoon-style indoor swimming pool, health spa and workout room, tennis courts and a convention center. Deluxe to ultra-deluxe.

Anchored on the lake's North Shore, the **Hyatt Regency Lake Tahoe Resort & Casino** (111 Country Club Drive, Incline Village, NV 89450; 702-832-1234, 800-233-1234, fax 702-831-7508) is a resort resembling a medieval castle with sand-colored walls, red roofs and 458 guest rooms decorated with deep green carpeting, colorful flower-print quilts and maple-colored wood furniture that includes a four-poster bed and armoire. Some even have fireplaces. Resort amenities include an outdoor heated pool and spa, health club and private beach with boat rentals. Ultra-deluxe.

The alpine-style **Haus Bavaria Bed & Breakfast** (593 North Dyer Circle, Incline Village, NV 89450; 702-831-6122) is a rustic, split-level retreat set on a hilltop overlooking the Lake Tahoe. All of the inn's five guest rooms have full baths, balconies and Scandinavian-style wood furniture. Deluxe.

Not far away, the **Cal-Neva Lodge Resort Hotel & Casino** (2 Stateline Road, Crystal Bay, NV 89402; 702-832-4000, 800-225-6382, fax 702-831-9007) combines the comfort and convenience of a resort hotel with the rustic charm of a mountain lodge. Most of the 200 guest rooms are in the hotel's tower and feature sitting areas with club chairs covered with sateen upholstery, dark, polished-wood headboards and nightstands, deep teal carpeting with matching decorative wall coverings, patterned throw quilts and ceramic-and-brass table lamps. The most elegant rooms are in the hotel's chalet wing and cottages and feature stone fireplaces and antique furnishings. Deluxe to ultra-deluxe.

Another charming bed and breakfast is the **Rockwood Lodge** (5295 West Lake Boulevard, Homewood, CA; 916-525-5273), originally built in 1936 as a summer home for a well-to-do California dairyman. The five-room bed and breakfast retains the original rock and stone exterior and knotty pine interior, but now contains country antiques, feather beds, down comforters and Laura Ashley fabrics. Deluxe to ultra-deluxe.

The Incline Village area also has hundreds of rustic cabins, townhouses, charming chalets and spectacular lakefront homes available for rent. For a complete list of these specialized accommodations, contact the **Incline Village/Crystal Bay Visitors Bureau** (969 Tahoe Boulevard, Incline Village, NV 89451; 702-832-1606, 800-468-2463, fax 702-832-1605).

LAKE TAHOE AREA RESTAURANTS

One of the lake's best spots for fresh seafood is **Pisces** (55 Highway 50, Stateline; 702-588-3515) at Caesars Tahoe, where you can feast on Dover sole, Norwegian salmon and Maine lobster prepared by a chef who works in open view of diners. The restaurant's onyx table tops, marble columns and torch lamps on the wall don't exactly spell Cannery Row, but the seafood dishes are fresh and ably presented. Moderate to deluxe. Closed Sunday and Monday. You can also get some of the best Chinese food, from Hunan to Cantonese, at Caesars' moderate-to-deluxe **Empress Court**, where guests are ensconced in cloth-upholstered booths separated by etched-glass dividers. Some specialties include a tasty grilled squab salad and satay beef.

Another great seafood restaurant is the **Fresh Ketch** (2435 Venice Drive East, Tahoe Keys; 916-541-5683), an enchanting little affair overlooking the lake from the Tahoe Keys Marina. The house specialty is Long Island oysters, but you can also choose from fish, poultry and steak dishes. Moderate to deluxe.

For simple fare, the **Sierra Café** in the Hyatt Regency (111 Country Club Drive, Incline Village; 702-832-1234) offers moderately priced breakfast, lunch and dinner, including a dinner buffet, in a coffee shop setting that's made cozy by a floor-to-ceiling fireplace and a roomful of potted plants.

Take Harvey's Resort's elevator to the 19th floor to find **Llewellyn's** (Highway 50, Stateline; 702-588-2411), a long-time local favorite that serves up deluxe-priced continental cuisine and panoramic views of the lake. On weekends, the piano bar adds to the romantic ambience. You can come down to earth at the resort's **Sage Room Steak House**, which features a tasty Dungeness crab cocktail and hearty black bean soup. You can also indulge yourself with filet mignon, steak Diane, beef Wellington and flaming tableside desserts. Deluxe.

Right across the street, **The Summit** (Highway 50, Stateline; 702-588-6606), on the 16th floor of Harrah's, offers equally spectacular views plus candlelit dinners from a changing "American Progressive" menu. Ultra-deluxe.

The freshly baked breads and pastries at the Tahoe House (625 West Lake Boulevard, Tahoe City; 916-583-1384) attract locals from throughout the region.

Traditional Japanese dishes are showcased at **Samurai** (2588 Lake Tahoe Boulevard, South Lake Tahoe; 916-542-0300), which also features a sushi bar and private tatami seating. Moderate.

You can dine on seafood dishes and homemade pasta in the knotty-pine paneled dining room at the **Tahoe House** (625 West Lake Boulevard, Tahoe City; 916-583-1384). Moderate.

Another rustic getaway is **The Soule Domain** (Crystal Bay; 916-546-7529), a log cabin-style restaurant with a huge stone fireplace, and specialties that include filet mignon with shiitake mushrooms, laced with Gorgonzola and brandy, and tuna grilled with papaya-mango chutney. Deluxe to ultra-deluxe.

A popular hangout with the North Shore locals is **Captain Jon's** (Tahoe Vista Inn, 7220 North Lake Boulevard, Tahoe Vista; 916-546-4819), where the house favorites include poached salmon, roast duckling with blueberry or oyster sauce, and the fresh seafood salads. If you can't decide on a selection from the extensive wine list, try one of the fresh fruit daiquiris. Moderate to deluxe.

LAKE TAHOE AREA SHOPPING

Most of the lake's shopping is clustered in the South Lake Tahoe area. Although you would expect "mall" to be a four-letter word in this neck of the woods, there are a few reminders of city-life in the form of the **Boatworks Mall** (780 North Lake Boulevard) with several fine art galleries, the Bavarian-style **Cobblestone Mall** (475 North Lake Boulevard) and the **Roundhouse Mall** (700 North Lake Boulevard), which is located in a converted railroad depot built in 1890.

You'll also find shops worth exploring in the tiny resort communities of **Kings Beach, Incline Village, Zephyr Cove, Al Tahoe** and **Bijou**, the home of the Lake Tahoe Historical Society Museum and the *Tahoe Daily Tribune*, the area's only newspaper.

Lake Tahoe is home to a thriving arts community, with a number of galleries representing the works of local and visiting artists. A good spot for original works of art is **Arts Desire** (761 Northwood Boulevard, Incline Village, NV 89450; 702-831-3011) and **Hanifin's Arts & Antiques** (855 Emerald Bay Road, South Lake Tahoe, CA; 916-542-4663) for sculpture, paintings and antiques. For original wildlife and landscapes of the region, try **Heritage Graphics West** (Boatworks Mall, Tahoe City, CA ; 916-581-2208).

LAKE TAHOE AREA NIGHTLIFE

Besides a few bar bands and restaurant piano players, virtually all of the lake's after-dark action takes place in the major resort-casinos.

At Caesars Tahoe, the **Circus Maximus Showroom** (55 Highway 50, Stateline; 702-588-3515) frequently hosts big-name headliners such as David Copperfield, Julio Iglesias, Diana Ross and Reba McEntire. And the hotel's **Nero's 2000** nightclub, with its elevated dancefloor, Roman pillars and high-tech sound and lighting, is a great spot to dance the night away. Cover for both.

The **Grand Lake Theater** (Lake Tahoe Boulevard, Stateline; 702-588-6211; cover) in the Horizon Hotel features headliners such as Carrot Top, Donna Fargo and Jeff Foxworthy, while the hotel's **Aspen Lounge** offers varied entertainment, from jazz to rock to dance and karaoke. No cover.

Other places to find celebrity entertainment include the **South Shore Room** (Highway 50, Stateline; 702-588-6606) in Harrah's Resort Casino Hotel, with tickets available through the casino, and the **Emerald Theater** (Highway 50, Stateline; 702-588-2411) in Harvey's Resort Hotel & Casino, which hosts acts such as musical revues and stand-up comedians. Cover.

LAKE TAHOE AREA BEACHES

At South Lake Tahoe there are plenty of good spots to unfurl a beach blanket, including **Regan Beach** (at the end of Sacramento Avenue in Al Tahoe), which has grassy picnic areas, restrooms, a playground and wind-surfing rentals; **Baldwin Beach** (off Route 89 in Camp Richardson), which features picnic areas with barbecue pits and restrooms; **Zephyr Cove** (off Route 50 north of Round Hill), where you can picnic and launch a small boat; and **El Dorado Beach** (across from the South Lake Tahoe Chamber of Commerce, South Lake Tahoe), which has a lifeguarded beach, picnic grounds and boat ramp.

On the North Shore, try **Kings Beach State Recreation Area** (at the end of Coon Street, Kings Beach), which has a playground and restrooms; **Tahoe City Commons Beach** (near the fire station, Tahoe City), with grass picnic areas, fire pits, playground and restrooms; and **Meeks Bay Resort** (Route 89, 10 miles south of Tahoe City), which has a beach, picnic area, and a full-service marina that rents aquacycles and paddleboats.

The Sporting Life

GOLF

There are some excellent courses within a few miles of downtown Reno: **Lakeridge Golf Course** (1200 Razorback Road; 702-825-2200); an 18-hole private course, **Brookside Golf Course** (700 South Rock Boulevard; 702-856-6009); **Northgate Golf Club** (1111 Clubhouse Drive; 702-747-7577); **Washoe County Golf Course** (2601 South Arlington; 702-828-6640); and **Wildcreek Golf Course** (3500 Sullivan Lane, Sparks; 702-673-3100).

With an alpine backdrop, the courses at Lake Tahoe are among the most beautiful in the country. Among the better ones are: **Incline Village Golf Resort** (955 Fairway Boulevard, Incline Village; 702-832-1144); the par-58 **Incline Village Executive Golf Course** (690 Wilson Way, Incline Village; 702-832-1150); **Old Brockway Golf Course** (7900 North Lake Boulevard, Kings Beach; 916-546-9909); **Tahoe City Golf Course** (251 North Lake Boulevard, Tahoe City; 916-583-1516); **Bijou Golf Course** (3464 Fairway Boulevard, South Lake Tahoe; 916-542-6097); **Edgewood Tahoe** (180 Lake Parkway, Stateline; 702-588-3566); and the **Glenbrook Golf Course** (2070 Pray Meadow Road, Glenbrook; 702-749-5201).

TENNIS

In Reno you can walk through your backswing at the **Lakeridge Tennis Club** (6000 Plumas Street; 702-827-4500) with its 14 outdoor and four indoor courts; and at the **Reno Hilton** (2500 East 2nd Street; 702-789-2000), where you can play on three outdoor and five indoor courts. Fee for both.

Besides the courts at several Lake Tahoe public schools, you can play at the **Lakeside Tennis Club** (955 Tahoe Boulevard, Incline Village; 702-832-4860; fee) or the **North Tahoe Regional Park** (at the foot of National Avenue, Tahoe Vista; 916-546-7248).

HIKING

About 25 miles from Reno, **Mount Rose** has a five-mile trail through alpine wilderness that begins at the mountain's summit, just off Route 431. Closer to town, you can hike to **Jones and Whites Creeks** via an eight-mile loop that follows a jeep trail from its trailhead at Galena Creek Park, about 15 miles from Reno on Route 431.

Hiking opportunities at Lake Tahoe and the surrounding wilderness are virtually limitless. Marked trails range from easy two-mile hikes to

---

The Lake Tahoe Region boasts the largest concentration of ski areas in the country—all within an hour of each other.

---

overnight treks. Wilderness permits are required for some of the trails in the area. For a permit, maps and additional information, contact the **Lake Tahoe Basin Management Unit** (870 Emerald Bay Road, South Lake Tahoe, CA 96150; 916-573-2600).

FISHING

Lake Tahoe's deep, clear waters are famous for its game fish, including mountain whitefish and kokanee salmon, but notably its variety of trout—Mackinaw, brown, rainbow and brook. A valid California or Nevada fishing license is required to fish Lake Tahoe. Licenses can be purchased at sporting-goods stores and fishing shops around the lake. Contact the **Nevada Division of Wildlife** (Box 10678, Reno, NV 89520; 702-688-1500) for more information. Once you're properly licensed, try some of these South Shore hot spots: **Emerald Point**, at the mouth of Emerald Bay and close to the shore, for rainbows and brown trout; **East Shore**, between Zephyr Point and Glenbrook Bay, for most species; **Hobart Hole**, south of Elk Point near Nevada Beach, where the Mackinaw can be found at depths of 50 feet and more; **Agate Bay**, just off the Tahoe Vista and Kings Beach shorelines; **Crystal Bay**, along the Incline Village shoreline, where casting on the surface should net rainbow and brown trout; and **Tahoe Flats**, a couple miles out from the dam at Tahoe City for trolling for Mackinaw.

SKIING

Lake Tahoe is a skier's Valhalla. And the conditions are unbeatable: winter daytime temperatures range from 25 to 45 degrees, the sun shines more than 75 percent of the time, and the area's annual snowfall averages 350 inches. Elevations range from 6000 feet to 10,000 feet with vertical drops of up to 4000 feet. More than 150 ski lifts operate around Lake Tahoe during the ski season, which usually lasts from November through May, but has been known to extend to the Fourth of July.

The best of the area's world-class downhill resorts include: **Alpine Meadows** (916-583-4232), seven miles northwest of Tahoe City at the end of Alpine Meadows Road, off Route 89; **Boreal Ski Area** (916-426-3666), 10 miles west of Truckee off Route 80; **Diamond Peak Ski Resort** (702-832-1177) in the town of Incline Village; **Donner Ski Ranch** (916-426-3635), Route 80 to the Soda Springs exit west of

Truckee; **Granlibakken** (916-583-4242), at the end of Granlibakken Road one-half mile south of Tahoe City; **Heavenly Ski Resort** (702-586-7000), south of South Lake Tahoe's casino district, reached via South Benjamin Drive off the Kingsbury Grade; **Homewood Ski Area** (916-525-2992), six miles south of Tahoe City on Route 89; **Soda Springs** (916-426-3666), west of Truckee on old Route 40; **Squaw Valley** (916-583-6985), eight miles northwest of Tahoe City off Route 89; and **Tahoe Donner** (916-587-9400), three miles northwest of Truckee off Donner Pass Road.

Transportation

BY CAR

There's only one (reasonable) way to drive the 446 miles from Las Vegas to Reno: take **Route 95** north from downtown Las Vegas to the northern Nevada city of Fallon and turn west on **Route 50**. Continue to **Route 80**, which will take you into the Reno–Sparks valley.

BY AIR

The flight from Las Vegas to Reno's **Reno-Cannon International Airport** (702-328-6400) takes about 65 minutes. Airlines with flights into Reno include America West, American, Delta, Reno Air, Southwest, United and USAir.

The city of South Lake Tahoe has the lake's only commercial airport, **South Lake Tahoe Airport** (916-541-4080), located just south of the city on Route 50. Trans World Express flies directly into the airport, while most fly into Reno and are shuttled by Tahoe Casino Express.

BY BUS

Greyhound Bus Lines (155 Stevenson Street; 702-322-2970) services Reno via Las Vegas.

Greyhound also services South Lake Tahoe on a regular basis. The terminal (702-588-4645) is located at Harrah's Hotel Casino.

BY TRAIN

Amtrak's "California Zephyr" (800-872-7245) services Reno on its route between Chicago and San Francisco. The train stops in the middle of downtown at 135 East Commercial Row. For service to Lake Tahoe, take Amtrak to Sacramento, and transfer to Amtrak Bus Service. The bus goes to Harrah's Hotel Casino in Stateline, and the South Center "Y" Shopping Center in South Lake Tahoe.

CAR RENTALS

Rental cars available at the Reno-Cannon airport are **Avis Rent A Car** (702-785-2727), **Budget Car and Truck Rental** (702-785-2690), **Dollar Rent A Car** (702-348-2800) and **National Car Rental** (702-785-2756). **Alamo Rent A Car** (702-323-8306) and **Enterprise Rent A Car** (702-329-3773) offer free shuttle buses from Reno-Cannon airport.

At the South Lake Tahoe Airport, try **Avis Rent A Car** (916-542-5638) and **Hertz Rent A Car** (916-544-2327).

Index

HIDDEN GUIDES

Adventure travel or a relaxing vacation?—"Hidden" guidebooks are the only travel books in the business to provide detailed information on both. Aimed at environmentally aware travelers, our motto is "Adventure Travel Plus." These books combine details on unique hotels, restaurants and sightseeing with information on camping, sports and hiking for the outdoor enthusiast.

ULTIMATE GUIDES

These innovative guides present the best and most unique features of a destination. Quality is the keynote. They are as likely to cover a mom-and-pop café as a gourmet restaurant, a quaint bed and breakfast as a five-star tennis resort. In addition to selectively covering each destination, they feature short articles and one-line "teasers" that are both fun and informative.

THE NEW KEY GUIDES

Based on the concept of ecotourism, The New Key Guides are dedicated to the preservation of a region's rare and endangered species, culture, architecture and archaeology. Filled with helpful tips, they give travelers everything they need to know to respect and enjoy these exotic destinations.

ULYSSES PRESS To order direct, send a check or money order to:
Ulysses Press, P.O. Box 3440, Berkeley, CA 94703-3440;
to charge by credit card, call 800/377-2542 or 510/601-8301·

TRAVEL

_____ Hidden Boston and Cape Cod, $9.95

_____ Hidden Carolinas, $14.95

_____ Hidden Coast of California, $14.95

_____ Hidden Florida, $14.95

_____ Hidden Florida Keys and Everglades, $9.95

_____ Hidden Hawaii, $15.95

_____ Hidden Mexico, $13.95

_____ Hidden New England, $14.95

_____ Hidden Pacific Northwest, $14.95

_____ Hidden Rockies, $14.95

_____ Hidden San Francisco and Northern California, $14.95

_____ Hidden Southern California, $14.95

_____ Hidden Southwest, $15.95

_____ Disneyland and Beyond: The Ultimate Family Guidebook, $9.95

_____ Disney World & Beyond: The Ultimate Family Guidebook, $10.95

_____ Florida's Gold Coast: The Ultimate Guidebook, $8.95

_____ Ultimate Las Vegas and Beyond, $11.95

_____ The Maya Route: The Ultimate Guidebook, $14.95

_____ Ultimate Arizona, $11.95

_____ Ultimate California, $14.95

_____ Ultimate Maui, $11.95

_____ Ultimate Santa Fe and Beyond, $11.95

_____ Ultimate Washington, $11.95

_____ The New Key to Belize, $13.95

_____ The New Key to Cancún and the Yucatán, $13.95

_____ The New Key to Costa Rica, $14.95

_____ The Virago Woman's Travel Guide to New York, $13.95

_____ The Virago Woman's Travel Guide to Paris, $13.95

_____ The Virago Woman's Travel Guide to Rome, $13.95

FREE SHIPPING!

Total cost of books   = _____

Book rate shipping   = __FREE__

California residents add 8% sales tax.   = _____

Total enclosed = _____

NAME _____PHONE _____

ADDRESS_____

CITY _____STATE ____ZIP _____

About the Author

David Stratton has worked as a newspaper reporter and editor for eight years in California and Nevada, most recently as features editor for the *Las Vegas Sun*. He is currently staff writer, editor and graphic designer for a Las Vegas publisher of gaming books and a monthly game room magazine. A native of the Hawaiian islands, he moved to Las Vegas in 1989 after living in Southern California for 30 years. This is his first book.

About the Illustrator

Glenn Kim is a freelance illustrator residing in San Francisco. His work appears in numerous Ulysses Press titles including *Hidden Southwest, The Maya Route: The Ultimate Guidebook* and *The New Key to Cancún and the Yucatán*. He has also illustrated for the National Forest Service, several Bay Area magazines, book covers and greeting cards, as well as for advertising agencies that include Foote Cone and Belding, Hal Riney and Jacobs Fulton Design Group.